A
RACE
AGAINST
DEATH

A
RACE
AGAINST
DEATH

PETER BERGSON,
AMERICA, AND THE
HOLOCAUST

DAVID S. WYMAN
AND RAFAEL MEDOFF

THE NEW PRESS
NEW YORK

Published in the United States by The New Press, New York, 2002
Distributed by W. W. Norton & Company, Inc., New York

LIBRARY OF CONGRESS CATALOGING-IN-PUBLICATION DATA
Wyman, David S.
A race against death : Peter Bergson, America,
and the Holocaust / David S. Wyman and Rafael Medoff.
p.   cm.
Text based on a twelve-hour interview with Hillel Kook (Peter Bergson) includes
"Report to the Secretary on the acquiescence of this government
in the murder of the Jews" dated January 13, 1944.
Includes bibliographical references (p.) and index.
ISBN 1-56584-761-X (hc.)
1. Holocaust, Jewish (1939–1945)—Influence.   2. World War, 1939–1945—
Jews—Rescue—United States.   3. Refugees, Jewish—Government policy—
United States—History—20th century.   4. Jews—United States—Politics and
government—20th century.   5. Kook, Hillel, 1915—Interviews.   I. Title.

D809.U5 W96   2002
940.53'18—dc21
2002025538

The New Press was established in 1990 as a not-for-profit alternative to the large,
commercial publishing houses currently dominating the book publishing industry.
The New Press operates in the public interest rather than for private gain, and is
committed to publishing, in innovative ways, works of educational, cultural, and
community value that are often deemed insufficiently profitable.

The New Press, 450 West 41st Street, 6th floor, New York, NY 10036
www.thenewpress.com

Book design by Kathryn Parise
Composition by Westchester Book Composition

Printed in the United States of America

2   4   6   8   10   9   7   5   3   1

In memory of my brother Hollis
and Evelyn Grant Johnson
and Chuck Markels and Dave Jensen,
four of many kind guides along the way.
—David S. Wyman

For my wife, Carin: "She is robed in strength and
dignity, and she smiles at the future. She opens her
mouth with wisdom, and teachings of kindness are
on her tongue." (*Proverbs* 31:25)
—Rafael Medoff

CONTENTS

On the issue of the extermination of the Jews and our rescue work with the Emergency Committee. The Jews were being killed—it wasn't any more four million to save. We started off [in December 1942] by saying a memorial to two million dead Jews, save the others, while the figures were changing like in a race, so many killed and so many to go. You didn't really know if there were still Jews there, you hoped there were.

—*Hillel Kook (Peter Bergson)*
April 14, 1973

The problem is immediate. The problem is essentially a humanitarian one. It is not a Jewish problem alone. It is a Christian problem and a problem for enlightened civilization.

We have talked; we have sympathized; we have expressed our horror; the time to act is long past due.

—*United States Senate Committee on*
Foreign Relations, December 20, 1943

ACKNOWLEDGMENTS

The authors would like to acknowledge the valuable help of the following institutions and individuals.

The Agudath Israel Archives, *American Jewish History*, the Chicago Jewish Historical Society, the Jabotinsky Institute (Metzudat Ze'ev), the United States Holocaust Memorial Museum, the United States Library of Congress, the W.E.B. DuBois Library at the University of Massachusetts at Amherst, and the Weizmann Institute.

William Aurelio, Norton Bagley, Lon Carter Barton, Régine and Edward Barshak, Shmuel Bolozky, Maury Botton, Doron Bregman, Rosemary Brown, Lowell Cantrell, Blanche Cook, Judy Crichton, David Curtis, Irving Cutler, Judith Cohen, Samuel V. Daniel, Margaret Drain, Stuart Erdheim, John K. Fairbank, Yael Fischer, Frank Freidel, Marian Greenberg, Laurence Jarvik, Darlow Johnson, Joy Kingsolver, Nili Kook, Rabbi Moshe Kolodny, Archibald Lewis, Martin Ostrow, Robert Peck, David Pierce, Howard Quint, Baruch and Malka Robbins, Walter Roth, Pierre Sauvage, André Schiffrin, Merav Segal, Harry L. Selden, Jonathan Shainin, Amira Stern, Leslie Swift, Midge Wyman, and Bat-Ami Zucker.

PREFACE

"This is Strictly A Race Against Death," declared the headline of an advertisement that appeared in prominent American newspapers in the autumn of 1943. The Nazi slaughter of Europe's Jews was proceeding relentlessly, and a small band of Jewish activists in the United States was trying desperately to rouse the conscience of the nation and prod the Roosevelt administration to rescue Jews from Hitler.

The unlikely leader of these rescue advocates was the diminutive, 28 year-old nephew of the Chief Rabbi of Palestine. In the 1930s, as the clouds of war began to gather on the European horizon, Hillel Kook left his home in Jerusalem to help organize the unauthorized immigration of Jews from Europe to Palestine. After the outbreak of World War II, he traveled to the United States, where, under the name Peter Bergson, he initiated a series of political action efforts that sought to bring about U.S. intervention on behalf of Hitler's Jewish victims.

Kook spearheaded an extraordinary campaign of public rallies, hard-hitting newspaper advertisements, and lobbying in Congress that forced America to confront the Holocaust. Ads with headlines such as "How Well Are You Sleeping?," "Help Prevent 4,000,000 People from Becoming Ghosts," and "They Are Driven to Death Daily, But They *Can* Be Saved" startled Americans who were more accustomed to Jewish groups that spoke in reserved tones, if they spoke out at all.

Whether by mobilizing hundreds of rabbis to march on Washington just before Yom Kippur, or by recruiting Hollywood celebrities such as Ben Hecht, Edward G. Robinson, and Eddie Cantor to support the Jewish cause, Kook displayed an uncanny ability to take a largely-ignored issue and propel it to the forefront of public interest.

Kook's activities aroused fierce opposition. State Department officials urged the Department of Justice to have him deported from the United States. FBI agents infiltrated his organizations, surreptitiously opened his mail, and even sifted through his trash for information to use against him. The British government repeatedly pleaded with the Roosevelt administration to find a way to silence him.

Perhaps most disheartening, many prominent American Jewish leaders also worked hard to obstruct Kook's activities. Some regarded Kook as a dangerous rival who was usurping the place of the established leadership by taking away the support of grassroots Jews. Other Jewish leaders opposed Kook because they feared his vociferous public activity would provoke anti-Semitism. And Zionist leaders resented Kook's attempts to temporarily put the goal of Jewish statehood on the back burner in order to focus attention on the rescue issue.

Yet despite the many obstacles that his opponents created, Kook and his group succeeded in breaking through the wall of silence that surrounded news about Hitler's annihilation of the Jews. His campaigns significantly increased public awareness of the Nazi genocide. Most important, Kook's efforts led to the establishment, late in the war, of the War Refugee Board, a United States government agency charged with the task of rescuing Jews from the Nazi Holocaust. An estimated 200,000 Jews were saved directly or indirectly by the War Refugee Board.

In these pages, Kook finally tells his side of the story. Based on unpublished interviews, *A Race Against Death* explores, through Kook's eyes, the extraordinary events of those dark years.

It is the story of one man's appeal to the conscience of a generation, and his campaign for a moral reckoning in the face of the greatest tragedy mankind has ever known.

NOTE BY DAVID WYMAN ON
THE ORIGIN AND STRUCTURE
OF THE BOOK

This book is built around a twelve-hour interview granted to me by Peter Bergson (Hillel Kook) on April 13–15, 1973, in Amherst, Massachusetts. The interview was conducted as part of the research for my book *The Abandonment of the Jews: America and the Holocaust, 1941–1945,* published in 1984 under the supervision of André Schiffrin, then director of Pantheon Books. In 1985, after reading the parts of the interview that had been transcribed, Mr. Schiffrin offered to publish an edited version of it, supplemented by an introduction providing historical background and numerous explanatory footnotes that would appear with the introduction as well as with the text of the interview itself.

In 1985, however, because of the widespread notice that *The Abandonment of the Jews* had attracted, a great deal of my time began to be taken up by public lecturing. The lectures continued to absorb substantial amounts of time until 2000. By then I had delivered 425 speeches in forty states, Canada, and Israel. During the same years I devoted a large amount of time to two major scholarly projects to which I had committed myself before the prospect of publishing the Hillel Kook interview arose. The first was a set of thirteen volumes of the most important documents that I had used in *The Abandonment of the Jews.* It was published under the title *America and the Holocaust.* The second was to edit (and contribute a long chapter to) a thousand-page study of the responses of twenty-two nations to the Holocaust in the years since 1945. This book was titled *The World Reacts to the Holocaust.* For two years in the early 1990s, I was also heavily involved as academic adviser to the film *America and the Holocaust: Deceit and Indifference,* which was broadcast in 1994 by PBS as part of the prestigious American Experience series. Because of these activities, for many years I was able to give only limited attention to the Hillel Kook interview.

In 2001, an annotated excerpt from the interview appeared, under the title "The Bergson Group, America, and the Holocaust," in a special issue

of *American Jewish History* concerning America's response to the Holocaust. Dr. Rafael Medoff served as guest editor of the issue. Our discussions of the interview and its historical significance led to a decision to
work together to prepare the original interview for publication. The endur-
ing interest and commitment of André Schiffrin, who left Pantheon Books
in 1990 and subsequently founded an independent publishing company
called The New Press, made possible the realization of this project.

In addition to the text of the long interview with Hillel Kook, this volume incorporates several excerpts from four short interviews that I had
subsequently conducted with Kook and his close associate from the World
War II years, Samuel Merlin. Also included are a number of valuable
insights concerning Kook and his era that appeared in the full, original
transcripts of interviews that had been conducted for two documentary
films on America's response to the Holocaust. The films are *America and
the Holocaust: Deceit and Indifference* (1994), written, produced, and
directed by Martin Ostrow for American Experience; and *Who Shall Live
and Who Shall Die?* (1981), written, produced, and directed by Laurence
Jarvik. Through the kindness of Mr. Ostrow and American Experience, we
have included passages of relevance to this book from Mr. Ostrow's interviews with Max Lerner and Will Rogers, Jr. Through the kindness of Mr.
Jarvik, we have included excerpts from Mr. Jarvik's interviews with Hillel
Kook, Samuel Merlin, and Emanuel Celler. Each time material from one
of these additional interviews appears, the source is identified in a source
note.*

*The authors gratefully acknowledge the kindness of Martin Ostrow, American Experi-
ence, and the WGBH Educational Foundation of Boston, Massachusetts. The authors are
also grateful for the kindness of Laurence Jarvik. His film *Who Shall Live and Who Shall
Die?* is distributed by Kino International Corporation of New York City.

A
RACE
AGAINST
DEATH

CHAPTER

1

Introduction

AMERICA'S RESPONSE TO THE HOLOCAUST: A BRIEF OVERVIEW

In its response to the Holocaust, the United States fell far short of measuring up to America's basic human and democratic values. In the pre-Holocaust years (1933–1940), hundreds of thousands of European Jews could have reached safe haven if the United States and other countries had been willing to open their doors. The United States could have set the example by a temporary widening of its immigration quotas. Instead, even the small quotas that were legally available were not filled, except from mid-1938 to mid-1940. Then, in the worst years (1941–45), immigration was made even more difficult. And not until January 1944, fourteen months after it had incontrovertible evidence that genocide was occurring, did the United States government begin to take even limited steps toward rescue.[1]

The three main factors that lay behind America's failed response were the Great Depression, nativism, and anti-Semitism. In 1933, at the worst point in the Depression, unemployment in the United States reached 25 percent. Even by 1938 it was still above 15 percent. The decade of the 1930s was one of insecurity, fear, and anxiety. Many Americans worried that foreigners would enter the country and take their jobs. During World War II, when war production eliminated unemployment, there was still widespread apprehension that the Depression would return with the end of hostilities.[2]

Nativist attitudes, which were particularly widespread in the 1920s, remained prevalent in the 1930s and 1940s. A great many Americans disliked foreigners of any kind and wanted to end or significantly reduce the small flow of immigration that still existed. The issue was partly one of job competition, but many Americans also harbored fears about the cultural impact foreigners had on the United States.[3]

Anti-Semitism, already on the rise in the 1920s, increased dramatically in the 1930s and reached a peak in the late 1930s and the World War II years. By 1942, sociologist David Riesman described it as "slightly below the boiling point," and in early 1945, public opinion expert Elmo Roper warned that "anti-Semitism has spread all over the nation and is particularly virulent in urban centers."[4]

The pervasiveness of American anti-Semitism in that era is shown in a series of national public opinion polls taken from 1938 to 1946. The results indicated that over half of the U.S. population perceived Jews as greedy and dishonest, and that about one-third considered them overly aggressive. A set of surveys extending from 1938 through 1941 showed that between one-third and one-half of the public believed that Jews had "too much power in the United States." During the war years, a continuation of the survey saw the proportion rise to 56 percent. According to these and other polls, this supposed Jewish power was located mainly in "business and commerce" and in "finance." From late 1942 into the spring of 1945, significant Jewish power was also thought to exist in "politics and government."[5]

Other surveys from August 1940 on through the war found that from 15 to 24 percent of the respondents looked on Jews as "a menace to America." Jews were consistently seen as more of a threat than such other groups in the United States as "Negroes, Catholics, Germans, or Japanese" (except during 1942, when Japanese and Germans were rated more dangerous).[6]

If a threat actually existed, however, it was not *from* Jews, but *to* them. An alarming set of polls taken between 1938 and 1945 revealed that roughly 15 percent of those surveyed would have supported "a widespread campaign against the Jews in this country." Another 20 to 25 percent would have sympathized with such a movement. Approximately 30 percent indicated that they would have actively opposed it. In sum, as much as 35 to 40 percent of the population was prepared to approve an anti-Jewish campaign, some 30 percent would have stood up against it, and the rest would have remained indifferent.[7]

The polling results, taken as a whole, indicate that during the years of World War II anti-Jewish attitudes reached their highest point in U.S. history: approximately one-third of the American public was anti-Semitic. Parenthetically, public opinion surveys conducted in the United States after the war show that prejudice against Jews decreased strikingly between 1945 and 1960 and continued downward in the years that followed.[8]

The high levels of anti-Semitism of the late 1930s were closely connected with the insecurities and fears brought on by a decade of economic depression. Anxieties resulting from years of widespread unemployment led many to search for explanations, to ask who was to blame. The underlying negative image of Jews, deeply ingrained in Western society over the centuries, offered an answer to many Americans. And the widespread tensions and anxieties generated by the nation's involvement in World War II fostered a further increase in anti-Jewish attitudes. But certainly a contributing force in the spread of hatred toward Jews was the large number of anti-Semitic demagogues who held sway in America in that era. By 1940, more than one hundred anti-Semitic organizations were on the scene. Although they and their leaders always remained on the outer fringes of society, a handful of them drew substantial public attention despite their relatively small numbers.[9]

Among the leading anti-Semitic forces were William Dudley Pelley's Silver Shirts, which never numbered over 50,000 but whose leader annually sold about 1 million pamphlets and periodicals. The Reverend Gerald B. Winrod's Protestant group, Defenders of the Christian Faith, published the monthly *Defender Magazine* with a circulation of 100,000.

And the German-American Bund, the small but vociferous American Nazi movement, numbered about 25,000, including some 8,000 uniformed Storm Troopers. By far the most influential of the anti-Semitic demagogues was the Catholic priest Father Charles E. Coughlin, whose weekly tabloid *Social Justice* circulated to more than 200,000 subscribers and whose Sunday radio broadcasts were regularly heard by 3.5 million listeners along with an additional 10 million who tuned in at least once a month. Within a few months of America's entry into World War II, these main voices of organized anti-Semitism were effectively silenced. But their message of hatred and fear had by then reached millions of Americans.[10]

All four of these leading voices of hatred toward Jews emphasized a brand of political anti-Semitism that had circulated extensively in Western society since World War I. It focused on an alleged world Jewish conspiracy that secretly wielded vast international economic and political power. These "international Jews" supposedly manipulated the capitalist system through their stranglehold on international finance, and simultaneously controlled the Soviet Union as well as the international Communist movement. Their alleged objective was to increase their power to the point where they could rule the world. While the theory as a whole was too extreme for wide acceptance, parts of this mythology spread in American society: for instance, that the Jews were Communists and that they were at the same time capitalist manipulators intentionally imposing the Depression on the country.[11]

While there is no way to measure the specific impact of the anti-Semitic demagogues on American society, it seems very likely that their influence contributed importantly to the polling results cited above that pointed to 35 to 40 percent approval for a large-scale anti-Jewish campaign. In fact, the outlines of such a campaign began to take shape in 1938 as thousands of Coughlin followers formed Christian Front groups that distributed anti-Semitic propaganda and held frequent turbulent street meetings marked by the shouting of anti-Jewish slogans and the incitement of street fights. In 1940 seventeen Christian Fronters in Brooklyn were arrested after the Federal Bureau of Investigation discovered plans for a series of bombings and a program of anti-Jewish terror. Ultimately, none of the group was convicted, but by late 1940 the Christian Front had declined significantly.[12]

After the United States entered the war, anti-Jewish hatred again turned into violence, especially in several northeastern cities, where there were a great many incidents of teenage gangs beating Jewish schoolchildren. The worst and most persistent outbreaks—those in New York City and Boston—led to official investigations which were sharply critical of police negligence in dealing with the problem.[13]

Anti-Semitic attitudes were also found in the U.S. Congress, though they were not often openly expressed. The most flagrant incident occurred in February 1944 when John Rankin (Democrat—Mississippi), speaking on the floor of the House of Representatives, referred to Walter Winchell, a very well known news commentator of the time and a Jew, as "that little kike." Because Rankin was widely known to be a bigot, his comment might not have been totally unexpected. What in retrospect was most revealing was the almost complete absence of any rebuke. There was no outcry in the Congress. No outcry in the press. And none from the public. It was acceptable discourse.[14]

Troubling though the anti-Semitism of the thirties and forties was to American Jews, those who were hurt most by it were the Jews of Europe. Anti-Semitism in the 1920s had helped to bring the Immigration Act of 1924, which all but closed America's doors. But the anti-Semitism of the thirties and forties was crucial in keeping them closed. However, despite the strength of the anti-Semites, their victory in the struggle concerning American refugee policy was not a foregone conclusion. The opinion polls indicating 35 to 40 percent approval for a possible large-scale anti-Jewish campaign also showed that, if such a campaign had been launched, almost one-third of Americans would have actively opposed it. Clearly, a reservoir of sympathy for endangered Jews did exist in American society. And although many political, religious, and intellectual leaders, including President Franklin D. Roosevelt, turned away from the European Jewish catastrophe, a smaller number did try to mobilize this underlying concern and turn it into political pressure for American rescue action. The obstacles, however, were very great.[15]

During the spring of 1940, as the German war machine moved rapidly across western Europe, a near-hysteria swept America concerning the threat of Nazi spies and saboteurs infiltrating the United States. It was fueled by rumors that Germany's shockingly swift defeat of France had been significantly abetted by such internal subversion. The American media burst with stories about the supposed menace, publishing them under such sensational titles as "Enemies Within Our Gates," "Treachery in the Air," and "Hitler's Slave Spies in America." The threat of subversion was, of course, a legitimate concern. Care had to be taken to keep Nazi agents and collaborators out. But instead of adding reasonable screening precautions to the immigration procedures, the State Department greatly exaggerated the problem and used it as a device to cut in half the use of the already small quotas. In view of anti-immigration, anti-alien, and anti-Semitic attitudes current in the State Department, it is evident that the subversion issue was far from the only factor behind the new policy.[16]

Since his appointment as an assistant secretary of state in early 1940, Breckinridge Long* had been in charge of refugee policy. Long was virulently anti-alien as well as anti-Semitic. He kept President Roosevelt posted on his policies, and the president approved or at least accepted the steps that Long took. In an internal State Department memorandum in June 1940, Long outlined the methods used in implementing the drastic reduction of immigration: "We can delay and effectively stop for a temporary period of indefinite length the number of immigrants into the United States. We could do this by simply advising our consuls to put every obstacle in the way and to require additional evidence and to resort to various administrative advices which would postpone and postpone and postpone the granting of the visas."† The policy change was kept secret, but within weeks refugee aid organizations in the United States

---

*Breckinridge Long (1881–1958), an Assistant Secretary of State in the Wilson and Roosevelt administrations, assumed responsibility for immigration matters in 1940, and played a central role, from 1940 to 1944, in obstructing both Jewish refugee immigration to the United States and rescue initiatives.

†For the full text of Breckinridge Long's memorandum of June 1940, see the Appendix, page 203.

realized what had happened. They protested to President Roosevelt, to no avail.[17]

The 50 percent cut in immigration in mid-1940 was not the last of Long's changes. In the months that followed, he and the State Department concluded that there was increasing danger of foreign agents entering the United States disguised as refugees. In July 1941, Long further tightened visa procedures. Use of the quotas dropped to 25 percent (for a total of about 15,000 immigrants per year). This time, the State Department made the new procedures public. There were many protests. A small group of distinguished Americans asked to meet with President Roosevelt to request changes. The delegation, led by James G. McDonald, chairman of the President's Advisory Committee on Political Refugees and formerly League of Nations High Commissioner for Refugees, also included two leading Catholic prelates, the Most Reverend Joseph F. Rummel and Monsigneur Michael J. Ready; two Jewish leaders, Rabbi Stephen S. Wise and Paul Baerwald; Professor Joseph P. Chamberlain of Columbia University; and Hamilton Fish Armstrong, the editor of *Foreign Affairs* magazine. Roosevelt received the group, but the new policy remained in place.[18]

In the summer of 1941, as the new American visa policy took effect, the earlier German policy of forced emigration of the Jews was about to change to one of physical extermination. With the German invasion of the Soviet Union in June 1941, special mobile killing units (*Einsatzgruppen*) operating directly behind the front lines began systematically to destroy the hundreds of thousands of Jews in the newly conquered areas. For the most part, the method was mass gunfire, carried out at the sides of ditches. By the end of 1942, the *Einsatzgruppen* had killed more than 1.3 million Jews in eastern Poland, the Baltic states, and the western Soviet Union. The decision to extend the genocide policy to all the European Jews was probably reached during the summer of 1941, certainly by October 1941. To kill the Jews outside the eastern European regions where the *Einsatzgruppen* operated, six killing centers with large gas chambers were brought into operation by spring 1942. In the next three years, about 3 million Jews from across Europe were deported, mostly via freight train, to the killing centers to be put to death in the gas chambers.[19]

For many months, only scattered information about the mass killings arrived in the West. By mid-August 1942, however, strong evidence of systematic annihilation had arrived at the State Department. About two weeks later, but through different channels, the same information reached Rabbi Stephen S. Wise,* the foremost American Jewish leader of the era. Wise reported what he had learned to Undersecretary of State Sumner Welles, who asked him not to make the information public until the State Department had time to confirm it. Wise believed he had no realistic choice but to comply, for he could not risk alienating the one government department whose cooperation was most needed in the effort to help the European Jews. Only in late November 1942 did the State Department decide that it had obtained adequate confirmation. It then authorized Wise to make the dreadful truth public. The extermination news, now amply documented and confirmed by the U.S. government, received only minor attention in the American mass media. This pattern continued throughout the war, making it difficult for those who advocated government rescue action to build public support for it.[20]

On December 17, 1942, Great Britain, the United States, the Soviet Union, and eight other nations issued the Allied War Crimes Declaration. The declaration condemned Germany's policy of extermination of the Jews and pledged that the perpetrators would be brought to justice. Despite their condemnation, neither the British Foreign Office nor the U.S. State Department was willing to attempt to rescue Jews. The British recognized that any significant flow of Jews out of Axis Europe would place great pres-

---

*Stephen S. Wise (1874–1949), a Reform rabbi, was a charismatic orator, outspoken social activist, and the most prominent American Jewish leader during the first half of the twentieth century. He was one of the leaders of the American Zionist movement from its inception in the 1890s, and also co-founded the National Association for the Advancement of Colored People (1909) and the American Civil Liberties Union (1920). He founded the American Jewish Congress (1918) and the World Jewish Congress (1936), and chaired the American Zionist Emergency Council during the early 1940s. Wise's early and strong support for Franklin D. Roosevelt and the New Deal earned him greater access to the White House than any other Jewish leader, which increased his stature in the American Jewish community.

sure on them to reverse their policy of tightly restricting Jewish immigration
to Palestine. They had established the policy in the White Paper of 1939 in
response to Arab pressures. They were adamantly unwilling to modify it in
the years that followed.* The State Department also feared a large-scale
exodus of Jews from Nazi Europe because it would put pressure on the
United States to open its doors, at least to some extent. For both governments, the real policy, albeit unannounced, was the avoidance of rescue.[21]

Despite limited coverage by the major American news media, information about the mass killing of the Jews circulated in the United States and
Great Britain from November 1942 on. In Britain, Christian church leaders
and many members of Parliament joined Jews in calling for rescue action.
Pressures for governmental rescue action also arose in the United States as
the terrible reports spread. In addition to the minor coverage in the main
news media, the information was heavily reported in the Jewish press, both
Yiddish and English language. In early December, a Day of Mourning was
observed throughout the United States with special services held in synagogues and a memorial service broadcast nationwide by NBC Radio. A
meeting of five prominent Jewish leaders with President Roosevelt took
place a week later, bringing more publicity. The Allied War Crimes Declaration of December 17, 1942, was more widely publicized in the American
press than most developments connected with the Holocaust. Also in
December, one Jewish organization opened a campaign to break through
the news barriers by means of full-page advertisements in major newspapers. And on March 1, 1943, several Jewish organizations sponsored a "Stop
Hitler Now" mass demonstration in New York City that saw 20,000 people
fill Madison Square Garden with twice that number turned away.[22]

For a few months an effort to bring about American government action
was carried out by the Joint Emergency Committee on European Jewish
Affairs (JEC), a council of prominent mainstream Jewish organizations,

---

*In the White Paper of May 1939, Great Britain, which controlled Palestine under a
League of Nations Mandate, had reduced Jewish immigration to the area to 15,000 per
year. Actually, the British did not permit even that small quota to be filled. Even when Germany's systematic mass murder of the European Jews became known, the White Paper
continued in force, keeping Jewish refugees out of safe haven in Palestine.

including the American Jewish Committee, the American Jewish Congress, B'nai B'rith, the Jewish Labor Committee, Agudath Israel of America, and the American Emergency Committee for Zionist Affairs. The JEC developed eleven specific rescue proposals and brought them to public attention through a series of forty mass meetings held in twenty states during the spring of 1943. The committee sought help from sympathetic members of Congress. And it tried hard, but fruitlessly, to persuade the State Department to give serious attention to the eleven-point rescue program.[23]

In early December 1942, a campaign for U.S. government rescue efforts was also initiated by an organization called the Committee for a Jewish Army (CJA). The CJA had been formed a year earlier by a group of ten Palestinian Jews, then in the United States, who were connected with the Irgun Zvai Leumi, a Jewish underground militia based in Palestine. Called the Bergson group, after their leader Peter H. Bergson, these men had built the Army Committee into an effective political action organization. Once aware of the systematic annihilation of the Jews in Europe, they had worked to publicize the terrible news and to build popular and political support for U.S. government rescue action, centering their efforts on the call for a special rescue agency. The Committee for a Jewish Army pressed its cause with full-page newspaper advertisements, intensive lobbying in Washington, and a striking pageant called "We Will Never Die" that played to large audiences in several major cities. The CJA also sought to join its efforts with those of the Joint Emergency Committee but was turned down. A major issue was the strong antipathy of several mainstream Jewish leaders to the CJA's hard-hitting and sometimes sensational full-page newspaper ads. *Opinion,* a leading Zionist journal, characterized the ads as "glaring" and "garish," and accused the Army Committee of actions that were "gravely menacing to the unity and security of American Jewish life."[24]

Confronted with increasing calls for action in both Great Britain and the United States, the British Foreign Office and the State Department devised a stratagem for undermining the pressures for rescue. Representatives of the two governments met for twelve days in Bermuda in April 1943. The ostensible purpose of the conference was to look into ways to rescue the Jews who could still be saved. The findings of the Bermuda Conference were kept secret, but the diplomats announced that several recommendations for action had been sent on to the two governments. In reality, the Bermuda Conference recommended almost nothing in the way of rescue proposals. Nevertheless, its real objective was accomplished: It succeeded in dampening the pressures for action by giving the appearance of planning steps to rescue Jews. The Jewish leadership, however, was not deceived. The Joint Emergency Committee understood what had actually occurred at Bermuda and was devastated by the unmistakable display of indifference by the two great democracies. The JEC, its hopes dashed, never recovered its former momentum; it was disbanded in early November 1943.[25]

Despite the impact of the Bermuda Conference, the struggle for American government action persisted. By summer 1943, the Bergson group was the major group pressing for intervention. In July 1943, it sponsored a special Emergency Conference in New York City, where, working with such important leaders as New York City Mayor Fiorello La Guardia, Secretary of the Interior Harold Ickes, and newspaper publishers William Randolph Hearst and William Allen White, it developed several rescue proposals and discussed ways to persuade the American government to take the lead in carrying them out. A new organization, the Emergency Committee to Save the Jewish People of Europe, was formed to supersede the Committee for a Jewish Army. The new Emergency Committee continued and expanded the Army Committee's rescue campaign, using full-page advertisements, mass meetings, editorial support by newspapers, and lobbying in Washington. In October 1943, it organized a demonstration in Washington by four hundred Orthodox rabbis. Months of lobbying on Capitol Hill resulted, in November, in the introduction in Congress of a rescue resolution calling on President Roosevelt to establish a government rescue agency independent of the State Department. By the end of 1943, substantial support for the legislation was building in Congress.[26]

Meanwhile, in an unrelated set of developments, Treasury Department officials had found that the State Department not only had failed to pursue rescue opportunities, but had even obstructed rescue efforts that American Jewish organizations had attempted on their own. Treasury officials also learned that Breckinridge Long and the State Department had secretly cut immigration to less than 10 percent of the quotas. In addition, in early 1943 a critically important channel for the flow of Holocaust information out of

Axis Europe to the United States was blocked. This was arranged by middle-level State Department officials who instructed the American Legation in Switzerland to stop transmitting such information. The channel was reopened, but only after eleven weeks and then only by the chance intervention of a high official who was unaware of the stoppage. The Treasury officials revealed these and other findings to Secretary of the Treasury Henry Morgenthau, Jr., in a thoroughly documented reported entitled "Acquiescence of This Government in the Murder of the Jews."*[27]

Morgenthau carried the information to President Roosevelt in January 1944. Roosevelt, recognizing that an explosive scandal was imminent and realizing that the State Department's record would be debated within days when the rescue resolution reached the Senate floor, decided to avoid the impending crisis by accepting Morgenthau's recommendation that he establish a government rescue agency by executive order. The new agency was named the War Refugee Board (WRB).[28]

The War Refugee Board received little support from President Roosevelt and his administration. It became largely a Treasury Department operation in collaboration with private Jewish organizations. In planning its rescue programs, the Board worked closely with American Jewish groups, and most of its overseas projects were implemented by Jewish organizations in Europe. In addition, government funding for the War Refugee Board was very small. The Board expended $1,615,750 of government money, while American Jewish organizations provided more than $16,300,000 for WRB-sponsored projects. The fact is that 9 percent of this U.S. government agency's work was funded by the government and the other 91 percent by the private contributions of American Jews. In its sixteen months of action, the War Refugee Board played a crucial role in saving the lives of about 200,000 Jews. Approximately 15,000 were evacuated from Axis territory (as were more than 20,000 non-Jews). More than 10,000 Jews were protected within Axis Europe by WRB-financed underground activities. WRB diplomatic pressures, supported by its program of psychological warfare, were instrumental in saving 48,000 Rumanian Jews and 120,000 Jews in

---

*For the full text of the report to Secretary Morgenthau on the "Acquiescence of This Government in the Murder of the Jews," see the Appendix, page 187.

Budapest. (The extraordinary rescue work achieved in Budapest by the young Swede Raoul Wallenberg was carried out under the auspices of the War Refugee Board and it was funded by the American Jewish Joint Distribution Committee.) Nonetheless, as the board's director concluded years later: "What we did was little enough. . . . Late and little, I would say."[29]

KOOK, JABOTINSKY, AND REVISIONIST ZIONISM

Though sometimes overlooked in recent years, the indispensable part that Peter Bergson and his Emergency Committee to Save the Jewish People of Europe played in the emergence of the War Refugee Board was widely recognized at the time. This was true in the press as well as among political observers, including those who understood the situation best, Henry Morgenthau, Jr., and his associates in the Treasury Department. The man known in America as Peter Bergson was actually named Hillel Kook. Who was he and out of what background did he come?

Hillel Kook, born in 1915 in Lithuania, moved with his family to Palestine when he was a child. Before he was twenty, he had become an active member of the Irgun Zvai Leumi, the Jewish underground militia associated with Vladimir (Ze'ev) Jabotinsky,* founder and leader of the nationalist Revisionist Zionist movement. During 1938 and 1939, Kook worked in Poland for the Irgun, organizing the emigration of Jews from Poland to Palestine, in defiance of British restrictions on Jewish immigration to the

---

*Vladimir Ze'ev Jabotinsky (1880–1940), a Russian Zionist orator and activist, played a crucial role in bringing about the establishment, under British auspices, of a Jewish Legion that helped capture Palestine from the Turks during World War I. Troubled by what he regarded as the excessively cautious response of the Zionist leadership to Britain's shift away from the Zionist cause, Jabotinsky in 1925 established his own more militant wing of the Zionist movement, the League of Zionist-Revisionists. In 1935, Jabotinsky and the Revisionists seceded from the World Zionist Organization and established the New Zionist Organization, which advocated the immediate establishment of a sovereign Jewish state in all of the original territory of the Palestine Mandate (including what later became the Kingdom of Jordan) and mass European Jewish immigration to Palestine. Later, militant Revisionists in Palestine established an underground militia, the Irgun Zvai Leumi.

Holy Land. The outbreak of World War II in September 1939 halted his activities in Poland, and Kook, at Jabotinsky's suggestion, went to the United States, arriving on July 7, 1940.[30]

Several other Irgunists who had been working in Europe also moved to the United States, joining one member who was already there. Over the next several years this group of ten men constituted a small, American-based wing of the Irgun. They did not conduct underground activities in the United States, however, and throughout the war they were almost completely isolated from the Irgun in Palestine. Kook, who was the leader, adopted the name of Peter H. Bergson while in the United States. Consequently, these men and the broader movements they initiated were referred to as the Bergson group or the Bergsonites.[31]

The roots of Kook's career as a political activist reach back to the post–World War I divisions within the Zionist movement over British policy in Palestine. The League of Nations had granted England a Mandate, or temporary trusteeship, of Palestine on the basis of the British pledge, in the Balfour Declaration, to facilitate the establishment of a Jewish national home there. Within a short time, however, there were indications that London was backtracking. Jabotinsky and other Jews were jailed by the British authorities for taking up arms against Palestinian Arabs who launched anti-Jewish riots in Jerusalem in April 1920; Jewish requests to establish a self-defense militia were refused; and, in 1922, England barred Jewish settlement in the eastern part of Palestine, known as Transjordan. World Zionist Organization (WZO) President Chaim Weizmann[32] responded cautiously to signs of a pro-Arab shift in British policy, restricting his expressions of concern to private conversations with British officials, and remaining optimistic that London was still committed to building a Jewish homeland. This cautious approach was supported by the growing Labor Zionist movement in Palestine, which favored gradualist settlement activity as the way to build a Jewish homeland. Most American Zionists likewise emphasized the physical and economic development of the Jewish settlements in Palestine. Political Zionism—the drive for Jewish statehood—was to be held in abeyance indefinitely, pending the economic buildup.[33]

Jabotinsky, by contrast, favored dramatic acts of public pressure. He thought in grand terms, such as creating a full-fledged army, forming alliances with world powers, and establishing a sovereign Jewish state on both sides of the Jordan River. Jabotinsky believed deeply in the power of ideas and the influence of public relations. His opponents criticized him for favoring "words over deeds," but in Jabotinsky's view, "words"—ideas and principles— would motivate Jews to act for Jewish statehood, and would secure the international sympathy needed to move toward statehood. His disciples, Kook foremost among them, learned well from Jabotinsky and in subsequent years would put great emphasis on the power of rhetoric, whether in newspaper advertisements, congressional resolutions, or speech making.

Frustrated by what he considered the excessive caution of Weizmann and other Zionist leaders, Jabotinsky resigned from the Zionist Executive, the movement's ruling body, in early 1923. During the next two years, Jabotinsky established his own Zionist youth movement, Betar, as well as a separate faction within the World Zionist Organization, known as the World Union of Zionists-Revisionists. (The name signified Jabotinsky's belief that Zionist policy urgently required revision.) Eventually, in the summer of 1935, the Revisionists formally seceded from the WZO and became the "New Zionist Organization."

Most American Zionist leaders supported Weizmann's leadership of the world Zionist movement. They also felt comfortable with Weizmann's allies, the Labor Zionists, who favored creating a Jewish homeland based on socialist principles. The Laborites dominated the leadership of the WZO-affiliated Jewish Agency, which had been established in conjunction with the British government, in 1923, to assist in building the Jewish national home.* The Labor Zionists' focus on agricultural development

---

*The League of Nations Mandate for Palestine, which was granted to Great Britain in 1922, called for establishing a "Jewish agency" that would be "a public body for the purpose of advising and cooperating with the administration of Palestine in such economic, social, and other matters as may affect the establishment of the Jewish national home and the interests of the Jewish population in Palestine." The Agency was responsible for the educational and social services to the Jewish community in Palestine, in addition to being the representative of organized Zionism and Diaspora Jewry in discussions with Great Britain and the League of Nations concerning the creation of the Jewish national home. The Mandate authorities did not recognize the Jewish Agency as having any governmental authority in Palestine, but the Agency was widely viewed by the Jews of Palestine as their de facto government.[34]

projects appealed to American Zionists, many of whom thought of Palestine as a twentieth-century version of America's own westward expansion. American Zionist publications brimmed with accounts of heroic pioneers draining Palestine's swamps and making the Middle Eastern desert bloom, and they often compared the Palestine enterprise to the efforts of the settlers who built America. The ability to present Zionism in American terms made it more palatable to those American Jews who worried that their Zionist sentiments might be seen as un-American. This gave the Labor Zionists a significant advantage over the Revisionists in seeking the sympathies of American Jewry.

Labor Zionist leaders from Palestine periodically visited the United States to further cement their relationship with American Jewish leaders. Jabotinsky, too, undertook speaking tours of the United States in 1926 and again in early 1935. But he failed to forge close ties to the leaders of the major American Jewish organizations, in part because he had no substantial movement of his own in the United States to cultivate relations and carve out a niche for Revisionism in the U.S. Jewish community. Emotionally and intellectually, many prominent American Jews thus came to regard the Revisionists as outsiders, even as unwanted intruders, rather than as a legitimate part of the Jewish scene. This atmosphere of unfriendliness would help mar future relations between the mainstream American Jewish leadership and those of Jabotinsky's disciples, such as Kook, who would seek to make their mark on the American scene during the 1940s.

Shortly after the start of World War II in September 1939, Jabotinsky, then in London, had proposed the establishment of an independent Jewish army, based in Palestine, which would fight side by side with the other Allied armies under the Allied command. Its ranks would include Palestinian Jews, stateless Jewish refugees from Axis Europe, and Jews from nonbelligerent countries. Jews from Britain or other Allied countries were expected to join the forces of their own nations. An independent Jewish armed force would enable Jews, the people most victimized by Hitler, to fight back in their own units, under their own flag and leadership.

During World War I, Jabotinsky had successfully lobbied the British government to establish the Jewish Legion, which assisted the British conquest of Palestine and contributed to London's decision to issue the Balfour Declaration. With the onset of a second world war, Jabotinsky hoped the resurrection of a Jewish army would likewise serve both military and political ends. If a Jewish fighting force aided the Allies against the Nazis, presumably England would be more favorable toward Jewish postwar demands for a state in Palestine. The Zionist fighters, toughened by their experience on the battlefield, could then become the nucleus of the Jewish state's own army.

The British government quickly rebuffed Jabotinsky's new army proposal. With pro-Axis sentiment spreading throughout the Arab world, London feared the establishment of a Jewish army would drive the Arabs closer to the Nazis and lead to a renewal of Palestinian Arab violence. Furthermore, the British expected the Zionist movement to launch a full-scale campaign for Jewish statehood after the war, and were uneasy at the prospect of the Jews having a full-fledged army at their disposal. As a British Foreign Office report would later summarize it: "A Jewish nation supported by a Jewish Army under its own banner is only one step removed from the full realisation of political Zionism."[35]

Jabotinsky traveled to the United States in March 1940, four months before Kook arrived, intending to launch a major campaign for a Jewish army. He chose America because of Washington's presumed influence on London. The British were anxious to obtain American support for their war effort, a situation that could give the Roosevelt administration leverage on England concerning the disposition of Palestine. The challenge for Jabotinsky and the Revisionists was how to convince America's leaders of the need for a Jewish fighting force. A second reason for Jabotinsky to launch his campaign in the United States concerned the potential influence of the American Jewish community. Jabotinsky hoped to mobilize American Jewish wealth and political power on behalf of the Jewish army cause. The Revisionists also sensed the opportunity to fill a vacuum that had been left by the major Zionist organizations, which in recent years had consciously limited their political action campaigns for fear of rousing accusations that Jews were trying to drag America into overseas conflicts. At the 1939 convention of the Zionist Organization of America (ZOA), President Solomon Goldman acknowledged that the ZOA had "virtually no propaganda department . . . not even a publicity department or a public relations staff. . . . We have not until this day developed a steady flow of publications on Palestine. . . . We have made only the most occasional and fragmentary use of the radio. We have no Palestine films to speak of. . . ."[36]

Jabotinsky and his followers encountered formidable obstacles in their attempts to solicit political and financial support from American Jews. To begin with, they faced the same difficulties as the major Zionist organizations: the hardships of the Depression years left many American Jews less able to support Zionism financially; the American public's anxiety about being drawn into overseas conflicts made some Jews nervous about associating with controversial foreign causes; and American Jewry's instinctive sympathy for England in its conflict with Nazi Germany bred a reluctance among some Jews to challenge London's Palestine policy.

Beyond these general factors, Jabotinsky's appeal was limited by the simple fact that the political, social, and economic outlook of Revisionist Zionism did not fit well with the views of many American Jews, especially liberal Jewish leaders and intellectuals. The Labor Zionists favored socialism, and their trade union in Palestine, the Histadrut, frequently initiated workers' strikes. Jabotinsky denounced the Histadrut's advocacy of class struggle between Jewish workers and the Jewish bourgeoisie, which he feared would weaken the national effort to build a Jewish state. Violence repeatedly erupted between striking Histadrut workers and the Revisionist youths who were hired to replace them.[37] "The kind of a world that [Jabotinsky] wants is not, I believe, the kind of world that you and I want," Felix Frankfurter, the Harvard law professor (and future Supreme Court Justice), warned Rabbi Stephen S. Wise, the foremost leader of organized American Jewry. "The economic and social outlook" of the Revisionists would countenance "the abandonment of our liberties" for the sake of profits, he contended.[38] Jewish immigrants to America benefitted significantly from their labor union membership, and many of them had participated in strikes at one time or another. Moreover, prominent American Jews, including many Reform rabbis and leaders of liberal Jewish organizations, were actively involved in labor rights issues as part of the New Deal and the interwar progressive agenda. Without the protection of the Histadrut, one leading Jewish magazine warned, Revisionism would bring "the abuses of western capitalism" to the Holy Land and spoil the ideals "which have made Palestine a laboratory for social progress."[39] Revisionism's anti-labor image inevitably impaired its search for American Jewish support.

Jabotinsky's emphasis on the need for Jewish military preparedness further complicated his efforts to attract American Jewish support. The European nationalist movements of the 1920s and 1930s were well-known for their glorification of militarism, which made it easier for opponents to charge that Jabotinsky's interest in Jewish armed self-defense mirrored the style of European fascists. Labor Zionist activist Marie Syrkin denounced Revisionism as comparable to "German or Italian fascism," and Stephen Wise's son James, editor of the monthly journal *Opinion*, criticized what he considered the "fascist tendencies" of the Revisionist movement.[40] In a stinging public attack on Revisionism in 1935, Stephen Wise denounced its "militarism" and advocacy of "social exploitation" as evidence that it had become "Fascism in Yiddish or Hebrew."[41] Although Jabotinsky in fact denounced totalitarianism and championed liberal democracy, it was hard for the Revisionists to escape the impressions created by their emphasis on the need for Jewish military force and their clashes with Histadrut strikers.[42]

THE JEWISH ARMY CAMPAIGN

Hillel Kook, who reached the United States in July 1940, soon became acquainted with the obstacles to winning mainstream American Jewish support for any projects related to the Revisionist agenda. Kook immediately joined the handful of Irgun Zvai Leumi emissaries from Palestine who, under the name "American Friends of a Jewish Palestine," had been working since 1938 to raise money to buy arms for the Palestine underground and help fund its program of moving Jews from Europe to Palestine. Their efforts encountered strident opposition from major Zionist organizations. The Emergency Committee for Zionist Affairs (ECZA), a coalition of mainstream Zionist groups, in 1940 issued a twenty-six-page booklet, *Revisionism: a Destructive Force,* which asserted that these "viciously Fascist" activists were raising funds to sponsor ships that "resemble concentration camps in that passengers were hung to the mast and were refused food in retaliation for criticism or complaints."[43]

After Jabotinsky died, in New York in August 1940, Kook and his Irgun comrades decided to forge an entirely different political path, one that would shed the taint of being associated with a Jewish underground militia and concentrate on issues that might attract broad public support. They severed all formal connections to the American wing of Jabotinsky's Revisionist movement, which was known as the New Zionist Organization of America (NZOA).[44] Setting aside fund-raising for the Jewish underground and unauthorized immigration to Palestine, Kook and his colleagues began to focus exclusively on the Jewish army issue. In December 1941, with their ideas fully crystallized, they closed down the American Friends of a Jewish Palestine and established in its stead a new organization, the Committee for a Jewish Army of Stateless and Palestinian Jews. Kook also decided to adopt the name Peter H. Bergson while in the United States, in order to spare his family—which included some of the most prominent rabbis in Palestine*—any embarrassment that might ensue from association with his forthcoming political activities.[45]

Bergson's dynamic personality made him the natural leader of the new group. Samuel Merlin, an Irgun member who had recently arrived from Rumania, emerged as Bergson's right-hand man and chief propagandist. Irgunists Alexander Rafaeli and Yitshaq Ben-Ami† were also key members

---

*Among several of Kook's relatives who were religious leaders were his uncle, Abraham Isaac Kook (1865–1935), who had served as chief rabbi of Palestine, and his cousin, Yehuda Zvi Kook (the chief rabbi's son), who was a leading rabbinic scholar and head of his father's religious seminary, the Mercaz HaRav yeshiva in Jerusalem.

†Samuel Merlin (1910–1996), who was born in Moldavia, had served as secretary-general of the Revisionist movement in Poland and worked with Kook and other Irgun members organizing unauthorized European Jewish immigration to Palestine from 1938 to 1939.

Alexander Rafaeli (1910–1999) earned his PhD in political science at the University of Heidelberg, graduating shortly after Hitler's rise to power. He joined the Irgun and helped organize unauthorized immigration to Palestine before being sent to the United States in May 1940. Rafaeli at first went by the name "Hadani," one of several aliases he had used previously while on underground missions for the Irgun. After a brief time in the United States, however, he resumed using his real name. Rafaeli was a member of Bergson's inner circle and played a key role in its activities until late 1943, when he began his service in the

of the group. "We accepted [Bergson's] suggestions as the next thing to commands," Ben-Ami later recalled. "Though we were on a civilian mission involving public relations and political activities, we still considered ourselves a unit of a liberation army, and we kept a strict hierarchical discipline within our ranks just as we had in Eretz-Israel."

> It was the ultimate source of our strength. Our attitude was the same as that of all nations in time of war—accept discipline or accept defeat. Not that everything went smoothly among us. We never lacked for arguments. We disagreed, sometimes vehemently, about policies, tactics, and specific courses of action. But eventually a consensus always emerged, and when it did, we all adhered to it regardless of whether or not it led to bruised egos. It enabled our small disciplined group to achieve the impact we eventually had.[46]

Bergson's first Jewish army rally, which drew 4,000 people to the Manhattan Center in June 1941, featured as its keynote speaker the best-selling author and Dutch expatriate Pierre van Paassen,* who subsequently accepted Bergson's invitation to assume the chairmanship of the army campaign. Bergson was convinced that having a prominent non-Jew as head of the project would demonstrate to Washington and London that the army idea had significant support beyond the American Jewish community.[47]

United States Army. In 1947, he returned to working full-time for the Bergson group. (Alex Rafaeli, *Dream and Action: The Story of My Life* [Jerusalem, 1993].)

Irgun member Yitshaq Ben-Ami (1913–1985) was sent by Jabotinsky to the United States in 1938 to raise funds for Revisionist immigration efforts. He established the American Friends of a Jewish Palestine, and subsequently served as a member of Bergson's inner circle on the Committee for a Jewish Army, the Emergency Committee to Save the Jewish People of Europe, and the Hebrew Committee of National Liberation.

*Pierre van Paassen (1895–1968), Dutch-born but a resident of Canada since age sixteen, was a prominent journalist in the United States during the 1920s and 1930s. He wrote a popular syndicated column, served as a foreign correspondent in Europe and the Middle East for American newspapers, and authored a best-selling autobiography, *Days of Our Years* (1939), which helped alert Americans to the dangers of Nazism. He chaired the Committee for a Jewish Army from 1941 to 1942, but later severed his ties to Bergson under pressure from mainstream Jewish leaders.

Bergson used van Paassen's name to attract an array of prominent supporters. Each new celebrity endorsement facilitated endorsements from others; during its initial months of activity, the Committee for a Jewish Army was printing up new letterheads every four days. The supporters included two well-known theologians, Reinhold Niebuhr and Paul Tillich; a number of Hollywood personalities, such as Eddie Cantor and Melvyn Douglas; and a number of U.S. senators and representatives. One of their strongest backers was Senator Claude Pepper (Democrat—Florida), who agreed to address one of the first Jewish army meetings, in California. Peter Bergson and Ben Hecht,* who picked up the senator at the Lakeview Country Club in Los Angeles to take him to the meeting, had to wait in the lobby while Pepper finished his meal because of the club's prohibition against Jews entering the dining room—a reminder, in fact, of the era's atmosphere of anti-Semitic discrimination, which made it harder to convince American Jews to support controversial initiatives such as the Jewish army campaign. But where Jewish support was lacking, the Bergson group more than made up for it with the backing of prominent non-Jewish political figures. At their Washington rally on December 4, 1941, the Jewish army campaigners read aloud telegrams of support not only from Claude Pepper but also from Senators Guy Gillette (Democrat—Iowa), Edwin Johnson (Democrat—Colorado), and Styles Bridges (Republican—New Hampshire) and, most important, Secretary of War Henry Stimson.[48]

The Japanese attack on Pearl Harbor three days later further galvanized the Jewish army campaign. With America at war, Bergson's opponents could no longer claim that the project was an attempt to drag the United States into foreign wars. The Jewish army campaign could be presented as a patriotic endeavor, a way for Jews in Europe and Palestine to contribute to the Allied war effort. Furthermore, in late 1941 and for much of 1942,

---

*Ben Hecht (1893–1964) began his literary career as a reporter for the *Chicago Journal* and the *Chicago Daily News*, first gaining fame when he coauthored, with Charles MacArthur, the play *The Front Page* (1928), about life as a journalist. He went on to become one of the most successful Hollywood screenplay writers. In 1940, shortly before joining the Bergson group, Hecht was involved in "Fight for Freedom," an organization urging U.S. military action against Nazi Germany, and helped author the group's "Fun to Be Free" pageant.

the threat of German North African forces to Suez and the nearby Palestine Jewish community underscored the appeal and the logic of the proposal. Such a Jewish army would be immediately valuable in holding the Middle East; it could also permit transfer of some Allied forces from that region to other fronts.

Bergson forged ahead. "JEWS FIGHT FOR THE RIGHT TO FIGHT" declared the headline of the Jewish Army Committee's full-page advertisement in *The New York Times* on January 5, 1942. The ad featured 133 signatures, including those of three U.S. senators, fourteen members of the House of Representatives, eleven rabbis, five Christian clergymen, and various well-known authors, journalists, and entertainers. A call for Jews to take up arms on behalf of the Allied cause, especially coming so soon after Pearl Harbor, naturally resonated among many Americans. Additional ads demanding a Jewish army would follow—in the *Times* and elsewhere—each generating enough contributions to sponsor the next. (The list of prominent supporters grew steadily to include several dozen U.S. senators; over one hundred representatives; numerous governors, mayors, and labor leaders; and over two hundred college presidents.) Jewish political advertising of this sort was a significant innovation. Jewish organizations usually sponsored newspaper ads only to announce specific events, and even then only in the Jewish press. The Bergson group was venturing into unknown territory, by splashing a controversial political message across the pages of America's largest daily newspaper, where it would be read primarily by large non-Jewish audiences— "just as you would advertise Chevrolet motor cars or Players cigarettes," marveled Bergson aide Eri Jabotinsky (son of Revionism's founder).[49] Although a newcomer to the United States, Bergson had already grasped a basic principle of American political advocacy: A controversial cause needed to secure substantial public backing in order to gain the attention of the White House or Congress. The Jewish army issue had to be taken out of the back pages of the Yiddish press and brought to the attention of the broader American public.

Bergson studiously avoided any direct public criticism of the British during the Jewish army campaign. The Jewish Army Committee's newspaper ads extolled the virtues of a Jewish fighting force and the contributions it might make to the Allied cause, but refrained from challenging

England's refusal to create a Jewish army or its ongoing near-closure of Palestine to Jewish immigration. (Issued in 1939, a British White Paper directive limited Jewish immigration to Palestine to 15,000 per year.) Bergson feared that attacks on Great Britain, an American ally fighting desperately against the Nazis, might alienate potential supporters. He also believed that this moderate approach stood a better chance of influencing British officials. Although some Revisionist activists took issue with this approach, insisting that the British should be directly challenged, the Bergsonites regarded their strategy as completely consistent with the principles of Jabotinsky. "Merlin often solved our internal debates by saying, 'If Jabotinsky were alive, he would do it this way. . . . The teacher was not with us, but his teachings were," according to Ben-Ami.[50]

The British soon became concerned that the Bergsonites were gaining supporters. Their ambassador in Washington, Lord Halifax (Edward F. L. Wood), was becoming more and more irritated by the ability of the "nucleus of extreme revisionist Zionists" to "conceal [themselves] from view by the outer rim of misguided humanitarians of every stripe and colour who form the bulk of the membership of the movement." The Jewish army campaign "appeals to the average American, Jew and Gentile alike, with the apparently simple and moving plea that many thousands of Jews, anxious to fight and die in the war against Hitler, are being denied that elementary right by His Majesty's Government." Bergson's line resonated among Americans who already harbored negative feelings about England, Halifax reported to Foreign Minister Anthony Eden, adding, "I need not remind you that anti-British grievances still find fertile soil in American public opinion." As a result, the campaign "has thus far been received sympathetically both by the American press in general and by the large collection of eminent Americans whom it has managed to persuade to sign its proclamations," Halifax complained to Eden. "The impressive list of names" on Bergson's advertisements "and the cumulative effect of the repetition of such manifestos over a period of many months, is bound to sink in."[51]

The State Department, too, was disturbed by the large number of congressmen and other prominent individuals who were signing the Jewish army broadsides. Wallace Murray, one of the State Department's pivotal

Mideast policy makers, feared the "agitation for the formation of a Jewish army" was already having an "alarming effect" by arousing anti-American feeling in the Arab world. Some State Department officials thought that granting the Bergsonites a meeting with the Foreign Office or Colonial Office might slow down their momentum, but the British rejected the idea on grounds that giving the Bergson group an audience would mean publicly recognizing its significance or legitimacy.[52] The British Embassy had a suggestion of its own for dealing with Bergson: It appealed—unsuccessfully—to U.S. Undersecretary of State Sumner Welles to take action against American government employees who signed Bergson's ads.[53]

The Jewish Army Committee's most notable advertisements were authored by Ben Hecht, the renowned journalist, playwright, and screenwriter, whose credits included such major successes as *Scarface, Wuthering Heights,* and *Gone With the Wind.* Hecht was a thoroughly assimilated Jew whose ethnic consciousness had been roused by Hitler's persecution of European Jewry. "Our mission in the United States would not have attained the scope and intensity it did if not for Hecht's gifted pen," Bergson aide Yitshaq Ben-Ami later recalled. "He had a compassionate heart, covered up by a short temper, a brutal frankness, and an acid tongue. Once he decided right from wrong on any issue, he mobilized all his faculties to fight for his beliefs with righteous fury."[54] Hecht's first meeting with Bergson was a memorable event for both of them. "I was an honest writer who was walking down the street one day when he bumped into history," Hecht wrote in his memoirs. A column he wrote for the liberal New York newspaper *PM* in April 1941 caught Bergson's eye. In it, Hecht lambasted prominent American Jews who hesitated to speak out against the Nazi persecutions for fear of drawing attention to their Jewishness. Bergson immediately called for an appointment. At Hecht's favorite Manhattan hangout, the "21" Club, he met the man with the "small blonde mustache, an English accent and a voice inclined to squeak under excitement. He was Peter Bergson of Warsaw, London and Jerusalem."[55] Hecht's flair for catchy slogans and eye-grabbing headlines well suited Bergson's newfound interest in the use of newspaper ads to communicate his messages to the world.

A second early, and important, target of Bergson's Jewish army initiative was Capitol Hill. In February 1942, Bergson persuaded Representative Andrew L. Somers[56] of New York to introduce a congressional resolution endorsing the creation of a Jewish army. Here, too, Bergson was breaking new ground. As a general rule, American Jewish leaders were anxious to preserve their relations with the White House and thus did not seek congressional action on any issue without the president's approval. This was especially the case with the Roosevelt administration, to which American Jewry felt closer than to any previous administration. Strongly sympathetic to the New Deal and heartened by FDR's anti-Nazi rhetoric—even though very little had been done to actually aid Hitler's Jewish victims—more than 90 percent of Jewish voters had supported FDR in 1936 and 1940. Stephen Wise, the Jewish community's most prominent leader, was a devoted Roosevelt supporter and enjoyed occasional access to the president. Bergson, however, felt no particular loyalty to the administration. In any event, although he knew the White House did not support the Jewish army idea, Bergson derived encouragement from the fact that several senior U.S. officials, most prominently Secretary of War Stimson, had expressed their personal sympathy for the proposal. Although the Somers army resolution never came to a vote, it carried a warning: Militant Zionists were ready to press their agenda on Capitol Hill, with or without the approval of the White House.[57]

Representative Somers, Bergson's first and most enthusiastic supporter in Congress, was the son of a militant Irish nationalist and felt a strong kinship with Jewish opponents of England. The British Foreign Office mocked him as "the less happy type of Irish-American Catholic demagogue."[58] When the Bergson group decided, in 1941, to assign its first full-time lobbyist to Capitol Hill, Congressman Somers volunteered the use of his office and secretarial staff. Rabbi Baruch Rabinowitz, who had recently resigned his Maryland pulpit to work full-time for the Bergsonites, was assigned the lobbying mission. His days were crammed with meetings with senators, representatives, and their aides. Frequently he spent "a good part of my nights," as he put it, ghostwriting speeches about Palestine or European Jewry for Somers and other sympathetic congressmen.[59]

Part of Bergson's initial aim was to ignite a public discussion about the army issue, and the Somers resolution, introduced in February 1942, together with the ad in *The New York Times* the previous month, did just that. Indeed, the *Times* itself further fueled the debate by running an editorial condemning the army proposal; the publishers of the *Times* feared talk of a "Jewish army" would arouse suspicions about Jewish separatism and nationalism. The rival New York daily *PM* responded with an editorial strongly endorsing the army idea.[60]

Mainstream Jewish organizations were less than enthusiastic about Bergson's Jewish army campaign. Much of the problem was their concern that the dissidents might begin to usurp their position as the spokesmen for American Zionism. "Stephen Wise will not tolerate any other Jewish organization working for Palestine and stealing honors and publicity from him," Merlin charged.[61] To complicate matters further, the mainstream Zionist leadership also advocated the establishment of a Jewish military force, albeit in a somewhat limited form. The Jewish Agency called for creating a militia (rather than a full-fledged army) that would be based in Palestine (rather than fighting on other fronts as well) and would be made up of Jews from Palestine (and not necessarily include stateless refugees from Europe). The similarities between the Agency's proposal and that of the Bergsonites made it harder for American Jewish leaders to oppose the Jewish Army Committee. And since many of the attacks on the army idea assailed the entire concept of Jewish nationalism or Zionism, mainstream leaders often found themselves offering what essentially amounted to a defense of the army concept. Indeed, the British Embassy in Washington reported to the Foreign Office in July 1942 that the Committee for a Jewish Army "is officially frowned upon by orthodox Zionists on account of its Revisionist connexions and objectives, but its activities naturally are not entirely unwelcome to them and they tend more and more to take up the Army cry. . . ."[62]

Another factor discouraging mainstream Jewish leaders from publicly opposing the Committee for a Jewish Army was the leadership's perception that Bergson was gaining widespread grass roots support in the Jewish community. By late 1941, leaders of the women's Zionist organization Hadassah were privately praising the Bergson group for having "brought in new ideas and taken the initiative," while the Zionist Organization of

America's executive committee acknowledged that "there seems to be a sentiment in the country in favor of a coming to terms with the Jewish Army Committee." Even Nahum Goldmann of the World Jewish Congress, who would soon emerge as one of Bergson's most passionate opponents, noted "the growing strength of the Jewish Army Committee and the participation of many Zionists and important local persons in the public meetings and dinners held under its auspices."[63] At the urging of Hadassah, the ZOA, and Goldmann, the leadership of the Emergency Committee for Zionist Affairs initiated merger talks with Bergson, but insisted on the right to appoint a majority of the Army group's board members. Bergson's compromise offer of 50 percent of the seats was rejected, and the talks ended unsuccessfully.[64]

In the case of the Jewish army, both the mainstream Zionists and the Bergsonites aimed at the same basic goals: a Jewish military role in the fight to defeat Germany and a greatly strengthened Zionist position in Palestine at the end of of the war. Yet the two campaigns were never able to collaborate. At least three additional sets of merger negotiations took place, lasting into October 1943. They also failed.[65]

FIRST RESPONSES TO THE HOLOCAUST

The underlying differences and animosities that divided the mainstream Zionists from the followers of Jabotinsky during the 1930s and 1940s are crucial for understanding the inability of the two sides to cooperate on the army goal. They are even more important for understanding the conflicts that divided the two groups when, starting in late 1942, they were confronted with their greatest test: how to respond to the systematic extermination of the European Jews. In fact, in the face of the unfolding Holocaust, when the need for American Jewish unity became most urgent, the divisions intensified between the mainstream Zionists and the Bergsonites.

At that time, American Jewry was the most powerful Jewish community in the world. Its full energies were desperately needed in the struggle to save as many European Jews as possible. Yet during that time the animosities between the Zionists and the Bergsonites became stronger, the divisions became deeper, and the opposition of the mainstream Zionist leadership toward the Bergson group's actions for rescue could accurately be termed obstructionist.

Beginning in late 1941, reports of mass Nazi atrocities against Jews reached the West. In October 1941, *The New York Times* reported massacres of ten to fifteen thousand Jews in Galicia. A number of American newspapers gave coverage to a March 1942 press conference by an official of the American Jewish Joint Distribution Committee, who had just returned from eastern Europe and estimated that the Nazis had already slaughtered 240,000 Jews in the Ukraine region alone. In June, *The New York Times* and other leading U.S. newspapers published excerpts from a report compiled by the Jewish Socialist Bund of Poland, which estimated that 700,000 Polish Jews had been annihilated by the Nazis, many in specially constructed gassing vans. During the summer of 1942, major American Jewish organizations, jarred by the news of the massacres although not yet fully comprehending the extent of the catastrophe, held a rally at Madison Square Garden and memorial meetings timed to coincide with the traditional Jewish day of mourning, Tisha B'Av.

The World Jewish Congress representative in Geneva learned, in August, of the Nazis' plan to systematically murder all of Europe's Jews, and forwarded the information to Stephen Wise, American Jewry's foremost leader. As per routine, the cable was first routed through the State Department, where officials considered it unbelievable and declined to pass it along to Wise. When Wise shortly thereafter received the cable through another source and asked the State Department if the information was accurate, Undersecretary of State Sumner Welles asked him to withhold public comment until its veracity could be further investigated. Wise assented. More than three months later, on November 24, 1942, Welles finally reported to Wise that the information was accurate: 2 million Jewish civilians had been massacred as part of an ongoing systematic Nazi annihilation plan. Wise was authorized to release the information to the media and did so that same evening. This historic announcement, informing the press for the first time of Germany's campaign to exterminate the European Jews, appeared in *The New York Times* the next day in a seven and one-half inch report on page 10. *The Washington Post* allotted the news less than three inches, buried on page 6. Coverage in the rest of the American press was similarly sparse.[66]

Even more important, as additional information became available in the weeks and months that followed, the press continued to treat the systematic murder of millions of Jews as though it were minor news. Information about the European Jewish catastrophe, though readily available, was almost never adequately covered in the American news media until the concentration camps were opened in the closing days of World War II.[67]

The failure of the press to inform the public severely handicapped all efforts to build pressure for government action to help the Jews. Proponents of rescue had to devise alternative ways to publicize the crisis in hopes of building public concern and thus political support for rescue action.

The news of the extermination, and the apathetic international response to it, jarred the Bergson activists. Two million Jews "had been butchered," and 4 million more "were yet to be fed to the lime kilns and bonfires," Hecht later recalled. Yet there were few voices "protesting this foulest of history's crimes."[68] The Bergson group moved rapidly to rearrange its agenda. The rescue of European Jewish lives became Bergson's top priority. The new approach was quickly evident. On December 5, 1942, eleven days after the U.S. government's confirmation of the ongoing annihilation of the Jews, the Committee for a Jewish Army ran a large display advertisement in *The New York Times*. Written by the popular author Pierre van Paassen, its first objective was to dramatize and spread as widely as possible the recently released extermination reports. The second was to press for rescue action. On February 8, 1943, another large advertisement ran in the *Times,* this one under the headline "ACTION—NOT PITY." Again, the focus was the ongoing annihilation of the Jews and the need for rescue action.[69]

The very next week, yet another large Bergson advertisement appeared in the *Times.* "FOR SALE to Humanity: 70,000 Jews," blared its shocking headline. Written by Ben Hecht, the advertisement cited media reports of a Rumanian offer to help evacuate into Allied hands some 70,000 Jews held in the Transnistria region, where they were in imminent danger of death by German armed forces. In return, Rumania asked to be paid transportation costs estimated at fifty dollars per person. Bergson's purpose was not to raise the funds for a Rumanian Jewish exodus, but rather to publicize the idea that large numbers of Jews could be saved, in Rumania and elsewhere, if the Allies would take advantage of opportunities to do so.[70] It was a calculated and forceful rebuttal to the Roosevelt administration's contention that an Allied victory over the Nazis was the only way to rescue the Jews.

Immediately, a barrage of protest came from the established Jewish organizations and press. They angrily charged the Jewish army committee with deliberately and deceptively implying that each fifty-dollar contribution would save a Rumanian Jew. Jewish spokesmen castigated the activists as irresponsible, unethical, and willing to edge "very close to fraud" in order to raise funds.[71]

Undaunted, the Committee for a Jewish Army pushed ahead with its publicity campaign. From that point on, the Bergson group centered its efforts on building public pressure for rescue action and lobbying members of Congress and administration officials to create support for government rescue steps. Although the Jewish army goal remained, the rescue issue now held top priority.*

Mainstream Jewish leaders, shocked by the magnitude of the slaughter in Europe but reluctant to take issue with a popular president in the midst of a war, initially accepted the Roosevelt administration's "rescue through victory" approach. An editorial in the B'nai B'rith journal *National Jewish Monthly* in early 1943 reflected this viewpoint: "There is only one way to stop the Nazi massacres, and that is by crushing the Nazis in battle." The Jewish leadership had sponsored a day of nationwide fasting and prayer in

*Jewish Agency officials in London continued to lobby periodically for the Zionists' proposal for a Jewish army in their meetings with British officials. In August 1944, Prime Minister Winston Churchill, moved by the slaughter of Hungarian Jewry and hoping to impress American public opinion, consented to the creation of a Jewish fighting force. The Jewish Brigade, which reached a strength of 5,000 soldiers, saw action during the final months of the war and then played an important role in helping survivors emigrate to Palestine at war's end. The Bergson group, which had done much to popularize the Jewish army concept from 1940 to 1942, could justly say that the birth of the Jewish Brigade was due in part to its political spadework.[72]

early December 1942, but hesitated to take further public action, prompting criticism from some in the Jewish media. "Is one day of mourning an adequate expression of the horror and despair that clutch at the hearts of all true Jews?," asked the *Jewish Spectator*. "It is shocking and—why mince words?—revolting that at a time like this our organizations, large and small, national and local, continue 'business as usual' and sponsor gala affairs, such as sumptuous banquets, luncheons, fashion teas, and what not. . . . How shall we feast while our brothers and sisters are perishing?"[73]

In February, Hayim Greenberg's bleak and scathing article, "Bankrupt," appeared in the Yiddish-language newspaper *Yiddisher Kemfer*. Greenberg, a leading U.S. Labor Zionist, charged that "American Jewry has not done—and has made no effort to do—its elementary duty toward the millions of Jews who are captive and doomed to die in Europe!" He was especially dismayed that "the chief organizations of American Jewry . . . could not in this dire hour, unequalled even in Jewish history, unite for the purpose of seeking ways to forestall the misfortune or at least to reduce its scope; to save those who *perhaps* can still be saved." What, he asked, "has such rescue work to do with political differences?" Actually, as Greenberg conceded in his article, a start had been made, during the last weeks of 1942, toward action, even united action. But it had petered out by January 1943.[74]

As early 1943 wore on without evidence that Allied victory was imminent, some Jewish leaders grew uneasy with the "rescue through victory" approach. Jarred by criticism from some segments of the Jewish media and grass roots, stunned by newly publicized details of the Nazi genocide, and aware of the army committee's plan to hold a rally at Madison Square Garden on March 9, Stephen Wise and the American Jewish Congress scheduled a March 1 mass meeting at the same location.

The March 1 "Stop Hitler Now" rally set off another wave of publicity and activity on the rescue question. Significantly, this mass meeting was cosponsored by the two giants of the American trade union movement, the AFL and the CIO, and by two small voices of Christianity and liberalism, the Church Peace Union and the Free World Association. As the meeting date neared, a full-page advertisement in *The New York Times* urged the public to attend and to insist that "America Must Act Now!" The public did come: Twenty thousand jammed Madison Square Garden, while 10,000 others stood outside, despite the winter cold, to listen to the speeches through amplifiers. Thousands more had dispersed after being turned away once the Garden was full. Police estimates indicated that, in all, 75,000 had come to the rally. The roster of speakers included AFL President William Green, New York City Mayor Fiorello La Guardia, and several other prominent figures, as well as Stephen Wise and World Zionist Organization President Chaim Weizmann.[75]

Indicative of a changing approach by the mainstream Jewish leadership was a list of eleven specific rescue proposals approved by the mass meeting and forwarded to the president. It included negotiations with Germany and its satellites to secure refugee emigration; increased immigration of refugees to Latin America, Great Britain, and (within existing quotas) the United States; opening the gates of Palestine and establishing "havens of refuge" in Allied and neutral nations; Allied financial backing for rescue measures, including financial aid to countries bordering Nazi territory to encourage them to accept additional refugees; and, in a recommendation that partly foreshadowed the focus of later rescue efforts, the establishment by the Allies of "an agency empowered to carry out [this] program."[76]

One immediate effect of the rally was a change in the editorial position of The New York Times, which had previously advocated the administration's 'rescue through victory' approach. In the wake of the demonstration, a Times editorial asserted that "the United Nations governments have no right to spare any efforts that will save lives." Editorials sympathetic to the March 1 rally appeared in other leading newspapers as well. In an indication of the administration's sensitivity to unfavorable publicity, the State Department on March 3 released previously secret information disclosing that the United States and Britain were planning a diplomatic conference to deal with the refugee problem.[77]

In an attempt to capitalize on the momentum created by the Madison Square Garden rally, the AJCongress and seven other major Jewish organizations established the Joint Emergency Committee on European Jewish Affairs (JEC), which set about organizing similar mass meetings around the country. The American Jewish Committee, which previously had refused to take part in public demonstrations, joined the JEC and cosponsored the rallies. Forty such demonstrations were held in twenty different states during the spring of 1943. In some cities, Christian church groups or local divisions of the AFL and the CIO cooperated in the rallies. Thousands typically attended these events; in some cities, the audiences reached 20,000 or more. Speakers included nationally known Jewish leaders, important regional Catholic and Protestant clergy, representatives of the AFL and the CIO, and prominent political figures.[78]

The Synagogue Council of America, prodded by student activists from New York's Jewish Theological Seminary, launched a campaign to have synagogues around the country hold memorial services for European Jewry during the traditional seven-week period of semi-mourning between the holidays of Passover and Shavuot, which in 1943 lasted from late March until early May. The campaign culminated in a May 2 "Day of Compassion," jointly sponsored by the Synagogue Council and the Federal Council of Churches, on which synagogues and churches from coast to coast held special memorial programs featuring speeches and prayers about the suffering of Jews under Hitler.[79]

The Bergsonites adopted a uniquely dramatic approach, organizing a pageant, "We Will Never Die," to publicize the plight of European Jewry. Striking a chord of humanitarian sympathy among the Hollywood elite, Hecht used his connections to recruit numerous prominent actors for the pageant's cast, including Paul Muni, Edward G. Robinson, and Stella Adler, with a score by Kurt Weill. Billy Rose served as producer of the pageant, and Moss Hart directed it. In three acts, lasting ninety minutes in total, "We Will Never Die" dramatized the major events of Jewish history, world Jewry's contributions to civilization, and the Nazi massacres. Its two opening performances at Madison Square Garden on March 9 were viewed by audiences totaling more than 40,000. When "We Will Never Die" was staged the following month in Washington, D.C.'s Constitution Hall, the audience included First Lady Eleanor Roosevelt, hundreds of members of Congress, cabinet members, Supreme Court justices, and members of the international diplomatic corps. "We Will Never Die" also played to packed houses in Philadelphia, Chicago, Boston, and finally, in July, at the Hollywood Bowl in Los Angeles. The pageant struck the first major blow at the wall of silence surrounding the Nazi genocide, and thus it played an important role in raising public consciousness about the plight of European Jewry. This was crucial to the initial phase of the rescue process: The public first had to be made aware of the dimensions of the slaughter before it would be seen as a problem requiring the attention of the American government.[80]

"We Will Never Die" also became the setting for the first significant conflict between established Jewish groups and the Bergsonites concerning the plight of European Jewry. About six weeks before the Madison Square Garden premiere, Hecht, hoping to obtain broad sponsorship of the event, organized a meeting of representatives of major Jewish organizations to unveil the project. Bergson told the meeting he would refrain from using the army committee's name in connection with the pageant if the other organizations would agree to sponsor it. But festering intracommunal tensions proved too onerous to achieve Hecht's goal; the gathering dissolved in acrimony and insults between rival groups.[81]

Later, when the American Jewish Congress announced its Madison Square Garden rally for the week before the presentation of "We Will Never Die," the Jewish army committee offered to stage the pageant as a joint project and to cooperate with the congress in its mass demonstration. The pageant's script was delivered to the congress to be examined for possibly unacceptable material. The congress rejected that proposal.[82]

Obstruction turned out to be more of a problem than noncooperation. With hopes of informing many more Americans of the European Jewish tragedy, the Committee for a Jewish Army pressed forward after the Hollywood presentation with arrangements to stage "We Will Never Die" in dozens of other cities.* Bergson supporters in Buffalo and Kingston, New York; Baltimore, Maryland; Pittsburgh, Pennsylvania; and Gary, Indiana, reported attempts by local mainstream Jewish organizations to bring about the cancellation of their showings. Local sponsors of the show in those cities were said to have been told that the pageant was the handiwork of

---

*For fuller information about the obstruction of efforts to present "We Will Never Die" in several additional cities, see the Appendix, page 207.

irresponsible extremists who were undermining the established Jewish leadership.[83] According to some accounts, Stephen Wise had even urged New York Governor Thomas Dewey to cancel plans to declare March 9, the date of the show's Madison Square Garden debut, an official day of mourning for European Jewry.[84] One Jewish journalist reported in April that almost from the start, the "most powerful single weapon yet produced to awaken the conscience of America" had, "because of the inexplicable intricacies in Jewish political life," been subjected to "action to wreck" it.[85]

Bergson shrugged off the Jewish establishment's opposition, but some members of his inner circle were more disturbed by the intra-Jewish fighting. "I can easily say that my struggle during those years was often harder, more tense and more depressing than the battles I was to know on the beaches of Normandy, in the flatlands of southern Holland and in Bastogne in Belgium," Bergson activist Alexander Rafaeli later recalled. "We fought against narrow minds. . . . The Jews were scared to demand help for European Jews and were frightened to fight against anti-Semitic politicians, primarily in the State Department." Rafaeli was amazed to encounter such fears among American Jews "in the middle of the 20th century, after the Jewish community had attained significant achievements and made an important contribution to the strength and welfare of the American republic."[86]

Although "We Will Never Die" did not directly criticize President Roosevelt, it helped reinforce a growing public perception that the Allies were doing less than they could to aid Hitler's Jewish victims. Certainly the British understood it that way. Their ambassador in Washington, Lord Halifax, complained to British Foreign Minister Anthony Eden that the Hecht pageant, which was "by implication anti-British," was "produced with great skill by Hollywood actors of the first water" and enjoyed "a highly successful tour of New York, Washington, Chicago, and other large towns."[87]

Meanwhile, the British Foreign Office, under pressure from members of Parliament and church leaders, had been urging the State Department to make some gesture on the refugee issue. Faced with the new stirrings in the Jewish community, as well as murmurs of discontent in Congress and the media over the Allies' apathetic response to news of the Holocaust, the

State Department moved to head off further public controversy by agreeing to an Anglo-American conference on the refugee problem. The twelve-day gathering, held in Bermuda in April 1943, produced little more than a reiteration of existing U.S. and British policy: tight restrictions on immigration to their own countries, no possibility of opening Palestine, and further preliminary exploration of such areas as the Dominican Republic and Cyrenaica (in Libya) as locales to which small numbers of refugees might one day be sent. The results of the Bermuda Conference were so meager, in fact, that the conferees decided to keep their recommendations secret to avoid risking embarrassment.[88]

The Roosevelt administration underestimated the anger and disappointment that the Bermuda fiasco would provoke in the Jewish community and beyond. Bermuda had raised hopes of Allied action to rescue Jews; the disappointment was all the worse because of the hopeful expectations it had created. The Bergson group set the tone. On the day the conference began, a Bergson ad in the *Washington Post* called on "the gentlemen at Bermuda" to take "ACTION—not 'exploratory' words." When the gathering ended, a Bergson group advertisement in *The New York Times* declared: "To 5,000,000 Jews in the Nazi Death-Trap, Bermuda Was a 'Cruel Mockery.'"[89] As a member of the U.S. delegation to Bermuda, Senator Scott Lucas (Democrat—Illinois) was particularly irritated by Bergson's criticism. From the floor of the Senate, he angrily denounced the Bergson activists as ungrateful "aliens" who were enjoying hospitality better "than they can get at any other place under God's shining sun," yet were "taking advantage of the courtesy and kindness extended to them" by attacking U.S. government policies. Lucas subsequently urged the State Department and the FBI to investigate if Bergson could be drafted and how he was raising funds for his newspaper ads.[90]

The debate over the Bermuda Conference was clouded, however, by a careless error in the composition of the "Cruel Mockery" advertisement. Bergson assumed that since the ad was sponsored by the Committee for a Jewish Army, he had license to print the names of the Committee's endorsers, including thirty-three U.S. senators, in a box alongside the text about Bermuda. But those senators had signed on in support of a Jewish army, not in opposition to Allied refugee policy; however only one, Harry Truman, resigned from the Committee in protest.[91]

One outcome of the Bermuda Conference was that its demonstration of the utter indifference of the British and American governments crushed the hopes of many proponents of rescue and made further efforts for government rescue action seem futile. The Joint Emergency Committee on European Jewish Affairs (JEC), formed in March by eight mainline Jewish organizations, had worked hard for several weeks to publicize the extermination of the Jews and had strongly pressed the State Department to take meaningful action for rescue. Within days of the close of the Bermuda conference, the JEC dropped into quiescence. Its public activities ceased, and its leaders met only three times from May until September. Several suggestions were discussed, including a march on Washington, a mass demonstration in New York City, and warnings to the Roosevelt administration of large-scale defections of Jewish voters in the 1944 election if rescue action was not initiated soon. But none of these steps was undertaken. Early in November, the Zionist organizations represented on the JEC succeeded in merging it into another Zionist-dominated rescue committee. Three of the JEC's four non-Zionist organizations dropped out, and the once hopeful united front on rescue was finished.[92]

THE EMERGENCY COMMITTEE AND THE RESCUE RESOLUTION

The Bergsonites, however, continued to splash their bold demands across full pages of the nation's major newspapers. While mainstream leaders still preferred a more cautious approach, the Bergson group was beginning to strike a responsive chord in the Jewish community. Grass roots dissatisfaction with the Jewish leaders' caution escalated during the spring and summer of 1943. An Orthodox monthly decried the Jewish establishment's "'sha-sha' policy," while the Independent Jewish Press Service urged Jewish leaders to "scrap our hush-hush mufflers and get ourselves a loud-speaker."[93] Even some of Bergson's political foes acknowledged that the activists seemed to have a better understanding of the needs of the hour and the sentiments of the Jewish masses. "They focused attention on the problems," the Labor Zionist journal *Furrows* wrote of the Bergson activists in a year-in-review essay at the end of 1943. By contrast with "the vacillations and temporizing of official Jewish leadership," the Bergson committees engaged in nonstop "advertisements and political agitation" to rescue European Jewry. "Their work succeeded in catching the legitimate Jewish organizations off guard and in demonstrating the inadequacy of Jewish leadership."[94] An internal survey by the Zionist Organization of America of 1942 and the first half of 1943 concluded that the conservative tactics of the American Zionist establishment had created a vacuum that "the irresponsible Bergson committees" were rapidly filling. "The popularity of these young men from abroad zoomed during this period of Zionist political inadequacy," it reported.[95]

In July 1943, the Bergson group did what should have been done at Bermuda, bring experts together to seek all possible ways to save European Jews. Its "Emergency Conference to Save the Jewish People of Europe" drew 1,500 delegates to hear panels of experts detail practical plans for rescuing Jews from Hitler—a blunt retort to the administration's claim that rescue could be achieved only through Allied military victory.* Significantly, the conferees consciously avoided discussion of the future status of Palestine. American Zionist leaders lambasted Bergson for his decision to put Palestine on the back burner, but he had become convinced that the rescue issue would never advance on the U.S. government's agenda if it was tied to the acrimonious Palestine controversy.[96]

The participation of prominent congressmen and labor leaders, as well as addresses by former President Herbert Hoover and New York Mayor Fiorello La Guardia, helped draw nationwide media attention to the conference. In addition to its consciousness-raising value, the gathering produced a new organization, the Emergency Committee to Save the Jewish People of Europe. It replaced the Committee for a Jewish Army as the primary vehicle for the Bergson group.[97]

The Emergency Committee attracted sympathy by appealing strictly

---

*For two views of the Emergency Conference to Save the Jewish People of Europe, see the Appendix, pages 211 and 213.

to the public's humanitarian instincts and deliberately avoiding political controversies such as the future of Palestine. Although mainstream Zionists chastised Bergson for downplaying Zionist principles, Bergson believed that finding the lowest common denominator was the key to attracting the support necessary to effect change. The Emergency Committee's simple plea to rescue the oppressed resonated across a broad spectrum of Americans, and that impressive range ,of support, in turn, increased the pressure on the Roosevelt administration to respond. A columnist for the left-wing political journal *New Leader* "nearly fell through the floor" when he "took a gander" at the Emergency Committee's list of sponsors. "Nestling cheek by jowl on one piece of paper," he marveled, were "Congressman James Domengeaux, bitter Southern reactionary," and "Erwin Piscator, left-wing producer," as well as "Lowell Thomas, Big Business propagandist," and Mary Van Kleeck, leading Communist Party fellow traveller," among other odd couples.[98] A cause capable of cutting so far across ordinary political lines could not be ignored by a president on the eve of an election year.

The Emergency Committee intensified the earlier campaign of national publicity and redoubled Bergson's earlier lobbying efforts. In August and September 1943, the frequency of the large newspaper advertisements was increased, while at the same time William Randolph Hearst ordered the thirty-four newspapers in his chain to print a series of editorials advocating the Emergency Committee's plans. Bergson's ability to attract so much attention and the impressive array of prominent Americans affiliated with his cause made it politically difficult for Secretary of State Cordell Hull to refuse Bergson's request for a meeting. On August 12, Hull reluctantly met with Bergson and two colleagues, American Labor Party leader Dean Alfange, who was cochairman of the Emergency Committee, and the famous sculptor Jo Davidson. The group's central demand, voiced to Hull and at meetings Bergson held subsequently with lower-level State Department officials, was that the government establish a special commission devoted to the rescue of Jews from Hitler. The idea was futher galvanized by the State Department's August 1943 announcement that it had created a commission to rescue famous works of art and architecture that were endangered by the hostilities in Europe. Hull was predictably noncommittal.[99]

Also sitting in on the meeting with Hull was Breckinridge Long, the assistant secretary in charge of refugee matters. Long, whose private diary reveals anti-Jewish prejudice, bitterly opposed the immigration of European Jews to the United States and used his office to obstruct rescue proposals. Given Long's prominence in the State Department, Bergson had little reason for hope of making much headway there.[100]

A simultaneous approach to the White House initially seemed promising. On the eve of Roosevelt's meeting with Winston Churchill in Quebec on August 19, Bergson announced he was sending a delegation, headed by Congressman Somers, to personally present the Allied leaders with a plea for rescue action. Full-page advertisements headlined "32 United Nations and One Forgotten People" appeared in the Quebec press. White House Secretary Stephen T. Early, hoping to head off embarrassing publicity over the refugee issue, sent Bergson a telegram offering a meeting at the White House if he would refrain from sending the Somers delegation to Quebec. Bergson managed to contact the delegation in Montreal, instructed them to return to the United States, and informed Early of his acceptance of the offer. Despite repeated calls and letters to the White House in the weeks to follow, however, the meeting never materalized.[101]

Bergson realized there was no alternative but to press ahead with the rescue campaign via publicity and Capitol Hill. On October 6, just days before Yom Kippur, the Bergsonites organized a march on Washington by more than four hundred rabbis to demand U.S. intervention to rescue European Jewry. The dramatic event attracted substantial media coverage, in part because Roosevelt refused to meet the protesters. Both Stephen Wise and Roosevelt's closest adviser on Jewish affairs, American Jewish Committee member Samuel Rosenman, had urged him to avoid the rabbis.[102] The Yiddish press, in reporting what some called FDR's snub of the protesters, published unprecedented criticism of FDR, and the Bergson group gained substantial new support both among grass roots American Jews and in Congress. British Embassy officials sarcastically dismissed the protest as "a 'March on Washington' in Pullman [train] cars," but they could not hide their growing irritation over the activities of "the indefatigable Mr. Bergson."[103] Additional protests soon followed. A week of prayer for European Jewry, organized by Bergson with the participation of six thousand churches, coincided with the Jewish High Holidays. A rally at Carnegie Hall on October 31 honored Denmark and Sweden for engineering the rescue of Danish Jewry.[104] Such events helped keep the plight of Europe's Jews in the limelight and maintain public interest in the rescue issue. The focus on Denmark and Sweden, like the convening of the rescue conference the previous July, was an attempt to buttress the argument that rescue was feasible. Instead of merely complaining about Allied apathy toward European Jewry, Bergson sought to draw positive attention to specific ideas for rescue and examples of nations that had successfully aided refugees.

Amidst the intensifying campaign for rescue came a new overture to Bergson from the Zionist establishment. This time, however, it came from Dr. Abba Hillel Silver, whose more forceful brand of Zionist advocacy had attracted a broad following among activist-minded grass roots Jews and, in August 1943, propelled him to the cochairmanship of the American Zionist Emergency Council (AZEC) as a counterweight to the more conservative Stephen Wise. But much had changed since the negotiations between Bergson and the establishment in 1941–42. In those days, Bergson's Jewish Army group was new, relatively small, and prepared to make substantial concessions to the established Zionist leadership, only to find that the establishment was not willing to compromise.[105] By the autumn of 1943, however, Bergson had become a force on the political scene, with the backing of numerous congressmen and celebrities. When Silver spoke of the need to "integrate" Bergson's work with that of the AZEC, Bergson responded with nothing more than "a general expression of good will and desire to avert controversy and conflict" with the AZEC.[106] Bergson and Silver went their separate ways.

If Bergson's success stimulated some Jewish leaders to consider cooperating with him, it provoked others to look for ways to undermine him. Stephen Wise, together with Nahum Goldmann of the World Jewish Congress, vigorously denounced Bergson during a meeting with Long on October 6. Goldmann met again with State Department officials in the months to follow, as did Morris Waldman, executive vice president of the American Jewish Committee. Bergson's success had stimulated these

Jewish leaders' fears that the dissidents were usurping the established leadership, and they labored to impress upon government officials that Bergson did not represent American Jewish opinion. They also expressed concerns that the Bergson group's criticism of the Allies might "lead to increased anti-Semitism" in the United States.[107] Their solution: Either draft Bergson or deport him. Officials at both the Justice Department and the State Department explored the suggestions, but ultimately advised that making a "martyr" out of Bergson would be worse than leaving him alone.[108]

Although Jewish leaders understood Bergson's rhetoric as critical of the Allies, he had in fact consciously refrained from publicly criticizing the popular President Roosevelt until late 1943. In November, the Bergson group crossed that line with a biting Ben Hecht full-page ad describing the ghost of his "Uncle Abraham," a victim of the Nazis, "sitting on the window sill two feet away from Mr. Roosevelt," waiting in vain for the president to take some steps to help save Europe's remaining Jews. The silence of the Allies was a death sentence for the Jews, the advertisement warned: "The Germans will think that when they kill Jews, Stalin, Roosevelt and Churchill pretend nothing is happening." According to Hecht, two days after the publication of "My Uncle Abraham Reports . . . ," financier Bernard Baruch, adviser to the president, complained to Hecht that FDR was "very upset" about the ad and pleaded for a moratorium on such attacks.[109]

The Bergsonites understood that if the president was upset, he must be paying attention to their protests, and if he was paying attention, then they were likely on the right track. "The administration was feeling our pressure," Ben-Ami concluded.[110] They pressed ahead with the next stage in their rescue campaign: congressional intervention. At Bergson's behest, a resolution was introduced in both the Senate and the House of Representatives on November 9, urging the administration to create a commission of experts "to formulate and effectuate a plan of immediate action" to rescue Jews from Hitler.* It was presented as a nonbinding resolution, since

---

*For the full text of the rescue resolution, see the Appendix, page 215.

it was unrealistic to expect Congress to compel the president, in wartime, to take a war-related step that the administration opposed. Bergson believed that even a nonbinding resolution would help increase the pressure on Roosevelt to intervene on behalf of the refugees.[111] The key sponsors of the bill were Senator Guy Gillette (Democrat—Iowa)—whom the British Foreign Office, explaining Gillette's support for Bergson, characterized as "a simple, confused but very honest Presbyterian"[112]—and Representative Will Rogers, Jr. (Democrat—California), who later explained that his Native American heritage sensitized him to the suffering of ethnic minorities, arousing his interest in the plight of the Jews.[113] "The Jewish problem has entered the realm of national American politics," a U.S. Labor Zionist journal remarked on the eve of the hearings on the Gillette-Rogers resolution. "It will be discussed when the resolution will be placed before Congress. The Revisionist group which won over a group of congressmen may rightly take credit for it."[114]

Bergson launched a fresh round of newspaper ads urging public support for the rescue resolution. Jarring headlines asked, "How Well Are You Sleeping?" and described the resolution as "A Race Against Death." William Randolph Hearst gave the campaign an important boost by instructing his newspapers to run editorials endorsing the resolution. Bergson also sponsored a series of radio broadcasts, some featuring American Labor Party leader Dean Alfange, urging passage of the resolution.[115]

The hearings in the House Foreign Affairs Committee, which began on November 19, included endorsements by former Republican presidential candidate Wendell Willkie, New York City Mayor Fiorello La Guardia, and other prominent figures. When Bergson's turn came to testify, he ran into ferocious questioning from Representative Sol Bloom,* the chairman of the House Foreign Affairs Committee and stalwart defender of the administration's policies on refugee matters. (Bergson was the only witness required by Bloom to testify under oath.) Bloom's grilling of Bergson focused in large part on Bergson's personal life, especially the fact that

---

*Sol Bloom (1870–1949), Democrat of New York, served in the House of Representatives from 1923 until his death. He served as chairman of the House Foreign Affairs Committee from 1939 to 1945.

Bergson was not an American citizen. Bloom also devoted a significant amount of time to chastising the Bergson group for sending a telegram to supporters urging them to help "force" passage of the resolution. During the course of the hearings, Bloom repeatedly argued that the financial costs of mass rescue were prohibitive, and that the Bermuda Conference, to which he had been a U.S. delegate, had already explored everything that could be done to help refugees.[116]

Stephen Wise testified on the last day of the hearings. Earlier he had sought behind the scenes to persuade the sponsors to withdraw the resolution. When that failed, he decided to appear at the hearings and criticize the resolution as "inadequate" because it did not urge the British government to immediately open the doors of Palestine to Jewish refugees. Wise sought to give the impression that he fully supported U.S. rescue action and merely wanted to correct a flaw in the wording of the resolution. The potential effect of his testimony, however, was to hurt the chances for its passage. The sponsors had consciously omitted the Palestine issue in order to attract the support of congressmen who were humanitarian-minded but reluctant to tangle with America's ally, Britain, in the midst of the war.[117]

As it happened, neither Bergson's appearance nor Wise's was decisive. Instead, a blunder by State Department official Breckinridge Long unexpectedly mushroomed into national controversy. Testifying, at his insistence, to a closed session of the hearings, Long presented an array of facts and figures that persuaded the congressmen the United States had already been doing all it could to help refugees. Afraid they would seem heartless if they simply voted down the resolution, several of the congressmen, with Bloom's support, decided to publicize Long's testimony in the hope of thereby justifying their decision to shelve the resolution without a vote. The plan backfired. When the testimony was made public on December 10, 1943, reporters and Jewish organizations discovered that Long had presented wildly exaggerated statistics about the number of refugees who had been granted entry to the United States. He claimed 580,000 had been admitted since 1933, when in fact not more than 250,000 had come, and many of them were not Jews.[118] The State Department now found itself the target of denunciations from mainstream Jewish organizations, the media, and a number of congressmen.[119]

Even though Bloom, as chairman of the House Foreign Affairs Committee, had succeeded in shelving the resolution for the time being, the Senate Foreign Relations Committee unanimously approved the measure on December 20, and it was slated to go to the full Senate for a vote early in the new year.[120] Despite the obstacles created by Bloom, Wise, and Long, Bergson had managed, through effective lobbying, public relations, and sheer determination, to force his issue to the top of the public agenda. But Bergson's success reignited the Jewish leadership's fury, and intra-Jewish disagreements once again burst into full public view. On December 29, while the rescue resolution hung in the balance, the American Jewish Conference issued an eight-page statement blasting the Bergson group as lacking "a mandate from any constituency," seeking to "undermine" major Jewish organizations, "refusing to accept the democratic discipline" of the Jewish Agency, making "rash and exaggerated claims," and "bringing confusion in the minds of well-meaning people who might otherwise be helpful to the truly representative bodies in organized Jewry."[121] The AJConference's denunciation reflected the variety of sentiments felt by Jewish leaders—especially by Conference cochairman Stephen Wise—in the wake of the rescue hearings: resentment that Bergson was usurping their position as the preeminent spokesmen on matters of Jewish concern; jealousy at Bergson's success in attracting widespread support among grass roots Jews, celebrities, and members of Congress; and a deep-seated conviction, as Zionists, that the status of Palestine should not be separated from the rescue issue.

THE WAR REFUGEE BOARD

These divisions within the Jewish community might have hampered the chances for progress on the rescue issue if not for the fact that in early January 1944, as the rescue resolution was coming to a climax in Congress, a series of events involving the State Department and the Treasury Department was nearing a crisis point. Over the previous several months, in a sequence of developments unconnected to the activities of the Bergson organizations, Treasury Department officials had learned that the State Department not only had done virtually nothing for rescue but had even impeded the rescue efforts that some American Jewish organizations were attempting on their own. Treasury officials also discovered that the State Department had quietly cut the use of the immigration quotas to less than 10 percent, had taken steps in early 1943 to stop the transmission of Holocaust information from Europe, and had delivered altered documentation to the Treasury Department in an effort to cover up the information cutoff. The Treasury officials conveyed these and other findings to Secretary of the Treasury Henry Morgenthau, Jr., and met with him on January 10 to consider how to proceed.[122] Harry Dexter White[123] was particularly blunt:

If you take the role which our Government has played and which it has permitted England to dominate in the decisions with regard to the whole problem of the Jewish question in Europe, this Government has played a role that is little short of sickening, and there is only one man who can alter it, and one only, and that is the President. . . .

Roosevelt has the power to alter the complexion of this whole treatment in Europe if he feels keenly enough that he wishes to do so.

England will put obstacles, and there will be other obstacles, but he can do it by himself. And he will never do it by himself—he will never pay any attention to the problem, unless he is brought to the point where he has to make a decision.

To get FDR to that decision-making point, White proposed that "the matter must be brought to the President's attention to just give him a survey and picture of what the United States hasn't done and what he has permitted England to do on this whole question, and the consequences of that action in the last two years. Most of it is his own responsibility." White acknowledged that bringing this information to FDR's attention "without indicting him in his responsibility is a delicate task," but it could be done, he argued, by presenting Roosevelt with a carefully composed memorandum on the subject.[124]

There was also an electoral angle, as Roosevelt adviser Ben Cohen pointed out in a discussion with the Treasury staff as to how best to approach the president on the issue. As Cohen put it, "There is also a factor which you don't want to put in the memorandum [to FDR] which will influence the President and influence [Secretary of State Cordell] Hull. We all know that during this political year minorities are being exploited. . . . [A]ll the politicians are trying to exploit the value of minority groups, and the situation has gotten to the point where something has to be done."[125]

Here was a cold political calculation that no president could ignore. Although Jewish voters were generally assumed to be in the president's pocket, the leading contenders for the Republican presidential nomination, Wendell Willkie and Thomas Dewey, were actively pursuing Jewish votes as early as the autumn of 1943. Willkie publicly endorsed the goal of Jewish statehood, while Dewey appeared at a Zionist rally in New York in November 1943 and called for the opening of Palestine to all Jewish refugees. In his diary, Vice President Henry Wallace worried about "how vigorously Willkie is going to town for Palestine." Wallace also noted the advice Winston Churchill had offered earlier that year when FDR had spoken of the need to maintain good relations with the Arab countries in order to have a bloc of friendly states in the Mediterranean region. Churchill replied that "there were more Jewish than Arab votes in the Anglo-Saxon countries and we could not afford to ignore such practical considerations."[126] Morgenthau and his aides were motivated by humanitarian sympathy for Hitler's victims, but the president was more likely to be motivated by the election-year danger of the congressional rescue resolution becoming, as Morgenthau put it, a "boiling pot on [Capitol] Hill" that could explode into a nasty scandal.[127]

On January 13, 1944, Morgenthau's staff handed him an eighteen-page memorandum carefully documenting what they had learned concerning the State Department's intentional obstruction of rescue. It was entitled "Report to the Secretary on the Acquiescence of This Government in the Murder of the Jews." Three days later, Morgenthau met with the president. He went with two significant assets: a potentially explosive Senate debate was in the offing, and public criticism of the administration's lack of rescue action was reaching a crescendo. Armed with a shortened version of the "Report to the Secretary," Morgenthau urged FDR to preempt Congress by establishing the rescue agency that the resolution was seeking. Roosevelt, recognizing that controversy was imminent and realizing that the State Department's record would be debated within days when the rescue resolution was slated to go to the floor of the Congress, decided to head off the impending crisis. He accepted Morgenthau's recommendation that he establish a government rescue agency by executive order and charge it with doing all that was possible, consistent with the war effort, to save European Jews. The new agency, formed on January 22, 1944, was named the War Refugee Board (WRB).* The creation of the WRB represented a major change in the previously abysmal American policy.[128]

Morgenthau and his staff, as well as several leading newspapers, acknowledged the link between Bergson's lobbying efforts, the rescue resolution, and the creation of the War Refugee Board. "The tide was running with me. . . . The thing that made it possible to get the President really to act on this thing [was] the Resolution [which] at least had passed the Senate to form this kind of a War Refugee Committee, hadn't it?" Morgenthau remarked at a Treasury staff meeting not long afterward. "I think that six months before [the rescue resolution] I couldn't have done it."[129] And again, "You know about the Resolution in the House and in the Senate by which we forced the President to appoint a Committee."[130] The *Christian Science Monitor* reported that the establishment of the WRB "is the outcome of pressure brought to bear by the Emergency Committee to Save the Jewish People of Europe, a group made up of both Jews and non-Jews that has been active in the capital in recent months," and an editorial in the *Washington Post* noted that in view of Bergson's "industrious spadework" on behalf of rescue, the Emergency Committee was "entitled to credit for the President's forehanded move."[131] Bergson had emerged as a political force, playing a central role in bringing about the Roosevelt administration's most significant response to Hitler's annihilation of the Jews.

The establishment of the War Refugee Board filled Bergson with opti-

---

*For the full text of the president's executive order establishing the War Refugee Board, see the Appendix, page 217.

mism about the possibility that many Jews would yet be snatched from the Nazi inferno. The Treasury Department aides who had been involved in exposing the State Department's obstruction of rescue, and who then became senior staff members of the War Refugee Board, recognized and appreciated the Bergson group's crucial role in the events that led to the board's creation. They maintained a warm rapport with Bergson and met with him frequently during the spring of 1944 to discuss his ideas for specific methods of rescue. But Bergson was soon disappointed to see the wide gap between what he proposed and what the board was able to implement.[132]

One handicap was that the board was not provided with anything approaching Cabinet-level status or powers. For example, all its overseas contacts and activities had to be funneled through the State Department and thus subjected to roadblocks and delays.[133] But the primary obstacle to the board's undertaking a comprehensive rescue effort was that from its inception, the administration allotted it virtually no budget, except for the salaries and administrative expenses of its small staff in Washington and its few representatives overseas. Consequently, the funds for the actual rescue actions that the WRB sponsored had to come almost entirely from private Jewish agencies. Clearly, the Jewish organizations lacked the resources needed to finance a full-scale government rescue program.[134] Beyond that, Bergson was convinced that the very concept of subjecting a government agency to the push and pull of private sector fund-raising was irreparably flawed and severely hampered the chances of the board ever having the kind of impact he had originally envisioned.[135]

In May 1944, the Bergson group acquired a former embassy building in Washington and declared it the headquarters of the newly formed Hebrew Committee of National Liberation. The Hebrew Committee, made up of the small Bergsonite core group of Palestinian Jews and patterned on the French Committee of National Liberation, set itself up as the government-in-exile for the Jewish state (yet to be established) in Palestine. At about the same time, the Bergsonites launched a partner organization, the American League for a Free Palestine, a mass-membership body for Americans, Jews and non-Jews, who wished to support the goals of the Hebrew Committee. Frustrated by what they considered the ineffectiveness of the regular Zionist movement, the Bergson group hoped its new committee would constitute a spearhead for Jewish nationalism. This echoed, to some extent, a long-standing Revisionist demand for Allied recognition of the Jews as a nation with a right to its own seat at the table when postwar claims would be considered. In creating the Hebrew Committee, Bergson did not intend to jettison the rescue issue. In fact, many of the Hebrew Committee's newspaper ads and press releases dealt with rescue. Bergson also hoped that the Hebrew Committee, like the French Committee, might open diplomatic contacts that he could use to help the rescue cause.[136]

What Bergson did not anticipate was the vehemence of the opposition that the creation of the Hebrew Committee would stir up among the American Jewish leadership. Previously the Bergsonites had presented themselves as independent, nonsectarian activist groups that did not presume to speak for anyone but their own membership. Now, however, Bergson declared that his new committee was the authentic representative of Palestine Jewry and those stateless European Jews hoping to immigrate to the Holy Land. This constituted a direct challenge to the authority of the World Zionist Organization and the Jewish Agency, which considered themselves the sole legitimate representatives of the Palestine Jewish community.*

Bergson inadvertently lent his critics additional ammunition by asserting that the new committee would distinguish between "Hebrews" and "Jews." It would apply the term "Hebrews" to Jewish residents of Palestine and European Jewish refugees, and use "Jews" to refer to Diaspora Jews only, indicating a religious preference with no implications of Jewish nationality. Bergson thought assimilated American Jews would welcome a formal separation of Palestinian and European Jews from their American brethren. It may be that some did quietly applaud it, but by 1944, sympathy for Zionism had become the dominant sentiment in the American Jewish community, and Zionist leaders were increasingly the community's

---

*For some of the reactions of the Zionist leadership to Bergson and the Hebrew Committee of National Liberation, see the May 1944 State Department document on this topic in the Appendix, page 229.

most prominent spokesmen. Mainstream American Zionist leaders, who were an integral part of the World Zionist Organization and the Jewish Agency, were outraged by Bergson's challenge to their authority, and horrified by the "Hebrews" versus "Jews" distinction, since it undermined the basic Zionist tenet of international Jewish solidarity.[137]

Most of the established organizations and the Jewish press condemned the young "adventurers" from Palestine for their effrontery and flamboyance. Bergson was forced to divert a considerable amount of his energy to responding to his critics. For instance, at the urging of Jewish leaders, the *Washington Post* ran a series of articles raising suspicions about the Bergsonites' finances. Though the *Post*'s charges were shown to be untrue and were retracted, Bergson's reputation was harmed. The attacks and the negative publicity hurt not only the Hebrew Committee and the American League for a Free Palestine, but they also took a toll on the Emergency Committee and its rescue activities. Longtime opponents of the Bergson group, especially the Zionists, used the opportunity to successfully pressure a number of important supporters to break with all Bergsonite undertakings, including the Emergency Committee.* In fact, the American Zionist Emergency Council systematized the effort. It used the Bergson organizations' letterheads and newspaper advertisements to collect the names of hundreds of their sponsors and then approach them through telephone calls, letters, and personal visits. In this way, prominent Bergson supporters, including actor Eddie Cantor, Professor Sheldon Glueck of Harvard University Law School, and a leading Catholic liberal of Chicago, Professor Francis E. McMahon, were convinced to resign from the Emergency Committee.[138]

It is true that the War Refugee Board made a very valuable contribution. But its achievements, as its director, John Pehle, readily acknowledged, were "little enough; late and little." They were significantly limited by the failure of President Roosevelt and the rest of his administration, other than the Treasury Department, to give the board the support it needed for

*For an example of the pressures applied to Emergency Committee supporters to break with the Bergsonite rescue effort, see the Appendix, page 225.

a major rescue effort. In fact, the president's executive order establishing the War Refugee Board mandated that all government departments provide that needed level of support. It was clear at the time, however, that strong and persistent public pressure would have to continue *after* the formation of the board for that support to materialize. Such pressure did not develop. The mainstream Jewish organizations were not strongly active on the rescue issue. And the group that had carried on the long fight for the rescue agency now found its impact blunted by intense and widespread assaults on it. In the end, rescue never became more than a very low priority in the Roosevelt administration.[139]

The Emergency Committee did not go under. It continued its efforts for rescue, but from a decidedly weakened position. In April 1944, *New York Post* writer Samuel Grafton, whose column ran in forty newspapers with combined circulations of over 4 million, wrote a series of columns proposing a "system of free ports for refugees fleeing the Hitler terror," comparable to the 'free ports' in which foreign goods could be temporarily stored without paying customs fees. Bergson, seizing upon the idea, launched a nationwide petition campaign and sponsored full-page newspaper advertisements calling for free ports for Jewish refugees. The idea was endorsed and promoted by the entire Hearst newspaper chain, as well as by many other leading periodicals, church organizations, and major labor unions. When the War Refugee Board's executive director, John Pehle, brought the idea to President Roosevelt in May, he went armed with an impressive book of press clippings about the free ports proposal. By the end of the summer, one such "port" was created at Oswego in upstate New York, and 982 European refugees (89 percent of them Jewish) were housed there for the duration of the war.[140]

Simultaneously, Bergson initiated newspaper advertisements and a congressional resolution calling for emergency refugee shelters in Palestine. The Bergsonites saw the shelters plan as a way to open Palestine for the immediate emergency without getting the matter entangled in the politically complicated issues of the White Paper and Jewish statehood. Those questions, they concluded, could wait until after the war. The War Refugee Board sympathized with this approach, and a number of members of Congress endorsed the resolution, but opposition from the State

Department and the mainstream American Zionist organizations blocked the resolution's advance. The State Department warned that passage of the measure would anger the Arabs and set off unrest in the Middle East; the Zionist groups feared that sending Jews to Palestine with the understanding that they might have to leave after the war would establish a precedent that could impair the Jewish claim to Palestine.[141]

The free ports campaign was undertaken in the context of the crisis in Hungary. In late March 1944, German forces occupied that country; in mid-April, the Nazis began concentrating the large Hungarian-Jewish population into central locations; on May 15, mass deportations to Auschwitz commenced. Since the rapidly unfolding Hungarian tragedy was reported in considerable detail in the West while it was still happening, the Bergson activists were able to respond quickly to the new developments. The Bergsonites formed alliances with Christian Hungarian-American societies and clergymen. One result was that leading Christian Americans of Hungarian descent telegraphed the Pope and President Roosevelt urging action to save the Jews in Hungary. They also dispatched messages to prominent Hungarians calling for an end to mistreatment of the Jews. Their statements were beamed into Hungary by U.S. Office of War Information radio, as were excerpts from special services in support of the Jews that were held in Hungarian-American churches.[142] It was also in response to the Hungarian catastrophe that the Emergency Committee to Save the Jewish People of Europe sent a letter to President Roosevelt in July urging the Allies to bomb the gas chambers in the extermination camps. The committee was the first organization to make this recommendation to the U.S. government.[143]

After the end of World War II, the Emergency Committee disbanded while the American League and the Hebrew Committee focused full-force on the campaign for Jewish statehood. Using the familiar tactics of newspaper advertisements, lobbying Congress, soliciting the support of celebrities, and staging dramatic theatrical productions, the Bergson activists helped in the buildup of public and political pressure on Britain to withdraw from Palestine. Following the creation of Israel on May 15, 1948, Bergson reassumed the name Hillel Kook and took up residence in the new Jewish state, where he was elected to its first parliament.[144] After serving one term, he returned to the United States and worked in several private business ventures before settling permanently in Israel in 1970. He passed away on August 18, 2001.

Confronting the Holocaust

*When Hillel Kook first arrived in the United States, shortly after the out-
break of World War II, he devoted his attention to the cause of creating a
Jewish army to fight against the Nazis. But when it became known, in late
1942, that Nazi Germany had a campaign underway to annihilate all of
European Jewry, Kook quickly changed his focus to the problem of rescuing
Jews from Hitler. In this chapter, he recalls the shock of realizing what was
happening in Europe and describes his first attempts to publicize the need
for rescue, through unconventional methods such as pageants and newspaper advertisements. Kook discusses both the support he received from unexpected sources as well as the unfriendly response of the major Jewish
organizations to his rescue campaigns. Along with Kook's remarks, this
chapter includes some reflections by Kook's close coworker of those years,
Samuel Merlin, as well as recollections by two of his important allies, Congressman Will Rogers, Jr., and the historian and author Max Lerner.*

WYMAN: When were you first aware that there was systematic extermination?[1]

KOOK: When Rabbi Wise was quoted in the *Washington Post* story, in
November of 1942.[2] That morning was the most traumatic day in
my life. When I read it in the *Post*.

W: What was your reaction?

K: I ran to see [Adolf] Berle, in the State Department.[3] My first thought was disbelief. I hoped it was not true. I ran to see Berle. I went, I told his secretary I'll wait until he can see me. And he saw me. I said, is it true? And he said, yes, unfortunately. They've known it for some time. They told Rabbi Wise he should make a statement and they had to urge him to make a statement.[4]

W: How widely known do you think this information became to the public in general?

K: The fact that the *Washington Post* didn't put it on the front page speaks for itself. It was on an inside page. It *became* known, there's no question.

W: Given a few more months, do you think the population in general was aware?

K: Oh, yes.

W: Including non-Jews, too, right across the board?

K: I don't know. I lived in Washington and New York. The press here—we ran some of those ads. But of course we didn't run them in Tallahassee.

W: Do you think that Jews were particularly well aware?

K: Yes, I would think so.

W: Do you think that people in the government were certainly aware?

K: No question about it. We tried to mobilize government counteraction. This wasn't pogroms. Here was a decision of a major European nation, a very mighty military power, to declare a war of extermination against the Jews at a time when the other major nations—the United States, England, and Russia—were fighting that nation, Germany. And my reaction was that this isn't something we can do. The only thing we can do is to get the government to act. Our whole activity was zeroed and concentrated on producing government action. In two ways—one, by lobbying, and the other by building public opinion.

In the time of the period we are talking about now, after the news came out concerning the extermination of the Jews.[5] Nothing! I wasn't *acting* as a lost fellow, we *were* lost. We were hit with this thing by shock. And we felt something ought to be done, and we knew that [the mainstream Jewish organizations] are much more powerful than we are. It wasn't a question here that we had ideas, we hadn't any ideas, we'll take anybody's ideas. When it came to questions of what should we do in Palestine we had some maybe different ideas than [the Zionist leadership]. But on this we had no preconceived notions, there was no ideology, there was nothing.

I arrived here in 1940. The American Friends of a Jewish Palestine* was operating and had a two-room office and one secretary, but it didn't have the money to pay her. And, slowly, slowly we started plodding along. Jabotinsky died, and then this whole thing sort of— even we were affected by the war, the war wasn't going well. The whole world looked very bleak.

And then we started working on the Committee for a Jewish Army. We started early in '41. We didn't succeed in really launching the committee in a big way till late '41. It took us a whole year to get together a few respectable names, to launch a public thing in Washington and get someplace. Slowly we started gaining supporters, and people, and things started happening. I started going down to Washington. One day I got a phone call from a man called Emanuel Neumann,[6] who was then working for the Emergency Committee for Zionist Affairs [later known as the American Zionist Emergency Council]. I'd known him briefly in Palestine, he was an American who was in the Jewish Agency executive and one of the Zionist parties. We met and he says, "You look familiar," and so on. He had started hearing things from congressmen, and he started getting questions, you know, "Is [the Committee for a Jewish Army] okay? Is it this? Is it that?" they asked. Suddenly, we became a factor in Washington, politically. And we started meeting. He said, "Look, you guys are young, you have energy, you are just what the Zionist movement needs. Why can't we work together?" I said, "Who says we can't work together?" "You're for a Jewish army," he said, "I'm for it." I said, "Fine. Let's try and get it. We are

---

*The American Friends of a Jewish Palestine was established in 1938 by a small group of Irgun Zvai Leumi emissaries sent to the United States by Jabotinsky to raise funds for the immigration of European Jews to Palestine in defiance of British restrictions.

working for a Jewish army. If you're for it, now let's talk." And he initiated some conversations, but nothing happened.

Dr. Neumann was then the Zionist movement's man in Washington. He also originated the meeting between Ben-Gurion and me at his home, in mid-1942. To try to hammer out—just he, and Ben-Gurion, and I met, and after a few minutes he left. We were supposed to meet for half an hour. We stayed there six hours. At the end of which Ben-Gurion told me I was crazy. [laughter]

W: It took him six hours!

K: Yes. But, it had a very profound effect on him. He knows it. There remained a kind of a contact between us. Basically, what he did in 1948 was what we tried to tell him in 1942 was to be done. We said, "Look, you have to declare independence. You can't say there *ought* to be a Jewish state." Jabotinsky and Weizmann used to debate. Jabotinsky wanted the Zionist Congress to pass a resolution that the aim of Zionism was a Jewish state. And they said that this was too extreme, this would alienate people. They were afraid to say what the purpose was. They didn't say they were against a Jewish state. But they said that the Zionist Congress shouldn't formulate it that harshly. Then Ben-Gurion came here with the aim of getting a Zionist convention— it was at the Biltmore Hotel, it's called the Biltmore Resolution—to do what Jabotinsky said should be done four years earlier. So I told him, "Look, this is a debate that is cold dishwater. It's last week's pudding." Whatever the expression is in English for such an expression. There's one in Yiddish. I said, "This isn't the issue anymore. The issue is: If we want a country, if we want independence, we have to declare it and ask for recognition. Nobody is going to do it for us." You know, like anybody else. And he thought this was crazy. That's what finally happened, obviously.

So there were—this was the first contact with Zionists. Then there started to be a series of contacts. The first big meeting was in 1942, early, when we were already sort of in full swing with the Committee for a Jewish Army, running ads which shook them. Full-page ads then was an unheard-of thing. They thought this was obscene. For political—for

Jews! There were Jews on the obituary page of the *Times* or something, you know. Suddenly, an ad? So, they thought it was a disgrace.

At one point somewhat later on, there was a meeting between Roosevelt and Wise, in which Roosevelt very sharply told Wise that our work—all this yelling about the Jewish army and this thing—will bring the Arabs to an uprising. And that it would then need ten divisions from the war to overcome the Arab uprising and that this may endanger the whole war effort. And therefore, if the Zionists won't find ways to hush us up, he will have to take very stern measures against the Zionist organizations, United Palestine Appeal, and all these things. I don't know whether Roosevelt said it, that's what Wise reported. So Wise called a kind of an emergency meeting of all the Zionist pooh-bahs, all the big *machers*, as we say in Yiddish, and invited us, and we were put on the carpet, we were being given a thrashing. And Wise says that there are only half a million Jews in Palestine, and there are nearly 5 million Jews—so may the Lord help them—in this country, and what right do we have to endanger the 5 million Jews here, and this and that. So this was part of a pattern of contacting us in order to get us not to act, which continued throughout the years of the extermination.

And Wise, typical to what I call the ghetto Jewish leadership, which wasn't restricted only to the ghetto, surrendered without a word. He didn't ask Roosevelt who made the report, what report? I mean, it didn't even dawn on him to question him. To me it didn't make sense. I mean, I know the Middle East a little bit, as a student, and this figure of ten divisions is just a lot of nonsense. I mean, because the whole Lawrence business is good for a movie. Not for ten divisions then, and where are the Arabs coming using ten divisions? So we went—

W: He, after castigating your group or telling you to dampen it down—

K: We told him we wouldn't.

W: Your first ads about rescue were still in the name of the Committee for a Jewish Army, and they included the creation of a Jewish army as one of your demands. What really was the purpose in such an army?

K: To fight the Germans.

W: Because of the threat of attack on Palestine, because they were coming across North Africa?

K: No, because we felt that the Hebrew nation was a belligerent in the war. Germany was fighting—if Germany won the war, we would be obliterated, not in the sense of the Holocaust, which we didn't foresee, but Germany was more our enemy than the enemy of the British, let's say. And we felt that it was our moral duty and practical survival necessity to fight the Germans. We felt that an army—it was a purely political thing—an army should consist of the Jews of Palestine. You see, Palestine was neutral under law. A mandated territory is neutral. Jews in Palestine could volunteer, they couldn't be drafted.

W: Why wasn't that satisfactory, to volunteer for the British army? It's the same objective, it's the same force, the same enemy.

K: Well, because—for the same reason that a Frenchman doesn't want to fight in the Portuguese army. Eventually what happened is that the British agreed to establish the Palestinian units.

W: That's putting the cart before the horse. At first there was no Jewish army, and there is an enemy that needs to be defeated. Why not join the British army? Just as many Americans joined the Canadian forces before the United States got in the war.

K: Why? Because the United States could have been in the war and didn't want to.

W: And so if you wanted to fight in the war, you had to go to Canada. So you didn't have a Jewish army, so why spend your efforts on a Jewish army when you can join the British one?

K: We wanted to have a Jewish army because we felt we were a Jewish nation. We're talking about survival, as a nation, not as individuals. Also the Holocaust. I said that we wanted a Jewish army because we felt—

W: Was the thought in your mind that, come the end of the war, if we have an armed forces it's going to be very useful—and, of course, the British knew this—

K: Absolutely, absolutely. No question about it. Who do you think is the army of Israel today, or was? All the people who were in these units.

W: This was never mentioned in the publicity.

K: Well, you don't—why should you go and say that? To annoy the British? Make it difficult for them? But no—I mean, the Committee for a Jewish Army was an open, political, Zionist move, linked with the future liberation of Palestine and getting the British out of there. No question about it. But how do you advance it in time of war? You shape it down. You don't cheat. The British knew it. That's why they were against it. I think that in a practical sense, as the war became more desperate, and as the Holocaust developed, we relented. When the Holocaust came, I said, "To hell with a Jewish army."

W: That became a minor—

K: And the British—exactly, exactly. So when the time became hot enough, there was no reason not to say, "Look, we are willing to fight. We want to fight on our terms. Give us the dignity of fighting in our own name." Why should I change my name in order to go and fight the common enemy? When the war became very hot, the position of the Jews became desperate. We dropped the issue and accepted the compromise that the British offered. They did offer a compromise. So in a sense, the campaign was successful. And the compromise was Jewish Palestinian units in the British army. We said, "Fine." About 5,000 people served. Not 200,000, as we had called for.

W: Can you tell a little more about the attempts at unified action with the mainstream Zionists in the campaign for a Jewish army?[7]

K: Twice we reached an agreement [with the American Zionist leaders]. We worked out a draft agreement where we will run a committee for a Jewish army together. But their representative, Judge [Louis] Levinthal,[8] wrote a letter saying that they wanted to postpone submission of the agreement that the subcommittee had reached. Then he said he could not bring it before the executive committee as planned, but it would be delayed. And then it petered out. I just know it died. After a little while, it became obvious to *me* that there was no bridge.

W: I got the feeling from researching the records that they felt they had to absorb your group into the Zionist movement; otherwise, they didn't feel you'd act responsibly.

K: Fundamentally, they thought we were a nuisance. They just thought what is the best way to get rid of us, by attacking us or by trying to swallow us. At some point, they thought of trying to swallow us, by swallowing us meaning we will be a couple of guys who instead of $25 a week will get $125 a week and we will get some expenses and will be happy. They tried to make functionaries out of us. It was stupid! If ever they realized that we are not little guys who are working for their own ego and position as Jewish charity bureaucrats. They called us irresponsible. If you have some other motivation, you are irresponsible, as far as they saw it. "Responsible" means do nothing. I always asked them, by the way, to quote something irresponsible we did. It used to drive me bats. Because I really am a very cautious person; as a matter of fact I have a tendency to procrastinate because I am cautious. I check because I am an explosive person and I know it, so I recheck myself. I didn't trust my first reaction, in those days when I was working. Now when I talk, I let myself go because it's not that important.

In eight years of activity, what did we do that was irresponsible? And to hear this day after day that we were irresponsible. And they believed in it. To them, as I said, irresponsible is someone who is not a Jewish bureaucrat, who was not elected by somebody to some of their goddamned committees. They said that to run a full-page ad in *The New York Times* for the Committee for a Jewish Army was irresponsible. Within two years they were running ads in *The New York Times* about everything, even internal Jewish things—any damn parochial, Jewish thing which really doesn't belong in *The New York Times* is there. And *that's* "responsible."

W: But beyond the question of the Jewish army, after the genocide became known did you ever make overtures to the established Jewish organizations about working together for rescue? It seems to me that with what you had to offer in terms of techniques and skills and what they had to offer in terms of membership lists, organizational structure, and funding, that if you could have worked together you could have been very effective. Did you approach them, or they approach you?

K: We tried. And we didn't succeed. I felt a terrible sense of frustration. In December 1942—we thought we might be able to do something about the gruesome tragedy of the Jews of Europe. That was one month after the Wise announcement, when we were groping for a way to do something. After the story in the *Washington Post*, the first thing we did was try to go to them and were flabbergasted when we couldn't move them. We said look, something has to be done—there's a fire! Something has to be done about saving the Jews. And we got involved in the same kind of tedious negotiations which weren't so terrible when we were doing it for a committee on a Jewish army. That was sort of to be expected then. I could negotiate with them in the days of the Jewish army. I could not negotiate with them for any length of time when they started with matters of rescue. There was too much of a gap.

K: Once, though, I thought I broke through, in a meeting in Proskauer's* home. But we didn't. Did you see a poem that Ben Hecht wrote and Arthur Szyk[9] did a lot of designs around?[10] It appeared finally as an ad in various newspapers.† It was written in late 1942, because it was at the time of Christmas. It was a very sarcastic poem. It says, "Oh, Jews, don't be bothersome, the world is busy with other news. Burn Jews . . ." and so on. And the last stanza said, because it was based on

---

*Joseph Proskauer (1877–1971), an attorney from Alabama, served as an appellate judge in the New York State Supreme Court from 1923 to 1930. Active in the American Jewish Committee since the early 1930s, Proskauer rose to its presidency in 1943, and continued the organization's traditional opposition to Zionism until the endorsement of the Palestine partition plan by the Truman administration, and then the United Nations, in the autumn of 1947.

†The advertisement appeared in modified form in *The New York Times*, September 14, 1943, 12, under the title "Ballad of the Doomed Jews of Europe." The key stanzas, the first and the last, follow:

> FOUR MILLION Jews waiting for death.
> Oh hang and burn but—quiet, Jews!
> Don't be bothersome; save your breath—
> The world is busy with other news.
>
> Oh World be patient—it will take
> Some time before the murder crews
> Are done. By Christmas you can make
> Your Peace on Earth without the Jews.

a story which was on the side, by Goebbels, saying that by Christmas the job of exterminating the Jews would be finished. And the last thing says, "Oh, world, don't be sad" or something, and then he says, "by Christmas you will have your peace on earth without the Jews." And then we had this straight text.

You know, most of the ads had an eye-catcher to get people to read. We had some expert advertising people helping us and they said, "Don't write this dull copy that nobody reads. The more dramatic the situation, the more you need to do something to get somebody to read it." We did all sorts. We sometimes did straight copy.

Well, the *Times* set the ad, and there was this business of a shortage of paper, so we had to wait a little. But we had it set meanwhile. And it leaked out. Apparently some frightened Jew read it, somebody who got frightened and thought that this will result in anti-Semitism. "What do you mean? You are attacking Christmas. How can you make a sneer of Christianity speaking of peace on earth without the Jews, and tie up Christianity with murder?" And, it got to—somehow it got to where it got. I get a telephone call from a man called Herman Shulman, who was president of the American Jewish Congress.[11] He introduced himself, I knew who he was, I didn't know him [personally]. He said that something very important has come up and he and Judge Proskauer, who was then president of the American Jewish Committee—and this was the most prestigious Jewish outfit you know. To them we couldn't even get. We tried and got to some smaller guys around in those days, some small functionaries, but we couldn't get to anybody on the top level. And he says that Judge Proskauer and he would like to see me at his earliest convenience, that Judge Proskauer was a little ill, and would I come to his home. We set an appointment for the same afternoon.

And I came there—he didn't tell me what it was about—and I thought, "Wow! Something's moving [on the rescue issue]." And they told me that they'd heard about this ad we were going to put in the *Times,* started making a long speech about how important it is not to print it. And I interrupted them, and I said, "Look, if you feel—I don't think you're right—but if you feel that this ad may do some damage, we won't print it." And they were flabbergasted because they must have heard of other meetings at which we weren't that easy to get along with. And I surprised them by saying, "Look, I understand that you think it's damaging. We won't publish it. I can assure you. We won't publish it because the subject is, unfortunately, not one, that this ad, or any one ad, is going to solve. I don't believe that this ad is going to save the Jews of Europe, so therefore, if you think it's going to hurt the Jews of America, we won't publish it. It's as simple as all that.

"But let's talk what *can* we do about saving the Jews of Europe. Now you've told me what we should not do, now let's talk about what can we do." And I sort of went on talking and Proskauer started crying, just started crying. And I really thought I got someplace, you know, he was already an older man then. Part of the thing was the contrast. He expected to find a brash, unreasonable guy—and he found a little fellow who was saying, "Look, there's a terrible situation going on, what can we do?" I mean I didn't know what to suggest. I said, "We don't know, we just do what we can. We don't know if it's good or bad. We just feel that sitting doing nothing is not the thing. So, we do. But you're a wiser man, you're an older man"—I don't remember exactly the words—"you tell me what to do. We have people, we have energy, we have mobilized a lot of people, we have writers."

At the time, we were in the middle of the rehearsals for the "We Will Never Die" pageant. Because I remember when I came and told Ben Hecht that I withheld the ad, he nearly blew his top. I went straight from there to rehearsal, I remember, the Capitol Hotel where we were rehearsing, he was rehearsing, Ed Robinson[12] and the other people who were commentators in the pageant. We decided—as it went on a little later, we sort of made it clear to them that if you don't do anything, we'll return to do the best we know how, which means publishing all sorts of ads, including this ad. We didn't do it as a threat, you know. But at the time I told Proskauer and Shulman, "It's not being published. I'm going to call the *Times* now, and I'll take it upon myself. I won't even consult with other people."

W: Did Proskauer have any answer? Did he just cry? Is that all?

K: No, no. We were talking and we decided to call a meeting of—he would call a meeting of leading organizations. I said, "We don't know how the organizations work and I realize that the American Jewish Congress is Zionist and the American Jewish Committee is non-Zionist." And I said, "Judge, whomever you feel should be called, you call as many organizations as you feel necessary. I would like to see all of them. And I'll take some people from our executive committee and we'll come, and let's sit and try and put our heads together and see what can be done." What brought him to tears was the presentation of a lost person. I mean, I didn't pretend that we had wisdom. I wasn't crusading for an idea. I was a guy yelling, "Help!" And this somehow got across because I said, "I don't know what to do." So, I just had a feeling that if we raise enough hell, we'll get the American government to do, and anyway the more you yell it certainly can't hurt. And we talked a little bit about the importance that American Jews should know somehow, and getting radio, and doing all sorts of things that they [the Jewish leadership] had access to.

Radio, by the way, is a thing we worked like dogs on, and managed to get one broadcast, thanks to James Warburg, who was of the Warburg family, who were big Jewish philanthropists, but he was not.[13] He was a kind of black sheep, who was a nonbusiness one. He was a writer, and during the war he worked in the Office of War Information. And somehow, through somebody I got to him and somehow penetrated and he gave us a few minutes on the radio. The energy that you had to put out! Imagine, that these guys [in the Jewish leadership] could pick up a telephone and get ten broadcasts like nothing.

Anyway, so Proskauer called a meeting—on a Sunday I think it was, at some club. And I remember that we really thought we had made a breakthrough. I had a sense of accomplishment that now things would start happening, because there was the president of B'nai B'rith, Henry Monsky,[14] and I think Abba Hillel Silver[15] was there, and also about fifteen other people, all very prominent Jewish leaders. We came there, and we spoke, and this, and that. And they wanted to hear again that we were withdrawing this ad. They were very concerned about it.[16] I think the next time I saw Judge Proskauer was, I don't know, sometime in 1946 maybe.

W: Were you able to raise the question of what can be done?

K: No. Later, we published the ad. We couldn't even get him on the phone anymore. We waited some months and published it, and published several others in between. But it didn't make sense, it didn't make sense.

W: The only issue in this meeting was the ad?

K: They wanted just to get a repeated assurance that it won't be published. We came with the suggestion that this group should immediately convene an emergency conference of Jewish organizations. And we said that we would join, that we would stop functioning as a separate organization.

W: Did they discuss that at all?

K: Yes. But they never did it. And then I sent them letters, and I tried, but they never did it.

W: You know they already had a sort of an organization going, the Joint Emergency Committee on European Jewish Affairs, which included representatives from the Zionist groups such as the American Jewish Congress, and the American Zionist organizations, and the American Jewish Committee, and the Jewish Labor Committee, and the Agudath Israel.[17] So perhaps their reaction to your suggestion was "We already have such a coordinated thing going."

K: But what we were talking about was to have a very energetic, concentrated effort on rescue. Something dedicated only to rescue. We outlined all sorts of practical suggestions there, you know. And we had this resolution in Congress already pending, and all sorts of things.

W: Now that was the group that held a mass meeting at Madison Square Garden a week before your pageant. Wise ran it. They filled the Garden, and they had a tremendous overflow, and they made the front page of the *Times*.[18] And they came up with a list of suggestions, too. One focused on the question of war trials, retributions to scare the Germans.

Beginning in late 1942, a lot of energy went into the idea of getting the government leaders—Roosevelt, Churchill, and Stalin—to threaten the Germans that they would face severe postwar punishment if they continued their atrocities against civilian populations. Several such declarations were issued, but only one, in December

1942, pointed out that the Jews were among the victims. To have the Jews specified in these declarations was one of the first things that the Jewish groups came up with, and of course your group pushed it, too. It was a psychological technique of threatening with retribution. Do you think this had any impact?

K: The fact that the Jews were not mentioned did harm to the Jews. The Germans could say, "Look, they don't really care about them." And we screamed about that. I think it would have helped. Again, on the theory that what you had to do was put a monkey wrench. Maybe it wouldn't have affected Hitler or Himmler, but it might have affected [less highly placed Nazi leaders such as] a Kurt Becher.[19]

W: They do think it affected Horthy and the Hungarian situation finally.

K: Yeah, it may have affected a lot of people, a lot of people underneath, and had a slowing effect. The chances are it wouldn't have changed the basic thing, because these were maniacs we were dealing with. But there were thousands of people involved in the murder process, and it could have slowed the pace of the massacre.

Authors' Note: Throughout the war, Jewish organizations sought official U.S. government statements threatening postwar punishment for war crimes against Jews. Except for the joint Allied War Crimes Declaration of December 1942, however, the word "Jews" was routinely omitted from Allied statements threatening retribution for war crimes. This policy of attempting to evade acknowledgment that Jews were the primary victims became a matter of public controversy after an especially stern war crimes warning was issued in November 1943 by the Moscow Conference of American, British, and Soviet foreign ministers. It specified several endangered peoples, but again failed to mention the Jews. This set off widespread criticism, including the Bergson group's "Uncle Abraham" advertisement.

In March 1944, at the urging of the recently formed War Refugee Board, President Roosevelt finally issued a strong war crimes retribution threat that specifically referred to the killing of Jews. In May, when the deportation of Hungarian Jews to Auschwitz was begun by the Nazis with the collaboration of the government of Hungarian regent Miklos Horthy, the War Refugee Board launched an intensive propaganda campaign aimed at the Hungarian government. At the WRB's request, the U.S. Office of War Information repeatedly beamed FDR's message to Hungary, as well as subsequent U.S. warnings of postwar punishment for Nazi collaborators, appeals from Hungarian-American leaders, and the texts of congressional resolutions concerning the plight of European Jewry. These messages were also publicized through the neutral press and radio. And Allied aircraft dropped them into Hungary in pamphlet form. The combination of this propaganda campaign, the growing indications that Germany would lose the war, and unfounded rumors of Allied air strikes on Hungary as retaliation for the deportation of Hungarian Jewry, finally persuaded Horthy, in early July, to halt the deportations, just before the largest Hungarian-Jewish community, that of Budapest, was to be seized.[20]

SAMUEL MERLIN RECALLS:

They tried to avoid the word "Jew." At Bermuda,* for instance, the word "Jew," as much as it was humanly possible, was avoided. They used words like "unfortunate people," "persecuted people," "helpless people," there was a whole vocabulary of words, I mean, not even euphemisms, just words in order to disguise the fact. Our task when the war broke out—we knew that Hitler was determined to destroy the Jews. Our first concern was to break, to destroy, the anonymity of the victim.[21]

W: Let's move to another topic.[22] How did you raise the funds needed for your work? Meetings, dinners, the pageants—?

K: Meetings, dinners, the usual. "We Will Never Die," which worried us sick in terms of financial responsibility—Billy Rose was the official producer, but he made me sign all the contracts.

W: You had to pay these people, like Billy Rose, Ben Hecht, and Moss Hart?

---

*The Anglo-American conference on refugees was held in Bermuda in April 1943. See pages 10–11 of Chapter 1.

K: No, no, no, no. They did it free. So did the actors. The actors, we paid
    expenses, which were considerable, though. Say Paul Muni, we paid
    his hotel. And for us this was a lot of money. We had to bring them in
    from Hollywood; we paid them expenses. Billy Rose was a terribly
    stingy bastard, but he never took a penny. He was a very fabulously
    wealthy man, and he never gave [us] a nickel. But he did a lot of work,
    he did a lot of work, and very good work.

    Hecht—I don't remember him contributing money, but he spent
    it—a lot of money on us. For a while in the beginning, you know, the
    only decent meals we got, he even writes about it in his book, he
    begins, you know, that we were hungry.* It was true. It wasn't true that
    day, but it was true in general principle. But he's a dramatist. I mean,
    there was a time when the only time I ate a good meal was when Ben
    Hecht invited me out to the Algonquin. And I wouldn't go and tell
    him, "Look, invite me," but if I happened to come, there was the
    weekly steak sort of, you know. Ben was a very generous man. He had
    no sense of money, he didn't know what money was. And he knew we
    had no money, and everything in sight he paid and signed.

W: Did you have any big donors for the Emergency Committee?

K: No. Never. It was mostly people who clipped out those coupons in the
    ads and mailed them in. One of the biggest amounts of money we ever
    got for the Emergency Committee was through the "We Will Never
    Die" pageant, which was a financial success, you see, because the sell-
    out of the first performance in New York City more than covered the
    costs. And left a little bit of a profit. We weren't sure we'll sell out, you

---

*"I ordered a third round of drinks for my guests [Bergson and a colleague, Jeremiah
Helpern], unaware that neither had eaten that day. They kept their eyes firmly averted from
the platters of fine food moving to and fro under their noses—for they were Hebrew heroes
trained in self-discipline." (Ben Hecht, A Child of the Century [New York, 1954], 516.)
Also: "I asked if they had any funds. 'No,' said Peter. 'We have not yet been able to achieve
our personal budget of five hundred dollars a month—for our food and lodging.' 'How do
you manage?' I asked. 'Merlin and I have a room together,' said Peter, 'and we do our own
cooking.' . . . A cause without nickels, without cohorts, or a roof over its head, and with an
army that numbered six men and a pretty girl!" (Ibid., 535.)

know, we didn't know what's going to happen. But then, when we did the second performance, that same night, this was all net profit.

W: And when you went to the other cities with it, then—

K: That—Washington *cost* money. We used the money we made in New York to spend the money in Washington. Washington was by invitation.

W: But you put it on in six cities, didn't you? Even out on the West Coast—in Hollywood?

K: Yes, yes, yes, yes. We put it on also in Philadelphia, Boston, and Chicago, and it covered itself in these cities.

W: What were some of the other techniques you used, both as the Committee for a Jewish Army and then as the Emergency Committee, to build support for government rescue action?

K: One area was the full-page advertisements.*

W: What papers did you carry them in, besides *The New York Times* and the *Washington Post,* and the *New York Post?* Did you place them on the West Coast, too?

K: Yes, oh yes. We had a strong—our really effective committees were in Los Angeles, Chicago; a little weaker one in Detroit; very strong one in Philadelphia; New York, of course, which was the headquarters. And in Washington, there was a very strong Emergency Committee.

Once we ran ads in Baltimore, you see in Baltimore there was a committee. And then occasionally some other town, some people would get together, I don't even remember. I wouldn't say that we didn't appear in others, but these were fairly regular. What happened is we would run an ad either in the *Times* or in the *Washington Post* because of its political effect. If it got a good reaction, which to us was mail, in terms of contributions, we'd then scratch together the money to run it in smaller cities, with the hope that it will cover half, a third, two thirds of what it cost. Some of them did a lot more than cover

*From 1942 to 1945, the Committee for a Jewish Army and the Emergency Committee to Save the Jewish People of Europe published more than seventy-five different large display advertisements, utilizing at least forty newspapers in some fifteen cities. Altogether, well over two hundred advertisements were placed.

themselves. But most of the times these things didn't cover themselves. The money came mostly from constant fund-raising efforts, which drained us something awful. We did all sorts of things. It was a fairly sizable organization, involving many hundreds of active people.

W: If you had an ad with a good response in a pilot newspaper, say the *Washington Post* or *The New York Times,* then you would place it, say, in a Chicago paper, or a Los Angeles paper?

K: Right, right. Sometimes, though, the local committees would choose to do that—if they could scratch together the money, they put it in, anyway.

WILL ROGERS, JR., RECALLS:*

I think the most effective technique of all of the methods we used was the ads. . . . They were hard-hitting and they had simple typography. . . . They carried tremendous impact. . . . I can remember when they appeared in the paper, even around the halls of Congress, there was conversation. . . . I would go down to the floor of Congress and they would be talking about it. "Look at this." Or, "Isn't this outrageous?" Or "Shouldn't something be done?" Very effective. Very effective.

W: Do you feel that there was a conspiracy of silence on this issue in the United States press?[23] Your ads and activities helped break through the curtain of silence. But do you think this silence was intentional?

K: We used the words "conspiracy of silence," but I don't think it was an active conspiracy. It was more like a passive conspiracy. I don't think people had meetings and said, "Let's not say anything about the killing of the Jews." But the accurate phrase would be more like Ben Hecht's ballad, you know, "the world is busy with other news."

---

*Will Rogers, Jr. (1911–1993), Democrat of California, served in the U.S. House of Representatives from 1943 to 1944. Both he and his wife were active in the Emergency Committee to Save the Jewish People of Europe.

The paragraph that follows is from the interview of Will Rogers, Jr., by Martin Ostrow, February 17, 1992, Tubac, AZ.

MAX LERNER RECALLS:*

I knew something about how the press varied in treating critical issues. I had been editor of *The Nation* for several years, and later on in 1943 I became an editor of *PM*, a very liberal daily newspaper, and from my knowledge of the press I knew that the establishment press was whitewashing the story of the Final Solution.

I have asked myself a good deal why a story like this did not get played by the establishment press, which after all was pretty professional. It was a big story. . . . One answer . . . is the hypersensitivity of *The New York Times*, because of its Jewish ownership, to the question of how it treated news affecting the Jews and their rescue. . . . A good newspaperman, no matter how skeptical he may be when he sees a dramatic story . . . is bound to react to it with a sense of "I would like to be the first really to deal with this; I would like to get a scoop on it; I would like to have my name associated with this." But there were no newspapermen at that time who really felt that way. It's interesting that the great columnists, for example someone like Walter Lippmann,[24] who responded to every important world event with great eloquence and great learning, Lippmann did not respond to this. Lippmann was a Jew, a self-hating Jew who wanted to hide his Jewish origins. . . .

So that between someone like Lippmann and the whole sensitivity of newspapers to charges of being too influenced by Jews, put all of those together and you get the answer of the dismal cloak of ignorance that was thrown over the whole story.

But the real news about what was happening did not come really through the newspapers. It came through the big dramatic ads which our committee, the Bergson committee, which had been written by Ben Hecht, which appeared in the newspapers, that is where most people

---

*Max Lerner (1902–1992) was a prominent voice in American journalism for nearly half a century. An outspoken liberal, he was the author of numerous books and magazine articles about contemporary affairs and ideas, as well as a syndicated columnist for the *New York Post* from 1949 to 1992.

The section that follows is from the interview of Max Lerner by Martin Ostrow, March 5, 1992, New York City.

really began to learn what the truth of it was and I was happy to be part of the effort for them to learn the truth.

W: How much of a role did William Randolph Hearst* play in your publicity efforts?[25]

K: He was a sponsor of the Emergency Conference. And he wrote editorials in regard to the extermination of the Jews, which [were published in his] forty-some papers, which is a lot of papers. His papers sold millions of copies. The *Mirror*, in New York, was selling more than 2½ million copies a day. In terms of public opinion, it was like Nixon—everybody talks against Nixon, but the majority voted for him. So Hearst represented a large segment of what is now called middle America, what Henry Wallace called the common man. He put his name on the editorials—he very rarely wrote signed editorials— and an editorial which he signed was a signal to the whole readership that this is a cause that he's interested in. His editorials ran on the front pages, not on the editorial page. And his papers gave us a lot of coverage, which induced others to give coverage. You know how it is, if the *Journal-American* in New York or the *Mirror* started giving these things coverage, then the other papers did something.

W: Did you ever see him yourself?

K: No, no, I never saw him.

MERLIN:[26] Hearst was the only newspaper owner who supported us without any qualifications or reserves. *All* his papers. He gave us pages after pages free. He gave us the whole editorial page— Hearst himself. He gave *orders* to print our material. So the

---

*William Randolph Hearst (1863–1951) was one of the most prominent figures in the American media during the 1930s and 1940s. His publishing conglomerate included twenty-eight newspapers, an array of radio stations and magazines, and film companies such as the Cosmopolitan Picture Studio. An outspoken anti-Communist as well as a sharp critic of the Roosevelt administration's New Deal policies, Hearst was immortalized as the main character in the movie *Citizen Kane*.

advertising agent called us: You are giving ads to everybody; why shouldn't you give once to the *Journal-American*. The *Journal-American* had a circulation of 6 million, 4 million, I don't know. At that time *The New York Times* had a circulation of only 600,000 during the weekdays. We felt somehow obliged to place an ad—the same ad that we placed in other newspapers. And it didn't bring any results. Well (I am speaking from memory, so I'm not sure), the same ad brought in from *The New York Times* $5,000. This ad [in the *Journal-American*] brought in less than $500.

W: *The New York Times* was your best source?

M: The best source was *The New York Times,* except Sundays. Sunday was the worst day. But we did a whole page on Churchill one Sunday. When Churchill visited the country. I thought it's a brainstorm of mine that we put it in the *Sunday Times*. It had a less than mediocre response.

W: That's interesting because this implies that working-class people who tend to read the Hearst papers were not interested, whereas people more toward an intellectual side who read *The New York Times* were the ones who were responsive.

M: Correct. The more solid people. There was *The Nation* and *The New Republic. The Nation* had a better circulation than *The New Republic* at that time, but we had better results from *The New Republic*. Next on the results which were satisfactory, in the sense that they covered the expenses plus, was the *New York Post*. When *PM* still appeared and we publicized in *PM*, it was less successful than *The New York Post*.

There was a time when *The New York Times* refused to publish our ads. This was a great controversy. They said that our facts may not be proven. All kinds of things. By the way, Gay Talese, in *The Kingdom and the Power,*[27] the book about *The New York Times,* tells the story that at a certain time they refused to give our ads. We argued with them. We negotiated. Talese has it in the chapter about the owners of *The New York Times* as Jews—their complexes, their problems. *The New York Times* had, and maybe still has, a censorship department in the sense that they didn't take every ad automatically, especially if it had political connotations or political contents. So, there was a fellow there and I used to argue with him—sometimes a sentence, a phrase, a word, and this and that. And we were always under pressure. We wanted the ad to go in the same day, which means tonight for tomorrow's paper. And then at a certain point, they stopped. They said we aren't going to take any more of your ads. They gave all kinds of reasons. That we make political statements without substantiating them, especially against the British.

So we thought that this is the end of the world. Without *The New York Times*—but, strangely enough, the *New York Post* picked up. And we started to give them very often. Sometimes every week an ad. Sometimes twice a week an ad. And what's interesting, it seems that people who used to read our ads in the *Times*, started to send in money in response to the ads in the *Post*, though they never did it before. Our ads were an event.

W: Did any other papers give you trouble?

M: No. All the papers around the country were after us. Tremendous. They wanted the ads first of all for the money. But not exclusively. It was also a matter of prestige.

Hillel Kook in 1948

Vladimir Ze'ev Jabotinsky during the 1930s

Chaim Weizmann, left, with Stephen S. Wise, during the 1940s

Senator Guy Gillette, left, with Ben Hecht, during the 1940s

Scene from the pageant "We Will Never Die," 1943

Hundreds of rabbis marching in Washington, D.C.,
October 1943, to urge U.S. rescue of European Jews

Left to right: Senator Guy Gillette, Congressman Will Rogers, Jr., Hillel Kook, and Eri
Jabotinsky, in 1944

Yitshaq Ben-Ami in the 1940s

Left to right: unidentified man, Congressman Andrew Somers, Hillel Kook, and Senator James Murray, in the 1940s (The man in the back is unidentified.)

Left to right: William B. Ziff, Dean Alfange, Congressman Sol Bloom, Herbert S. Moore, and Congressman Joseph C. Baldwin discussing the Gillette-Rogers rescue resolution, 1943

Samuel Merlin in the 1940s

Congressman Emanuel Celler in the 1940s

Baruch Rabinowitz, lobbyist for the Bergson group, speaking during the 1940s

War Refugee Board staff members, March
1944; from right to left: John Pehle, Josiah
DuBois, Albert Abrahamson

Hillel Kook in 1988

David S. Wyman with Hillel Kook in 1988

THIS IS STRICTLY A RACE AGAINST DEATH!

Is There Something You Could Have Done to Save Millions of Innocent People—Men, Women, and Children—from Torture and Death?

With the irresistible advance of the heroic Russian armies, regaining their native soil, the monstrous treatment the Germans mete out to Jews receives new confirmation. Stories of horror which must shake the conscience of humanity—if civilization is to survive—are being published by, eyewitnesses. One of these horror stories is reproduced on this page. Have courage and read it!

Perhaps you will recoil. It may disturb your sleep at night. But it may also fill you with anger, with zeal to do something to stop such atrocities, to rescue the Jews who survive.

Not because they were Poles or Dutchmen, not because they were peasants or officers—just because, and only because, they were Jews, more than two million men, women and children have been deliberately murdered by the Germans.

To those of my people who fight for the right to die with their boots on—my pride, my love, my devotion...

Arthur Szyk

New York, Dec. 1942.

"We shall no longer witness with pity alone . . ."

A Proclamation

ON THE MORAL RIGHTS OF THE STATELESS AND PALESTINIAN JEWS

WE, free people of America, a nation proudly fighting under its own flag against the enemies of freedom and civilization in this global war for survival, proclaim to our valiant allies, the British Commonwealth of Nations, to the free peoples everywhere in the world, as well as to our godless enemies:

That we shall no longer witness with pity alone, and with passive sympathy, the calculated extermination of the ancient Jewish people by the barbarous Nazis.

We proclaim the right of the Jews of the old world to live in freedom and equality, enjoying the rights and privileges of all other human beings.

We proclaim our belief in the moral right of the disinherited, stateless Jews of Europe and of the stalwart young Jewish people of Palestine to fight—as they ask to fight—as fellow-soldiers in this war, standing forth in their own name and under their own banner, fighting as The Jewish Army.

We proclaim our belief that to allow these Jews to fight now is a vital contribution to victory and an immediate moral necessity for the cause of world freedom.

Hundreds of thousands of Jews have perished as helpless martyrs in the war which Hitler is waging on Christian civilization. The Jews were not only the first victims of Hitler's aggression, but the most persecuted, the most tortured. No other people have suffered, comparatively, so much loss of life.

The Jews have been made to pay for every surge of heroism in enslaved countries, for every offensive operation of the United Nations, for every Axis setback, political or military.

Every footstep of the Jew in Europe is stained with his own blood. The Jews have had a hundred Rotterdams. They have seen the horror of a thousand Lidices.

Hitler decreed the extermination of the Jewish people as a prelude to his attack on all Christianity. The Nazi anti-Christ moved with the sure and unerring instinct of a somnambulist when, of all his potential adversaries, he first singled out the Jew for attack as the least-guarded part of our weakened democracy.

Attacking "the Jew" has always been a wedge—military, diplomatic or ideological—driven into the ranks of Hitler's opponents prior to piecemeal subjugation and annihilation.

These first victims of Hitler's aggression cannot conceive democracy denying to them participation on the battlefield in this crusade against barbarism. Two-hundred thousand Palestinian and stateless Jews in the Middle East and elsewhere are ready to give battle and fight to the death. But they have been

ACTION—NOT PITY
CAN SAVE MILLIONS NOW!
EXTINCTION OR HOPE FOR THE REMNANTS OF EUROPEAN JEWRY? — IT IS FOR US TO GIVE THE ANSWER

Daily, hourly, the greatest crime of all time is being committed: a defenseless and innocent people is being slaughtered in a wholesale massacre of millions. What is more tragic—they are dying for no reason or purpose.

The Jewish people in Europe is not just another victim in the array of other peoples that fell prey to Hitler's aggression. The Jews have been singled out not to be conquered, but to be exterminated. To them Hitler has promised . . . and is bringing . . . DEATH.

It is a satanic program beyond the grasp of the decent human mind. Yet, it is being carried out. Already 2,000,000 of the Jews in German-occupied Europe have been murdered. The evidence is in the files of our own State Department.

The Germans dared to undertake this process of annihilation because they knew that the Jews are defenseless; that the Jews are forgotten and deserted even by the democratic powers.

The Germans believe that the United Nations, indoctrinated by twenty years of anti-Jewish propaganda, are to a great extent apathetic and indifferent to the sufferings of the Jews. They believe that for crimes committed against the Jews, no retaliation on behalf of the Governments or armed forces of the United Nations will be carried out. They know that there is no instrument of power and force on this earth with which the Jews can fight back, to avenge their dead and save the remaining millions.

Of what avail are the statements of sympathy and pity and promises of punishment after the war? Since the perpetrators of these slaughters are to be punished for the murders they have already committed, then they can lose no more by further murder.

Such mere statements of sympathy and pity are to the Germans proof that their judgment of Democracy's attitude toward the Jews is justified, and in their criminal minds they understand them as "carte blanche" to go on with the slaughter.

What can be done?

What is necessary is to impress the Germans that the Governments of the United Nations have decided to change their present policy of passive sympathy and pity to one of stern and immediate action; that they consider the cessation of atrocities against the Jews as an immediate aim of their military and political operations. Under this premise rigorous United Nations' intervention to save European Jewry would become a matter of course. Exactly as it would be if it were American or British civilians who were being killed in a systematic campaign by the Nazis, the whole of the forces of these great democracies would be utilized to find an immediate and effective solution.

The inauguration of such a new policy on behalf of the United Nations would logically result in enabling all those Jews who have managed to escape the European-German hell to fight back. The first dictate, therefore, would be the immediate approval of the demand for a Jewish Army of the Stateless and Palestinian Jews—an army 200,000 strong.

Suicide squads of the Jewish Army would engage in desperate commando raids deep into the heart of Germany. Jewish pilots would bomb German cities in reprisal.

A Jewish Army would imply a call to arms of all Stateless Jews living in North Africa so that they may participate in the imminent invasion of the European continent.

A Jewish Army would immediately give a decisive moral relief to the agonized Jews of Europe. Their psychology of despair and helplessness would be transformed into one of hope for revenge and survival. A Jewish Army would give a meaning to their sufferings—to their death.

They will then realize that they cease being helpless victims and become partners in the global struggle for a better world, in which their survivors will live in freedom and equality as all other human beings.

The Jews of _Palestine_ and the _Stateless_ Jews want to fight . . . AS JEWS. They want to prove to Hitler, and to the world, that the Jews can be more than "the persecuted people". . . that Jews can die in other ways than through murder. They want the right to fight for the world's freedom, under their own banner. To die, if needs be, but to die _fighting_.

Of course, these are not all the practical proposals which the human mind is capable of conceiving. It is unfair to ask for a single solution to such a disastrous problem. What we must realize is that it is our duty not to resign ourselves to the idea that our brains are powerless to find any solution; not to resign ourselves to the idea that the forces of Democracy are too weak to enforce such a solution.

Remember when a few thousand British soldiers were put in chains by the Germans? How swift the retaliation? . . And how practical . . .

The Germans chained no more British soldiers.

Remember when a tiny town in Czechoslovakia was horribly "punished"? How swift the hurricane of world-indignation that answered . . .

There have been no more Lidices.

Remember when small and encircled Sweden opposed vigorously and stubbornly the expulsion of Norwegian Jews. The Germans abandoned their plan.

The Jews of Norway are still there.

The American sense of justice and decency and American ingenuity must also find ways to overpower the diabolical plan to exterminate the Jewish people. It must find a way now, before millions more perish.

It is, therefore, our primordial demand that an inter-governmental commission of military experts be appointed with the task of elaborating ways and means to stop the wholesale slaughter of the Jews in Europe. This must be done now—before the greatest homicidal maniac extends his policy of extermination to other peoples; before he dares introducing poison gas and bacteriological warfare.

Remember that for years the Germans rehearsed on the Jews what they later practiced on other peoples.

Therefore we have decided to launch an all-out campaign to save European Jewry. We will spare no efforts and have no rest until the American public will be fully informed of the facts and aroused to its responsibilities.

We believe in the overwhelming power of public opinion, as the greatest, if not the only, power in democracy. Governments in democratic countries like the United States and Great Britain can act only when they feel sure that they are backed by a powerful movement of public opinion. We plead with everyone to help and to co-operate in this sacred campaign we have launched. Join in this fight—write to your Congressmen, contribute to our work, so that this message may be carried to every city and hamlet in the United States as is being done in Great Britain. We are part of the collective conscience of America; this conscience has never been found wanting.

NO AMERICAN CITIZENS are wanted as soldiers in the Jewish Army. They fight in the Armed forces of the United States, where millions of men of all creeds have joined the struggle.

I want to support your campaign to save European Jewry by action—not pity, and to help publicize your messages through the press, radio and public meetings throughout the country. I am glad to enclose my check in the amount

$. . . . .

Name . . . .

Address . . . .

PLEASE MAKE YOUR CHECK PAYABLE TO THE COMMITTEE FOR A JEWISH ARMY OF STATELESS AND PALESTINIAN JEWS, 535 FIFTH AVE., N. Y.

Committee for a Jewish Army
of Stateless and Palestinian Jews
NATIONAL HEADQUARTERS · NEW YORK, 535 Fifth Ave. · MUrray Hill 2-7237

FOR SALE to Humanity
70,000 Jews
Guaranteed Human Beings at $50 a Piece

Roumania is tired of killing Jews. It has killed one hundred thousand of them in two years. Roumania will now give Jews away practically for nothing.

SEVENTY THOUSAND JEWS ARE WAITING DEATH IN ROUMANIAN CONCENTRATION CAMPS:

Roumania Will Give These 70,000 Jews to the Four Freedoms for 20,000 Lei ($50) a Piece. This Sum Covers All Transportation expenses.

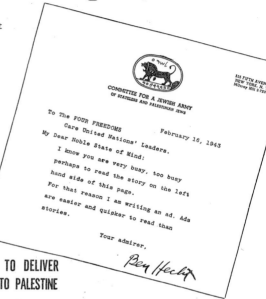

To The FOUR FREEDOMS
Care United Nations' Leaders.

February 16, 1943

My Dear Noble State of Mind:

I know you are very busy, too busy perhaps to read the story on the left hand side of this page.

For that reason I am writing an ad. Ads are easier and quicker to read than stories.

Your admirer,

Ben Hecht

ROUMANIA OFFERS TO DELIVER THESE 70,000 ALIVE TO PALESTINE

Attention Four Freedoms ! ! !
NO SPIES WERE FOUND AMONG THE 300,000 JEWS WHO CAME TO PALESTINE SINCE HITLER ASSUMED POWER IN GERMANY
THERE WILL BE NO SPIES SMUGGLED IN AMONG THESE JEWS.
(IF THERE ARE YOU CAN SHOOT THEM)

Attention Humanity ! ! !
PALESTINE'S ARABS WILL NOT BE ANNOYED BY THE ARRIVAL OF 70,000 JEWS THE ONLY ARABS WHO WILL BE ANNOYED ARE THE ARAB LEADERS WHO ARE IN BERLIN AND THEIR SPIES IN PALESTINE.

Attention America ! ! !
THE GREAT ROUMANIAN BARGAIN IS FOR THIS MONTH ONLY !
IT IS AN UNPRECEDENTED OFFER!
SEVENTY THOUSAND SOULS AT $50 A PIECE!
The Doors of Roumania Are Open! Act Now!

The four million Jews of Nazi-held Europe can be saved from the fate of their two million brothers already exterminated.

The Germans have dared to undertake this process of annihilation because they knew that the Jews are defenseless and forgotten.

The great, humanitarian people of the United States and Great Britain must be made aware of the facts.

To that end the Committee for a Jewish Army of stateless and Palestinian Jews has launched an intensive campaign to arouse the conscience of humanity and to demand that something be done NOW, WHILE THERE IS STILL TIME, to save the remaining Jews of Europe.

The principal demand of the Committee is that the United Nations immediately appoint an inter-governmental committee to formulate ways and means of stopping this wholesale slaughter of human beings.

You are part of the collective conscience of America; this conscience has never been found wanting. Join in this fight! You can help spread this message to your friends. You can write to your Congressmen. You can make contributions for the further distribution of messages like these to all the people of the United States. In this way, you, with the force of your indignation, of your wrath, and of your action, you can help save European Jewry!

Committee for a Jewish Army

of Stateless and Palestinian Jews

National Headquarters • New York, 535 Fifth Ave. • MUrray Hill 2-7237

I want to support your campaign to save European Jewry by action—not pity, and to help publicize your messages through the press, the radio and public meetings throughout the country. I am glad to enclose my check in the amount of

$ . . . .

Name . . . .

Address . . . .

PLEASE MAKE YOUR CHECK PAYABLE TO THE COMMITTEE FOR A JEWISH ARMY OF STATELESS AND PALESTINIAN JEWS, 535 FIFTH AVE., N. Y. C.

To 5,000,000 Jews in the Nazi Death-Trap Bermuda Was a "Cruel Mockery"

When Will The United Nations Establish An Agency To Deal With The Problem of Hitler's Extermination of a Whole People?

SOMEHOW, through invisible, underground channels, one ray of shining hope might have penetrated the ghettos of Europe. A rumor might have spread and grown into a whisper among the agonized Jews of Hitler's hell. A whisper telling of deliverance from torture, death, starvation and agony in slaughter-houses. This ray of hope and this whisper were expressed in one word: Bermuda!

The rumor told of representatives of the United States and Great Britain, the leading champions of the United Nations, the protagonists of the Four Freedoms, assembling to save the hunted and tortured Jews of Europe. On the deliberations of this small convention on an Island in the Atlantic were focused all the hopes of the doomed Jews of Europe; those, too, of the free well-meaning people the world over. Men and women of good will everywhere at last believed that the United Nations had decided to do something about the unprecedented disaster of a people put to death.

Wretched, doomed victims of Hitler's tyranny! Poor men and women of good faith the world over! You have cherished an illusion. Your hopes have been in vain. Bermuda was not the dawn of a new era, of an era of humanity and compassion, of translating pity into deed. Bermuda was a mockery, and a cruel jest

THIS is not our definition. It is the definition of the London Sunday "Observer"—one of the most influential and important newspapers in Great Britain.

Not only were ways and means to save the remaining four million Jews in Europe not devised, but their problem was not even touched upon, put on the agenda, or discussed. More than that—the name "Jews" was banished from the vocabulary of this convention, as PM's foreign editor, Alexander Uhl, reports: "It was regarded as almost improper to mention even the word Jew."

But not only the attention of the victims of Nazi atrocities and of their friends the world over was concentrated on the meeting at Bermuda: Hitler, too, was concerned with the United Nations' reply to his challenge to the extermination of the Jewish population in Europe. Alas! To him Bermuda was again convincing proof that the United Nations were neither ready nor willing to answer his threat with action. They were continuing to give him "carte blanche" in his extermination process, exactly as in the pre-war days they permitted him to deal with Jews in Germany, with Austria and Czechoslovakia, thus paving the way for aggression, invasion, and war.

Can it be possible that the United Nations do not understand that should Hitler succeed in exterminating the Jews as a people, they by their silence will pave the way to the extermination of the Czechoslovak, Polish, Greek or even the French peoples?

Now we are witnessing a variety of attempts to justify the Bermuda failure, to wrap it in secret formulae, such as "no dealing with Hitler," or "not to interfere with the prosecution of the war," or "not to undertake anything which should prolong the war," etc. All this is just throwing sand into the eyes of public opinion. All this has nothing to do with the real facts and the harrowing truth.

The facts, plain and simple, are the following:

(a) This is a specific problem of Jewish disaster. Hitler did not (as yet) decree the extermination of all the peoples of Europe, he decreed the extermination of the Jewish people in Europe and this process of extermination is unabated and steady. Two million or more have been put to death already!

(b) Five million Jews in Europe still live. The governments of Roumania, Hungary and Bulgaria, all satellites of Germany, are willing to release their Jews any time the United Nations are willing to take part in the deliverance. By doing so, they hope to find grace and pardon in the eyes of the United Nations whom they consider as the inevitable victors in this world struggle.

(c) The United Nations have taken no advantage of these offers. They have not done so for one reason: the British government has prevented them, fearing that public opinion will demand that these refugees be admitted into Palestine—a practical place of salvation only a few days away from the Axis countries by short water route, train or even bus, where the new Hebrew Nation awaits them with open arms.

The Jewish Problem Is Not a Refugee Problem

With the Bermuda Conference a thing of the past, not having even discussed the problem of the extermination of the Jewish people in Europe, now, more than ever, it is clear that we are dealing not only with a *refugee problem*, but with the *Jewish problem* of Europe. These two problems should not be confused. They are entirely distinct. Democracy cannot connive with the slaughter of millions of innocent civilian people—the Jews in Europe. There are ways and means to stop Hitler's wholesale murder and to evacuate those who can be evacuated. *But no one has been assigned to deal with this tremendous problem.* What is necessary is that the machinery for action be created. The United Nations, which have uttered so many words of pity must now *do* something if these words of pity are to be more than empty lies. They must create a United Nations Agency composed of military and diplomatic experts, which should have full authority to define and effectuate a realistic and stern policy of action, to save the remaining millions of Jewish people. *This Agency or Commission will deal, not with refugees outside Hitler's reach, but with the Jewish people under his yoke today.*

A Program of Action (. . . Not Pity!)

There are two broad areas in which this Agency can begin to operate without delay or procrastination.

1. Immediate utilization of all existing possibilities of transfer of Jews from Hitler-dominated countries to Palestine or to any temporary refuge and the initiation of all further possibilities in this program.

2. The immediate creation of a Jewish army of stateless and Palestinian Jews, including "suicide" Commando squads, and Air Squadrons for retaliatory bombing, which will raid deep into Germany, thus participating as an entity in the war and bringing their message of hope to Hitler's victims.

Join the Crusade for Decency

The crime of Europe calls for the mobilization of every shred of righteousness and spiritual power left in the world. *On the field of battle soldiers die. On the field of massacre civilization dies.* The thunder of civilization against the swamp-like antics of the German government is alone capable of stopping the German crime against life. Such a thunder unleashed by our own representatives and by all the nations that serve the cause of God would strike terror into the souls of the German people.

Therefore we dedicate ourselves to this fight and we call upon every American to join hands with us in this crusade for humanity and decency.

Every citizen is part of the collective conscience of America; this conscience has never been found wanting. Demand action from your government against the German massacre of the Jews.

Ballad of the Doomed Jews of Europe

by Ben Hecht

FOUR MILLION JEWS waiting for death.
Oh hang and burn but—quiet, Jews!
Don't be bothersome; save your breath—
The world is busy with other news.

Four million murders are quite a smear
Even our State Department views
The slaughter with much disfavor here
But then—it's busy with other news.

You'll hang like a forest of broken trees
You'll burn in a thousand Nazi stews
And tell your God to forgive us please
For we were busy with other news.

Tell Him we hadn't quite the time
To stop the killing of all the Jews;
Tell Him we looked askance at the crime—
But we were busy with other news.

Oh World be patient—it will take
Some time before the murder crews
Are done. By Christmas you can make
Your Peace on Earth without the Jews.

●

You can prevent their doom

DEMAND OPEN DOORS TO PALESTINE

Do you remember all the high, brave words of the United Nations' statesmen—saying that the Jews of Europe, the Four Million Unmurdered Ones, must be saved and would be saved?

What has been done?

Nothing!

This isn't quite true.

One thing was done. The statesmen met, conferred, debated, and cut off all hope of escape for the surviving Jews of Europe.

Palestine had been the only land eager and ready to receive the Four Million Jews still surviving the great German murder campaign

The doors of Palestine have been closed in the face of the Jews.

Rather than offend the *amour propre* of some unreliable Arab politicians, the United Nations have condemned all the surviving Jews of Europe to death—by closing the only avenue of escape, Palestine.

The murder of the Jews is in full progress.

They are being exterminated at the rate of thousands a day.

If you are not too busy, and there are not too many things on your mind, if you believe there is something a little amiss with allowing Four Million human beings to be murdered in German lime kilns and gas chambers—Four Million who might be saved

—write to a Statesman, a Congressman, a Senator, an Alderman, a Judge, a Mayor, a President.

Ask them why the door has been closed.

Ask them whether the world profits more from catering to the political whims of a few Arabs than from saving the lives of millions of men, women and children who are dying because the doors are shut.

Help us to carry out the campaign we are launching to "save the Jews of Europe by opening the doors of Palestine."

COMMITTEE FOR A JEWISH ARMY OF STATELESS AND PALESTINIAN JEWS

National Headquarters, 535 Fifth Ave., New York 17, N. Y. Murray Hill 2-7237

This Committee, under the Chairmanship of Senator Edwin C. Johnson, is dedicated to the task of saving the lives and dignity of the Hebrew people of Europe and Palestine. It has gained the moral support of leaders from all walks of American life.

Seventy military authorities, 40 Senators, 210 Congressmen, 22 Governors, 115 government officials, 82 jurists and justices, 80 mayors, 314 clergymen and rabbis, 54 labor leaders, 290 columnists. 422 authors, newspapermen, columnists, 254 artists, 112 lawyers and attorneys. 98 doctors, and many hundreds more have endorsed the principles and objectives of this movement by signing the "Proclamation on the Moral Rights of the Stateless and Palestinian Jews."

A Report of Failure and a Call to Action

We failed to persuade Governments to take steps to save the Jewish people of Europe.
Now We Must Turn to Mass Action

The foremost duty of workers in a humanitarian cause is to be honest and sincere with themselves as well as with the public. Nothing is more harmful to the cause one serves than the normal urge to delude oneself with glimpses of success or victory; nothing is more dangerous than to be satisfied by mere words of sympathy and pity from high places. No matter how disagreeable it may be, we refuse to delude ourselves and we refuse to take words as a substitute for deeds.

No, we don't cherish any illusions; during the months between the closing session of the Emergency Conference to Save the Jewish People of Europe and today, nothing has been done by the Allied Governments to stop the slaughter or to alleviate the torments of five million people.

Two months have elapsed since the experts attending the Emergency Conference to Save the Jews of Europe worked out a program that would enable hundreds of thousands of Jews to escape the death sentence passed upon them by Hitler—death by starvation, death in gas chambers, death in front of machine-gun squads.

Two months have passed since this program was presented to our President, to Secretary of State Cordell Hull, to the leaders of both Houses of Congress, to the Ambassadors of the United Nations.

Meanwhile we took other steps

Our co-chairman, the courageous and dynamic Congressman Will Rogers, Jr., flew to England to submit and discuss this program with the British Government. Upon his return he frankly declared:

"I have seen and talked to many leading personalities here; Members of Parliament of both houses, and of all parties and affiliations. I have discussed the problem extensively with Under-Secretary of State for Foreign Affairs Richard K. Law, Mr. Eden being absent from London during much of my stay there, and with numerous other Government officials, as well as with our Ambassador to Great Britain, John Winant, and the newly appointed American Vice Director of the Intergovernmental Refugee Committee, Patrick Murphy Malin.

"All of them expressed deep sympathy as to the horrible plight of the Jews of Europe, but I must confess, and I feel it is my duty to state, that the sum total of all my efforts and the continuous efforts of the many British parliamentarians who are sympathetic to the cause, have up to now brought no results whatsoever. Despite the fine expressions of sympathy and understanding, no governmental action has been undertaken by any Government to even attempt, on some tangible scale, to rescue these people, though it has been established beyond a doubt that the vast majority of them could be saved now."

We sent delegates to Turkey and Palestine. Their cabled reports state authoritatively that it is possible to rescue the Jews of Europe if only the doors of the havens of refuge are unbolted by the United Nations. Hundreds of thousands could escape from the Balkan countries to Palestine if the discriminatory immigration restrictions of the White Paper are lifted and the Jews are freely admitted to their own homeland.

On this, too, there has been no official action

MASS PETITION MOVEMENT IS LAUNCHED

*W*E are not giving up the struggle. On the contrary, we appeal to you to join us in the fight. With the active help of all humane and public-spirited Americans we shall not fail. We must not fail. The lives of four million innocent and helpless human beings are at stake. Democratic governments cannot resist forever the pressure of public opinion. Ultimately they must yield. The voice of indignant Americans can make them do so before it is too late.

500 RABBIS GO TO WASHINGTON TO PETITION PRESIDENT

Upon the approach of the High Holy Days of the Hebrew New Year and the Day of Atonement, every Jew prepares the balance sheet of his own conscience, and in this particularly horrible year each asks himself whether he has done everything possible to discharge the heavy responsibility each man must bear for the slaughter of an entire people in Europe.

On Wednesday, October 6, 500 leaders of the Rabbinate, representing American Orthodox Jewry of close to 3,000,000 members of congregations and communities, are going to Washington to impress upon our Government the tragic plight of the Jews of Europe. They will be led by Rabbis Israel Rosenberg, president; Hiam I. Bloch, vice president; Juda L. Seltzer, executive director; and Reuben Levovitz, secretary, of Union of Orthodox Rabbis of the United States, and by Eliezer Silver, co-president Union of Orthodox Rabbis and president of Agudas Israel of America; Wolf Gold, vice president Union of Orthodox Rabbis and honorary president Mizrachi Organization of America; and Solomon N. Friedman, president Union of Grand Rabbis of the United States.

Following solemn services at the Lincoln Memorial for the two million Jewish victims, they will go to the White House and will also be received by Vice President Wallace as well as by a group of representative members of both Houses of Congress, headed by Majority and Minority leaders, Senators Alben W. Barkley and Charles L. McNary, to whom they will present the petition which pleads for the millions that are still alive.

PETITION

The extermination of an entire people arouses the decent instincts of mankind to demand that immediate and effective measures be taken to stop such barbarous action.

We, Americans, have always upheld the right of all men to "life, liberty, and the pursuit of happiness," and have engaged in two world wars on the side of humanity, civilization and democracy.

Therefore, we, the undersigned Americans, call upon the Executive and Legislative branches of our Government to create a special Intergovernmental Agency to save the Jewish people of Europe, with powers and means to act at once and on a large scale.

We also respectfully petition our Government to convey to the British Government, which was entrusted with the Mandate for Palestine, the conviction of Americans that it is against all justice that the Jews alone, of all peoples, are not allowed free entry to Palestine, and the desire of Americans that the doors of Palestine be opened to all European Jews escaping the death trap of Europe.

We hereby appeal to the President and the Congress of the United States, the guardians of America's humanitarian tradition, to take this action at once.

6,000 CHRISTIAN CHURCHES HOLD DAY OF INTERCESSION SERVICES

A call to "set aside Sunday, October 10, as a Day of Intercession, when the Christian Churches may lift up their voices to God on High beseeching Him to ameliorate the lot of the Jewish people and to usher in an era of enlightenment and justice," has been issued by the Rt. Rev. Henry St. George Tucker, Presiding Bishop of the Protestant Episcopal Church, the Rt. Rev. Francis J. McConnell, Resident Bishop of the Methodist Church, and the Rev. Dr. Henry Sloane Coffin, Moderator of the Presbyterian Church.

"Will you not join us in our day of special prayer by speaking of the plight of the European Jews from the pulpit and offering up words of intercession for them and urging immediate action to alleviate their lot?" reads the appeal. "Will not the members of your congregation form themselves into a committee to work with the Emergency Committee to Save the Jewish People of Europe?"

The fate of millions of human beings lies in the hands of the American people. If Americans call for action, they will get results. If they implement the prayers of the Day of Intercession by organizing committees in their communities to make known the will of the American people, they will save thousands of Jewish communities in France and Denmark, in Rumania and Hungary, in Bulgaria and even in Poland.

If YOU speak up, Governments will listen.

WE HAVE FAITH IN AMERICA

We know that the conscience and humanity of Americans will not accept a policy of inaction in a matter of life and death to millions of people. We have faith that the force of your indignation will enable us to carry out the plans for the rescue of European Jewry before it is too late.

We therefore call upon you for moral and material help in our fight. Add your name to the millions of signatures that will make this petition a powerful instrument of public opinion. Make your generous contribution to enable us to reach our fellow-Americans in every part of our great country. Let America's voice be heard and known.

EMERGENCY COMMITTEE TO SAVE THE JEWISH PEOPLE OF EUROPE
One East Forty-Fourth Street, New York 17, N. Y.   MUrray Hill 2-7237

EXECUTIVE BOARD

CO-CHAIRMEN:
Peter H. Bergson
Louis Bromfield
Ben Hecht

Rep. Max Lerner
Rep. Will Rogers, Jr.
Mme. Sigrid Undset

VICE-CHAIRMEN:
William Helis
I. A. Hirschman
Prof. Francis E. McMahon
Dean George W. Matheson
Herbert S. Moore

Fletcher Pratt
A. Hadani Rafaeli
Lisa Sergio
Rep. Andrew L. Somers
Dr. Maurice William

Dean Alfange
William S. Bennet
Konrad Bercovici
Io Davidson
Oscar W. Ehrhorn

TREASURER: Mrs. John Gunther

MEMBERS:
Stella Adler
J. J. Amiel
Bart Andress
Al Bauer
Y Ben-Ami
A. Ben-Eliezer
M. Berchin
Rabbi Philip D. Bookstaber
Bishop James A. Cannon, Jr.

Rep. Samuel Dickstein
Nathan George Horwitt
E. Jabotinsky
Rose Keane
Emil Lengyel
I. Lipschutz
Lawrence Lipton
Emil Ludwig
S. Merlin
Michael Potter

Victor M. Ratner
Curt Riess
K. Shridharani
Johan J. Smertenko
Arthur Szyk
Irving Taitel
Thomas J. Watson
Gabriel Wechsler
Alex Wilf

EMERGENCY COMMITTEE
TO SAVE THE JEWISH PEOPLE OF EUROPE
1 East 44th Street, New York 17, N. Y.

I hereby lend your efforts to obtain immediate United Nations action to save the Jewish people of Europe. I enclose my contribution to enable you to carry out this tremendous task in the sum of $................

NAME................

ADDRESS................

Please make checks payable to Mrs. JOHN GUNTHER, Treasurer

My Uncle Abraham Reports...

By Ben Hecht

I have an Uncle who is a Ghost.

But, he is no ordinary Ghost like so many dead uncles.

He was elected last April by the Two Million Jews who have been murdered by the Germans to be their World Delegate.

Wherever there are Conferences on how to make the World a Better Place, maybe, my Uncle Abraham appears and sits on the window sill and takes notes.

That's how I happened to be in Moscow a few weeks ago.

My Uncle Abraham sat on the window sill of the Kremlin and listened with great excitement, to one of the Finest Conferences he has ever attended since he has been a World Delegate.

He heard every word that Eden, Molotov and Hull spoke.

Last night my Uncle Abraham was back in a Certain Place where the Two Million murdered Jews meet. It is the Jewish Underground. Only Ghosts belong to it.

When the Two Million Souls had assembled, my Uncle Abraham arose and made his report to them as World Delegate.

"Dishonored dead," said my Uncle Abraham, "Fellow Corpses, and Ghosts from All Over. Of the Moscow Conference I have this to report. The Conference made a promise that the world was going to punish the Germans for murdering all the different peoples of Europe—Czechs, Greeks, Serbs, Russians, French hostages, Polish officers, Cretan peasants. Only we were not mentioned. In this Conference, which named everyone, only the Jew had no name. He had no face. He was like a hole in Europe on which nobody looked."

A Ghost from the Lime Kilns of Warsaw spoke.

"Why is this?" asked this Ghost, "why is it that we who are dead are without a Name in the Conferences of Fine People?"

"This I do not know," said my Uncle Abraham, "I can only report what exists. Jews do not exist, even when they are dead. In the Kremlin in Moscow, in the White House in Washington, in the Downing Street Building in London where I have sat on the window sills, I have never heard our name. The people who live in those buildings—Stalin, Roosevelt and Churchill—do not speak of us. Why, I don't know. We were not allowed by the Germans to stay alive. We are not allowed by the Four Freedoms to be dead."

A Woman Ghost from the Dynamite Dumps of Odessa spoke.

"If they didn't mention the two million murdered Jews in the Conference, isn't that bad for four million who are still alive? The Germans will think that when they kill Jews, Stalin, Roosevelt and Churchill pretend nothing is happening."

And from the Two Million Ghosts came a great cry.

"Why is this silence? Why don't they speak of Us?"

My Uncle Abraham raised his hand.

"Little Children," my Uncle Abraham spoke: "Be patient. We will be dead a long time. Yesterday when we were killed we were changed from Nobodies to Nobodies. Today, on our Jewish tomb, there is not the Star of David, there is an Asterisk. But, who knows, maybe Tomorrow—!"

This ended the Meeting of the Jewish Underground.

My Uncle Abraham has gone to the White House in Washington. He is sitting on the windowsill two feet away from Mr. Roosevelt. But he has left his notebook behind.

Statement on Atrocities
Signed by President Roosevelt, Prime Minister Churchill and Premier Stalin.

The United Kingdom, the United States and the Soviet Union have received from many quarters evidence of atrocities, massacres and cold-blooded mass executions which are being perpetrated by Hitlerite forces in many of the countries they have overrun and from which they are now being steadily expelled. The brutalities of Nazi domination are no new thing, and all peoples or territories in their grip have suffered from the worst form of government by terror. What is new is that many of these territories are now being redeemed by the advancing armies of the liberating powers and that in their desperation the recoiling Hitlerites and Huns are redoubling their ruthless cruelties. This is now evidenced with particular clearness by monstrous crimes on the territory of the Soviet Union which is being liberated from Hitlerites and on French and Italian territory.

Accordingly, the aforesaid three Allied powers, speaking in the interests of the thirty-two United Nations, hereby solemnly declare and give full warning of their declaration as follows:

At the time of granting of any armistice to any government which may be set up in Germany, those German officers and men and members of the Nazi party who have been responsible for or have taken a consenting part in the above atrocities, massacres and executions will be sent back to the countries in which their abominable deeds were done in order that they may be judged and punished according to the laws of these liberated countries and of the free governments which will be erected therein. Lists will be compiled in all possible detail from all these countries, having regard especially to invaded parts of the Soviet Union, to Poland and Czechoslovakia, to Yugoslavia and Greece, including Crete and other islands; to Norway, Denmark, the Netherlands, Belgium, Luxembourg, France and Italy.

Thus, Germans who take part in wholesale shooting of Polish officers or in the execution of French, Dutch, Belgian or Norwegian hostages or of Cretan peasants, or who have shared in slaughters inflicted on the people of Poland or, in territories of the Soviet Union which are now being swept clear of the enemy, will know they will be brought back to the scene of their crimes and judged on the spot by the peoples whom they have outraged. Let those who have hitherto not imbued their hands with innocent blood beware lest they join the ranks of the guilty, for most assuredly the three Allied powers will pursue them to the uttermost ends of the earth and will deliver them to their accusers in order that justice may be done.

The above declaration is without prejudice to the case of German criminals whose offenses have no particular geographical localization and who will be punished by joint decision of the governments of the Allies.

HELP Prevent 4,000,000 People from Becoming Ghosts

There are four million Jews still alive in Europe.

They can be saved. Experts agree on that.

Sweden and Denmark have just proved it by saving 6,000 Jews in a few days.

This Committee considers it a sacred duty to do all humanly possible to save them.

Our offices and representatives in Washington and in London, in Palestine and in Turkey, are steadily working in this direction, trying to get large-scale government action. This action will have to express itself in the creation of an Intergovernmental Agency to save the Jewish people of Europe and in declaring the doors of Palestine and other countries under United Nations control open for escaping Jews. For, it is now strictly a race for time against death.

Every day that passes dooms thousands who can be saved.

This Committee is asking the American people for a half million dollars with which it hopes—and believes—results can be secured effecting the rescue of the four million martyred Jews in Europe.

We need your financial help immediately. By your support will be determined the speed, scope and affectiveness of our work to save the Jewish people of Europe.

Emergency Committee to Save the Jewish People of Europe

One East Forty-fourth Street, New York 17, N. Y.   MUrray Hill 2-7237

EXECUTIVE BOARD

CO-CHAIRMEN:
Peter H. Bergson
Louis Bromfield
Dr. Max Lerner

Ben Hecht
Rep. Will Rogers, Jr.
Mme. Sigrid Undset

VICE-CHAIRMEN:
Dean Alfange
William S. Bennet
Konrad Bercovici
Jo Davidson
Oscar W. Ehrhorn
William Hells
Prof. Francis E. McMahon

Dean George W. Matheson
Herbert S. Moore
Fletcher Pratt
A. Hadani Rafaeli
Lisa Sergio
Rep. Andrew L. Somers
Dr. Maurice William

TREASURER: Mrs. John Gunther

MEMBERS:
Stella Adler
J. J. Amiel
Al Bauer
Y. Ben-Ami
A. Ben-Elizer
M. Berchin
Rabbi Philip D. Bookstaber
Bishop James A. Cannon, Jr.
Lester Cohen
Babette Deutsch
Rep. Samuel Dickstein
Nathan George Horwitt
E. Jabotinsky
Rose Keane
Emil Lengel
I. Lipschutz

Lawrence Lipton
Emil Ludwig
Gov. Edward Martin (Pa.)
Gov. J. Howard McGrath (R. I.)
S. Merlin
Michael Potter
Victor M. Ratner
Curt Riess
K. Shridharani
John J. Smetenko
Arthur Szyk
Irving Taitel
Thomas J. Watson
Gabriel Wechsler
Alex Wilf

- [By a ruling of the Treasury Department, contributions to this Committee are tax exempt]-

EMERGENCY COMMITTEE
TO SAVE THE JEWISH PEOPLE OF EUROPE
1 East 44th Street, New York 17, N. Y.

I hereby join your efforts to obtain immediate United Nations action to save the Jewish people of Europe. I enclose my contribution to enable you to carry out this tremendous task in the sum of

$..

NAME..

ADDRESS..

Please make checks payable to Mrs. JOHN GUNTHER, Treasurer.

HOW WELL ARE YOU SLEEPING?

Is There Something You Could Have Done to Save Millions of Innocent People—Men, Women, and Children—from Torture and Death?

With the irresistible advance of the heroic Russian armies, regaining their native soil, the monstrous treatment the Germans mete out to Jews receives new confirmation. Stories of horror which must shake the conscience of humanity—if civilization is to survive—are being published by eyewitnesses. One of these horror stories is reproduced on this page. Have courage and read it!

Perhaps you will recoil. It may disturb your sleep at night. But it may also fill you with anger, with zeal to do something to stop such atrocities, to rescue the Jews who survive.

Not because they were Poles or Dutchmen, not because they were peasants or officers—just because, and only because, they were Jews, more than two million men, women and children have been deliberately murdered by the Germans.

The Jews of Europe have suffered more fatalities from atrocities than all the European Nations combined. In the face of such a tragedy it is folly, indeed it is sinful, to debate whether Jews are a religion, a nation, or a race—to insist on calling them "refugees"—and thus to remain passive to their disastrous plight, ignoring it and surrounding it with silence.

They are a specific group of human beings whom our common enemy has publicly threatened to exterminate entirely. This Committee believes it is an inescapable duty of all Americans to actively oppose Hitler in this respect also, and to do all that is humanly possible to save the four million Jews who are still alive in Europe.

These Four Million Can Be Saved!

Experts agree on that. Sweden and Denmark have just proved it by saving six thousand Jews in a few days.

They are safe for only one reason: the doors of a neighboring country were unlocked.

And because of that fact, the escaping Jews found the resources and energy to reach these doors of safety. What Sweden did so simply, so humanely, other nations are being urged to do, *must* do if their consciences are to be clear for the peace to come!

Read what this committee has already accomplished, what its further plans are.

Our Program of Action!

AT THE EMERGENCY CONFERENCE HELD IN NEW YORK, ON JULY 20-25, 1943, EXPERTS FROM ALL PARTS OF THE UNITED STATES FORMULATED A PROGRAM OF EFFECTIVE ACTION THAT CAN AND MUST BE TAKEN NOW TO SAVE THE JEWISH PEOPLE OF EUROPE. THEY URGED THE GOVERNMENTS OF THE UNITED STATES AND THE UNITED NATIONS TO ADOPT A PLAN EMBRACING THE FOLLOWING OUTSTANDING MEASURES:

1. To create a Governmental Agency specifically charged with the task of saving the Jewish people of Europe.
2. To seek guarantees from the Axis-satellite countries, through the International Red Cross, neutral countries, or the Vatican, to insure Jews the same treatment given to other nationals.
3. To relieve the starvation and disease which are decimating the Jewish people in Axis-held territory.
4. To insist that the Axis-satellite countries, which now seek to gain the goodwill of the victorious Allies, withhold their Jews from Hitler's slaughter-houses and permit them to leave their borders.
5. To urge neutral countries—Sweden, Ireland, Portugal, Spain, Switzerland, and Turkey—to grant the Jewish people temporary asylum.
6. To request neutral countries to grant transit facilities to all Jewish people passing from Axis-controlled lands to any United Nations territory, regardless of whether the persons involved be refugees, immigrants, or repatriates.
7. To obtain from the Governments of the United Nations temporary asylum with the understanding that after the war these refugees will be removed from their territories if they are not wanted.
8. To insist that Great Britain, pending this tragic emergency, open the doors of Palestine, where 600,000 Jews have expressed their desire to share their homes and food with their suffering brothers, thus putting an end to the discriminatory immigration laws that exclude many Jews from their own country.

Nazi Massacre Of Kiev's Jews Told by Witness

Victims Stripped, Lined Up at a Gulley, Shot; Babies Merely Thrown In Alive

German troops massacred Kiev's Jews during the first days of the Nazi occupation of the now-liberated Ukraine capital, robbing them of their clothes and jewelry and lining them up naked at the edge of a gulley, where they were shot, the Russian Tass News Agency reported yesterday.

Tass quoted an eyewitness story written for the Moscow newspaper "Izvestia" by Dmitri Orlov, a resident of Kiev:

"Several days after the Germans entered Kiev (on Sept. 20, 1943) I went to Lvovskaya Street. An incessant procession of people was streaming through it, and both sidewalks were lined with German patrols . . . The Germans were driving the Jews to Babyi Yar gulley, beyond the city.

"I also stealthily made my way to that place. I was able to stand the sight of what I saw there only for ten minutes, and after that everything went black before my eyes.

"The Germans forced the people to undress, and then methodically gathered their clothes and loaded them on trucks. In separate trucks they put underwear.

"Then they tore from the naked people—there were men and women among them—rings and watches, if they had any, and ranged them as if in a factory, the cold or from mortal terror, at the edge of the gulley and shot them.

"The Germans did not waste any bullets on little children, but simply hurled them alive into the gulley.

"Those who were waiting their turn stood silently. Some sang or even laughed. I could see that those who laughed were already insane.

"And this thing lasted three days. All those whom the Germans had not yet, as yet, driven to their death knew what was in store for them. The old men put on mourning clothes and gathered in their homes for prayer. Then they went to Lvovskaya Street. The invalids were supported by others, and some were even carried. And all of them were killed."

THIS COMMITTEE CAME INTO EXISTENCE TO ACHIEVE THE RESCUE OF THE JEWS OF EUROPE

Here is Part of Its Record:

Our offices and representatives in Washington and in London, in Palestine and in Turkey, are urging the respective governments to undertake large-scale action to save the four million Jews in Europe's death trap.

We brought the problem of the Jewish disaster to the masses of American people by nation-wide advertising in the leading newspapers in this country and through national radio-broadcasts, as well as through books, periodicals, and leaflets.

We organized mass expressions of public opinion demanding immediate action, through a mass petition movement, mass rallies and dramatic pageants.

We organized the pilgrimage of five hundred Rabbis to Washington.

We requested and obtained the week of compassion and prayer by six thousand Christian Churches.

We initiated the movement to pay tribute to Sweden and Denmark.

We organized the protest against the omission of the Jewish disasters from the Moscow statement on atrocities.

Now, we are able to state with satisfaction that the President, at his press conference on November 6, and Secretary Hull, in his historic appearance before the joint session of Congress, specifically mentioned their concern with the Jewish tragedy. The 'ring of silence around the catastrophe of the Jewish people was broken.

More than that. In all our activities, we put forward as the first and most immediate demand, the creation of a specific Governmental Agency with the task to effectuate the rescue of the millions of Jewish people still alive in Europe.

Now a Bipartisan Resolution Has Been Introduced in the Senate and House Demanding the Creation of Such an Agency

This resolution recommends to the President: *"...The creation by the President of a commission of diplomatic, economic and military experts to formulate and effectuate a plan of immediate action designed to save the surviving Jewish people of Europe from extinction at the hands of Nazi Germany."*

This resolution was introduced by leaders of both Parties: in the Senate by Senator Guy M. Gillette and eleven of his colleagues; in the House by Congressman Will Rogers, Jr. (D) of California, and Joseph Clark Baldwin (R) of New York.

The hearings of the Foreign Affairs Committee of the House have just opened. Prominent men from all walks of American life are testifying, urging this resolution's passage. Wendell Willkie declared this resolution of "paramount importance. *The urgency of the situation demands immediate action. The bill deserves the wholehearted support of every American.*"

You Can Do Your Part, Too!

Wire or write to your Senator and Congressman. Write also to the members of the Foreign Affairs Committee of the House. Demand their co-operation!

You can do your part, too, to carry out our tremendous plan of activities. You can help us mobilize public opinion from coast to coast. You can help us keep alive our headquarters in Washington, London, Palestine, and Turkey to continue our work for a people in deepest agony and despair. For each day thousands that can be saved. *This is strictly a race against death!*

This Committee is asking the American people for substantial financial support with which it will be enabled to carry on its work for the rescue of the Four Million martyred Jews in Europe.

We need your financial help *immediately*—NOW! You can sign your name below and enclose your contribution to speed the effectiveness of our work to save the Jewish people of Europe. Whatever you give is evidence of your conviction that human life is worth saving!

EMERGENCY COMMITTEE TO SAVE THE JEWISH PEOPLE OF EUROPE

One East Forty-fourth Street, New York 17, N. Y.   MUrray Hill 2-7237

EXECUTIVE BOARD

CO-CHAIRMEN:
Peter H. Bergson   Louis Bromfield   Ben Hecht
Rep. Will Rogers, Jr.

VICE-CHAIRMEN:
Dean Alfange   William Helis   A. Hadani Rafaeli
William S. Bennet   Prof. Francis E. McMahon Lisa Sergio
Konrad Bercovici   Dean George W. Matheson Rep. Andrew L. Somers
Jo Davidson   Herbert S. Moore   Dr. Maurice William
Oscar W. Ehrhorn   Fletcher Pratt

TREASURER: Mrs. John Gunther

MEMBERS:
Stella Adler   Nathan George Horwitt   Michael Potter
J. J. Amiel   J. Jabotinsky   Victor M. Ratner
Al Bauer   Rose Keane   Curt Riess
Y. Ben-Ami   Emil Lengyel   Arthur Rosenberg
A. Ben-Eliser   J. Lipshutz   K. Shridharani
M. Berchin   Rabbi Philip D. Bookstaber John J. Smertenko
Rabbi Philip D. Bookstaber Lawrence Lipton   Andrew Syzk
Bishop James A. Cannon, Jr. Emil Ludwig   Irvin Taitel
Lester Cohen   Gov. Edward Martin   Thomas J. Watson
Babette Deutsch   Gov. J. Howard McGrath Gabriel Wechsler
Rep. Samuel Dickstein S. Merlin   Alex Wilf

┌──[By a ruling of the Treasury Department,]──┐
│   contributions to this Committee are tax exempt   │

EMERGENCY COMMITTEE
TO SAVE THE JEWISH PEOPLE OF EUROPE
1 East 44th Street, New York 17, N. Y.

I hereby join your efforts to obtain immediate United Nations action to save the Jewish people of Europe. I enclose my contribution to enable you to carry out this tremendous task in the sum of $............

NAME ....

ADDRESS ....

Please make checks payable to Mrs. JOHN GUNTHER, Treasurer

The New York Times, Friday, December 17, 1943 - Page 31

TIME RACES DEATH
What Are We Waiting For?

This is a message of reassurance and clarification to all those who have been disturbed by the report of Breckinridge Long, Assistant Secretary of State, made in a closed session of the House Foreign Affairs Committee which is holding hearings on the Resolution recommending the President to create a special commission to save the surviving Jewish people of Europe. This report has been interpreted as a move to *kill* or *suspend* the rescue resolution.

We who are dedicated to the task of saving the Jewish people of Europe from annihilation at the hands of Nazi Germany do not share the fears that the report released by Representative Sol Bloom (chairman of the House Foreign Affairs Committee) will have this effect. First, because we refuse to believe that it is the intention of anyone in the State Department to stand in the way of putting an end to the martyrdom of the Jewish people. And what is more important, because we know that *an aroused and united American public wants the Resolution passed.* We are confident that it will be passed.

Jewish Disaster Not a Refugee Problem

Mr. Long's report, however, is likely to befog the issue and to cause confusion in the minds of many people. Therefore some clarification is necessary.

Mr. Long's statement contained some interesting statistics on the activities and endeavors of the State Department to alleviate the plight of refugees during the past decade. But this has nothing to do with the Jews who are facing death now in Hitler's Europe.

The Baldwin-Rogers Resolution is not concerned with refugees—those comparatively lucky people who have escaped death. For these refugees there exists the Intergovernmental Committee on Refugees; a committee which does not, and was never intended to deal with the problem of saving those who are still facing death in German-Occupied Europe. The Commission as demanded in the Baldwin-Rogers Resolution is concerned with the fate of those who are not yet refugees.

Mr. Long's statistics on immigration into the United States—right or wrong—have no bearing on the Resolution in Congress. The practical measures for saving the Jews who are in Europe now do not include mass evacuation from Europe to the shores of America. There are more accessible territories under the control of the United Nations, such as Cyprus, Palestine and North Africa, as well as Turkey and other neutral countries in Europe, which can absorb vast numbers of the people now trapped in the ghastly ghettos and execution camps of Poland.

Irrelevant Statistics

But Mr. Long's statistics are incorrect. He has included in his figure of 580,000 refugees, admitted to this country since 1933, first, 378,468 aliens who were resident in the United States of America and who returned to this country after traveling or visiting abroad; also 112,692 immigrants from "non-quota" countries like Canada, Mexico, and the nations of Central and South America; also other similar categories of "non-quota" immigrants, like professors, ministers, etc.

Mr. Long's statistics are incomplete for they do not show that while in the ten and a half years between January 1, 1933, and June 30, 1943, only 476,930 immigrants out of the accorded quota of 1,500,000, were admitted to this country, and only 243,965 persons permanently left the United States. They do not show that since the war, when the need for refuge became desperate, less than 100,000 refugees were admitted to this country, and of course not all of them were Jews.

But the decisive fact remains that all these statistics are irrelevant to the Baldwin-Rogers Resolution. For the sake of thousands of human lives these arguments must not be raised to becloud the issue, to spread confusion and doubt.

This Resolution Must Pass

BECAUSE—this will prove that the slaughter of an entire people is no longer ignored by the United Nations; that at long last the Jewish disaster has received consideration from America, the leader of the United Nations.

BECAUSE—it will hearten and strengthen the tortured millions of men, women and children in the ghastly ghettos of Poland and the Balkans; it will offer them the hope of escape to safety.

BECAUSE—it will inform the world that the time when the United Nations were weak and humiliated and impotent has passed; that the satellite countries of Europe, fearful of the advance of our American armies, must seek grace from the democratic nations against the day of reckoning, and must therefore cease to participate in Hitler's barbarous program of annihilation.

But What Has Held Up Action?

President Roosevelt answered this when he declared that "the heart is in the right place, but it is a question of ways and means."

Now this Congressional resolution seeks to provide the ways and means. Nothing has been done till now to save the Jews of Europe because the machinery for action did not exist. Nothing will be done so long as this machinery is lacking.

Confusion and distortion must be brushed aside. The people of America demand action.

You too must raise your voice. You too must stand up and be counted.

Let Congress know that the American people join us in the fight to save the surviving Jews of Europe—a cause which represents not only human lives but is also a test case of humanity and civilization.

A United Public Opinion Demands the Immediate Passage of the Resolution to Save the Jewish People of Europe

Wendell Willkie: "... This resolution is of paramount importance. The urgency of the situation demands immediate action. Th bill deserves the wholehearted support of every American." (From a statement to the House Foreign Affai Committee.)

Mayor Fiorello H. La Guardia: "... An adverse vote in the House would be fatally misconstrued and misinterpreted by o enemies and the world and would add to the terrible toll of human lives. An expression Congress represents the viewpoint of the American people. I urge very definite consideration." (From his testimony before the House Foreig Affairs Committee.)

Alfred E. Smith: "I earnestly urge that the Foreign Relations Committee approve of the bill to effectuate a plan of immediate actio designed to save the surviving Jewish people of Europe from extinction at the hands of the Nazis." (Telegram Rep. Sol Bloom, Chairman, House Foreign Affairs Committee.)

Dean Alfange: "... In every speech Hitler has made, he never failed to attack the Jews. In no speech made by the United Nation statesmen was Hitler ever answered. The tragedy of the Jews has been our own apathy" (testifying before the Hous Foreign Affairs Committee, in his capacity as Vice-Chairman of the Emergency Committee to Save the Jewish People of Europe).

NATIONAL ORGANIZATIONS:

Representatives of the AFL and the CIO, representing many millions of American workers, appeared before the hearings of the Hous Foreign Affairs Committee urging the immediate passage of the resolution and promising support and cooperation with the rescue commi sion when it will be created. Among the many other organizations who demanded action upon the resolution was the Executive Committe of the National Republican Club.

THE PRESS OF THE NATION:

New York Herald Tribune: "... Certain it is that nothing will be accomplished to save Nazi-Europe's surviving Jews fro methodical extermination by doing nothing. The resolution calls for affirmation of the America position, assumption by America of leadership in doing whatever may be done to save lives now. We should not hesitate to lead in imperative a humanitarian cause." (From an editorial, December 1st, 1943.)

New York Post: "... The creation of the commission called for by the resolution is a first step, and a necessary one, to halt th greatest massacre in history, so let's have it." (From an editorial, November 23rd, 1943.)

New York World-Telegram: "... The problem is immediate. It is humanitarian, not political. It is as much a Christian as Jewish problem—more, in the sense that any solution depends on the conscience, the initiative and the action of so-called Christian governments.

"... We hope this resolution passes, and that the President moves promptly." (From an editorial, November 24th, 1943.)

New York Daily Mirror: "This is not a Christian or a Jewish question. It is a human question, and concerns men and women all creeds. The resolution should pass." (From an editorial, December 10).

Washington Post: "It is a rare occurrence in legislative history for a bill or a resolution introduced in either house of Congress t have multiple sponsorship and the backing of members of both parties. . . . The fact that so many distinguishe lawmakers are backing this resolution suggests the urgency of the move they recommend." (From an editorial, November 27.)

Washington Sunday Star: "... According to the Emergency Committee to Save the Jewish People of Europe—a group made u of distinguished Americans of different faiths—two main courses of action could be followed now The first of these would be for the United Nations, particularly Russia, Britain and the United States, to make clear that although the rece joint warning to the Nazis on atrocities did not specifically name atrocities against Jews, the warning was nevertheless all-inclusive. Th second would be to try to effect the transfer of Jews from Nazi-dominated countries to territories beyond Nazi control.

"In line with this approach to the problem, there are now pending in both houses of Congress identical resolutions. This (the resolutio is a helpful move serving to speed up the official adoption of a rescue program that is sorely needed. The plight of the European Jews cann be exaggerated; their lot is worse than that of any other group within the reach of Hitler." (From an editorial, November 28.)

Washington News: "... The issue is not sectarian. The sole object here is to rescue as many as possible of these Hitler victims pending complete Allied victory and the liberation of Europe from barbarism. . . . Americans cannot b indifferent in this terrible emergency." (From an editorial, November 24.)

Scripps-Howard Papers: "... The suggested commission would find ways to provide temporary refuge in nearby neutral and Allie territory for all those who can get out of Nazi-controlled countries. . . . The mere fact that the Unite States Government is concerned may have some effect in modifying the wholesale brutality, especially in such Nazi-satellite states as Rumania Hungary, Bulgaria and Vichy France, where there is growing realization that the Allies are winning the war and will hold criminals to account." (From editorials, November 25th, 1943.)

Hearst Newspaper Chain: "... There is little time to be lost. . . . Mr. Peter Bergson, Co-Chairman of the Emergency Committe to Save the Jewish People of Europe, declared before the House Foreign Affairs Committee tha '1,000,000 additional Jews would be murdered by the Nazis before the Armistice.' This is too ghastly to contemplate. What is required no is action." (From editorials, December 10th, 1943.)

Christian Science Monitor: "It was in 1933 that a war of annihilation against the Jewish people in Europe—some eight millio persons—was systematically begun by the newly risen powers in Germany. Today, ten years an more than three million victims later, the United Nations still have failed to take any direct decisive action to rescue the innocent subject of the Nazis' blood purge.

"An opportunity to redress, in a small degree, this sin of omission is offered in the resolution..." (From an editorial, December 9th, 1943.

Chicago Daily News: "Congress should pass without delay the Gillette-Taft-Baldwin-Rogers joint resolution for the establishment o a commission to devise and execute measures for the rescue of as many as possible of the 4,000,000 Jews in Axis-controlled Europe, most of whom may be massacred or starved. . ." (From an editorial, December 7, 1943.)

SENATORS AND CONGRESSMEN WHO INTRODUCED THE RESCUE RESOLUTION

SENATORS: Guy M. Gillette, Allen J. Ellender, Homer Ferguson, Joseph F. Guffey, Edwin C. Johnson, James E. Murray, George L. Radcliffe, Elbert D. Thomas, Robert A. Taft, Frederick Van Nuys, Sheridan Downey, Bennett Champ Clark.

REPRESENTATIVES: Will Rogers, Jr., Joseph Clark Baldwin.

EMERGENCY COMMITTEE TO SAVE THE JEWISH PEOPLE OF EUROPE

One East Forty-fourth Street, New York 17, N. Y. MUrray Hill 2-7237

EXECUTIVE BOARD

CO-CHAIRMEN:

Peter H. Bergson, Louis Bromfield, Ben Hecht, Mme. Sigrid Undset

VICE-CHAIRMEN:

Dean Alfange
William S. Bennet
Konrad Bercovici
Jo Davidson
Oscar W. Ehrhorn
William Helis
Prof. Francis E. McMahon
Dean George W. Matheson
Herbert S. Moore
Fletcher Pratt
A. Hadani Rafaeli
Lisa Sergio
Rep. Andrew L. Somers
Dr. Maurice William

TREASURER: Mrs. John Gunther

MEMBERS:

Stella Adler
J. J. Amiel
Al Bauer
Y. Ben-Ami
A. Ben-Elizer
Theodor Benwahum
Rabbi Philip D. Bookstaber
Bishop James A. Cannon, Jr.
Lester Cohen
Babette Deutsch
Rep. Samuel Dickstein
Nathan George Horwitt
E. Jabotinsky
Rose Keane
Emil Lengyel
I. Lipshutz
Lawrence Lipton
Emil Ludwig
Gov. Edward Martin
Gov. J. Howard McGrath
S. Merlin
Michael Potter
Victor M. Ratner
Curt Riess
Arthur Rosenberg
K. Shridharani
Johan J. Smertenko
Arthur Szyk
Irvin Taitel
Thomas J. Watson
Gabriel Wechsler
Alex Wilf

WON'T YOU HELP?

This Committee considers it a sacred duty to do all humanly possible to save the Jew people of Europe. Our offices and representatives in Washington and in London, in Pa tine and in Turkey are steadily working in this direction, trying to get large-scale governm action. But we need your financial help.

We operate solely through voluntary contributions. By your support will be determi the speed, scope and effectiveness of our fight to save the Jewish people of Europe.

EMERGENCY COMMITTEE
TO SAVE THE JEWISH PEOPLE OF EUROPE
1 East 44th Street, New York 17, N. Y.

I enclose my contribution to enable you to carry out your tremendous task in sum of $________

NAME ________________

ADDRESS ________________

[By a ruling of the Treasury Department, contributions to this Committee are tax exempt]

3

Building a Coalition for Rescue, from Capitol Hill to Hollywood

Kook sought congressional support for his rescue campaign, as a means of pressuring the Roosevelt administration to intervene on behalf of European Jewry. In this chapter, he recounts how he and his colleagues went from door to door on Capitol Hill in 1943–44, pleading the Jews' case. Kook describes his group's success in persuading members of Congress, intellectuals, and celebrities to join his coalition for rescue. Neither the continued opposition of the Jewish establishment nor the investigations of him by the Federal Bureau of Investigation and the Internal Revenue Service convinced Kook and his comrades to desist from their activities. As with Chapter 2, the interview with Kook is supplemented by recollections of these events by Congressman Will Rogers, Jr., author Max Lerner, and Kook's associate Samuel Merlin.

WYMAN: What kinds of tactics or techniques did you use to build support for your rescue campaign?[1] How, for example, did you enlist major celebrities, Jews and non-Jews? The other Jewish organizations didn't do it much. How did you get a guy like Ben Hecht or the congressmen and senators?

KOOK: Well, the congressmen and senators and government officials is one thing and the intellectuals is another thing. [Attracting the support of] the congressmen and senators is a lobbying job, a very hard, tedious, persistent—I would compare it to the ladies who put over the temperance, they were the Temperance League—very similar. We simply ran around peacefully, quietly, a few guys and myself. They and I started running around—beaver work. Get an appointment and come in and talk, just running around the halls of Congress and government offices—my legs used to wear off—just plain hard lobbying.

WILL ROGERS, JR., RECALLS:[2]

When I first met Peter Bergson, he was just a stranger coming in the door. And my office was on the top floor, the fifth floor, of the old House Office Building. I assumed that he had just been walking around, banging on doors, and he happened to bang on my door at this particular time. I don't remember the exact details, but I do recall sitting down there and talking to him about the Jewish position in Europe. Now I knew a fair amount about it because it had been in the papers. We knew the Jews were under attack, the Germans were killing them, the Poles were throwing them out, and all this kind of thing was going on.

But I was just like anybody else—all right, what could I do about it? I couldn't do anything about it. Peter Bergson stimulated me, I think more than that, he stimulated my wife and she began to talk about it, and I began to talk about it and I began to be more interested. And then when he had a meeting, I tried to avoid any meeting with him if I could help it—I didn't want to be in public, making speeches, but slowly it dawned on me that it was my duty to go out and speak against the destruction of the Jews. Bergson never made the appeal on the Jewish basis. And I wouldn't have accepted it on that basis, either. It was a humanitarian, a worldwide basis. The Jews were being kicked around in Europe. The United States should do something about it, and the other people should do something about it, whether the victims were Jews or Cherokees or whatever it was.

K: Months it took, you know, how many meetings to go to, get to this one to introduce you to this one to get you to this one.[3] Reminds me of the way I met Adlai Stevenson. One day, Jo Davidson, the sculptor,[4] asked me, "Do you know Adlai Stevenson?"[5] And I said I didn't know who he was. So he says, "He's a lawyer from Chicago, and he's this and that, and he's an assistant to [Frank] Knox, Secretary of the Navy.[6] Would you like to meet him?" I said, "Sure I'd like to meet him." We were then working on the Committee for a Jewish Army.

So I go to see Stevenson, and I talked to him about the importance of having a Jewish army. And he says to me, "Mr. Bergson, why did you come and see me? I am Assistant Secretary of the Navy." So I looked at him and I hit it right—later, when he became a public figure, I knew him and his door was open to me—so I looked at him and I said, "If I knew—if you could introduce me to the Special Assistant to the Secretary of War, I would appreciate it very much, because I would much rather talk to him. But I don't know him. Jo Davidson knows *you*." I mean, I wasn't being funny, you know. I said it very seriously. And he liked it, the frankness. He had a sense of humor. I wasn't being humorous. I said, "Because I'm here. Because I'd talk to anybody. We are trying to do something."

You know what happened? The first statement by an important person for a Jewish army was from Frank Knox. Stevenson is the guy who got it, as a result [of our connection]. Later on, he brought Knox to the "We Will Never Die" pageant. When we were talking about the extermination I went to see him again several times. Again he said, "What can I do?" And I said, "Well, maybe you can raise it in Cabinet." And then I asked him if he'd come to the pageant. I said it was important. And he came, when it was in Washington. Stevenson and Knox came. He brought him. But the effort, the time and energy that you consumed, it was like marching up an enormous mountain, carrying God knows what.

We began this lobbying in 1940. The Jewish organizations weren't interfering with us then because nobody knew about it, they weren't paying any attention. In our ignorance we weren't smart enough not to go to the guys who were with Stephen Wise and the main organizations. It would have avoided a lot of trouble. Later on, I understood that and I left [Senator Robert] Wagner,[7] for example, alone, because I knew that everything I do with Wagner will go back [to his friends in the mainstream Jewish leadership] and I didn't want any pressures. So, Wagner was doing what he was doing there and I didn't go to him. In the beginning, we went to him and he joined the Committee for a Jewish Army, too.

Then later we got smarter and we started looking for senators from states where there were no Jews. And we found them on the merit of the cause. [Senator Guy] Gillette we found this way.* [Senator Elbert] Thomas we got.[8] The three main senators we had were Thomas of Utah, Gillette of Iowa, and [Edwin] Johnson from Colorado.†

Then we got an another ally. Did you see the thing where [Senator] Scott Lucas‡ attacked me bitterly? [Lucas acted in response to the Bergson group's advertisement in *The New York Times* in which it described the Bermuda Conference as a "Cruel Mockery."[9]] This was our biggest crisis. At that point, Johnson got scared. And Johnson called me in and he said—he was very somber—and he said, "Maybe I shouldn't do this, but I feel I should." He says, "I don't mean

---

*Guy Gillette (1879–1973), Democrat of Iowa, served first in the United States House of Representatives (1933–1936), and then in the Senate (1936–1945 and 1949–1955). He was an early supporter of the Committee for a Jewish Army, and also sponsored the Gillette-Rogers resolution of 1943, which led to the establishment of the War Refugee Board. During the period 1945–1948, when he was not in the Senate, Gillette served as president of Bergson's American League for a Free Palestine.

†Edwin Johnson (1884–1970), Democrat of Colorado, served in the United States Senate from 1937 to 1955. His active role in the Bergson group included serving as national chairman of the Committee for a Jewish Army; introducing an unsuccessful 1943 resolution urging the participants in the Bermuda Conference to act quickly to rescue Jews from Hitler; cosponsoring the Emergency Conference to Save the Jewish People of Europe; and cosponsoring the Gillette-Rogers rescue resolution.

‡Scott Lucas (1892–1968), Democrat of Illinois, served first in the United States House of Representatives from 1935 to 1939, and then in the Senate from 1939 to 1951. He was Democratic Whip (1947–1949) and majority leader (1949–1951). He was one of the three U.S. delegates to the ineffectual Anglo-American Bermuda Conference on Refugees held in April 1943. Lucas spearheaded the public criticism of the Bergson group for its unauthorized use of names of senators in its advertisement castigating the failure of the Bermuda Conference. Lucas was not mentioned or directly alluded to in the ad, but he took it as a personal attack.

you to think I have lost confidence in you, which I haven't, but I want you to know that the FBI is listening to your telephone. And they're doing it with a court order they got on Lucas's instructions." Since Johnson and I were talking on the phone frequently, the FBI apparently felt that they should tell him.* He was the chairman of the Committee for a Jewish Army, and all that. Yeah, because they were afraid of him.

Johnson said, "I hope I am not doing something which is against the interests of my country by telling you." And I said to him, "Senator, if you think that—" He also said, he was a very frank man, he said, "They've been doing it for quite a while now, so that if there is anything wrong, they already know it. But you might as well be careful, personally, because they're going to try and deport you." He probably thought I shouldn't say something personal, I don't know, if there was anything wrong with my personal life, a morality charge or something like that. And I said to him, "Senator, if you feel that anything they could hear by overhearing would be a problem, I think you should resign. If you have any doubts in me."

He got very upset. He said, "I didn't mean that at all. If I felt I should resign, I would resign. I don't feel I should resign. I'm just very concerned. Scott Lucas is a very powerful man, and he is angry as anything. He spoke for a couple of hours on the floor of the Senate. And he promised to come back. He said that you'll hear more." The culmination of the speech was that all these people who are doing all these terrible things, are headed by one who is not even an American, and who is a foreigner, and who is not even legally in this country. Which was a clear indication of things to come. And I was arrested later, by the way. They did sign deportation procedures. They did.

Then Johnson gave us some advice. There was a man called Senator Langer from North Dakota.[11] Langer was a very controversial man

---

*The FBI's surveillance of the Bergson group, which began in 1941, included periodically eavesdropping on the Bergson activists' telephone conversations, opening their mail, sifting through their trash, and planting informers inside their organization.[10]

in his state, a real fire-and-brimstone politician, who was arrested while he was governor on some charge. I don't know what. Eventually he was found innocent and was elected senator. And Lucas tried to unseat him after he came to Washington. Lucas tried to get the Senate to vote that he is not qualified to be a senator, to eject him—there is a procedure, I'm not too familiar with it.

And Lucas failed because the Senate is basically a club. Johnson told me this thing. Langer was a member of the Committee for a Jewish Army. We went down the list and anybody who would join, we enlisted. We didn't know if he was a bad senator or a good senator. We didn't care. Johnson said, "You know this about Langer?" And I said, "I heard of something." He said, "Well, Langer, of course, has never forgiven Lucas." So Johnson said the reason it's so difficult—this Lucas incident—is because Lucas put it on a personal basis. "He learned," he says, "from the way he couldn't unseat Langer. And he's now appealing to the same sentiment. He didn't make it a political issue, he made it a personal issue where senators are being used against another senator for political purposes. He made it a personal thing." He accused us of having used the names of senators in an advertisement without permission.

W: Lucas did?

K: Lucas, yes. The rest was immaterial—all his speech. The main issue was—you know what really was the thing, what we did? The fact is that none of the senators—first of all, we had been doing it all along and they were seeing the ads. We had this Proclamation of the Moral Rights of Stateless and Palestinian Jews. It was impossible to run an ad and everybody sign it, because mechanically, technically it was impossible.

W: One of your ads had two pages, and one page was full of little signatures. Must have been a thousand signatures.

K: That was the Proclamation. Only once we did that. That took months to put together. Now, from that Proclamation we used a quotation: "We shall no longer witness with pity alone," and we took a select list of names that did sign this declaration, yes. And we used to put it on the side of later ads with a sharp line setting it off from the rest of the ad.*

W: Yes. But the implication, the impression is that they are supporting what's in the main part of the current ad.

K: The impression was correct. They are supporting the general cause. Which they did. But there was no implication that they were supporting every word written, because underneath the main section there were other signatures. You see, if underneath we would only print "Emergency Committee," there would be some credence to the charge, but underneath there were three or four signatures; chairman, secretary, treasurer. In other words, it was clear there was one set of signatures on this, and another separate set. Why would there be different signatures?

W: Technically, yes. But the ordinary reader who sees that ad could well assume that all these names have endorsed that ad.

K: The Senators didn't feel that way.†

W: Well, a couple of them did. Truman did.

K: One. Truman. One, only. And he didn't charge us with anything, he just said, "I wish to resign from the committee as of now." Meaning he didn't put any aspersions on the past. He didn't say because you used my name—he just said—I talked to him and he said, "I like my friends," in his crisp little voice, "Scott Lucas is a friend of mine." I said, "Well, Senator, you know we are right and he is wrong." He says, "Yes, but he's a friend of mine, and I'm loyal to my friends, and I want to help Scott Lucas." He took it as a politician, one politician to another.

---

*"A Proclamation on the Moral Rights of the Stateless and Palestinian Jews," a two-page spread, including the printed signatures of more than 1,500 leading Americans. Described by Secretary of the Navy Frank Knox as a historic document, the advertisement ran in *The New York Times* on December 7, 1942, pages 14–15. It appeared after that in the *Chicago Daily News*, the *Los Angeles Times*, and the *Washington Post*. The full sentence that Kook quotes from is: "That we shall no longer witness with pity alone, and with passive sympathy, the calculated extermination of the ancient Jewish people by the barbarous Nazis."

†Thirty-three senators had by this time endorsed the Proclamation, and their names were included in the sidebar to the advertisement that had angered Senator Lucas. (More than 160 members of the House of Representatives had also signed the Proclamation by May 1943.)

This is what Johnson was afraid of. Precisely. And the thing that helped us was Langer. Langer came in—Johnson says you're not going to get anybody to speak here against Lucas, except Langer. And he says you should use Langer because, when he will speak, it will break—by there being one senator on each side, even though Lucas is much more important than Langer—it will break the "club" attitude, it will become an issue rather than a personal thing. What's bad about it is you put it on a personal basis.

We outlined strategy—he wouldn't see Langer, he said I should go and see Langer, which I did. And Langer was tickled pink, I mean he was just roaring to go. And he used to get up on the floor and start needling Lucas saying, "On such and such a date the senior senator from Illinois promised us to come back and inform us about the achievements at Bermuda, and I quote—" and he would quote him, and then say, "Well, it's been a week, it's been two weeks, it's been a month—" Lucas never came back, because he didn't have anything to come back with. Lucas, apparently, at that point really thought that a week later he will announce my arrest, or my something—he will have some real pay dirt.

W: He was really out to get you after that.

K: Oh, yes! He wasn't only out to get me—probably there were some of the Jewish leaders involved—

W: He felt that you had made a personal attack on him. Your ad was pretty rough, wasn't it?

K: It was a pretty rough subject.

In the ad we quoted the *London Sunday Observer*: "Bermuda was a mockery, and a cruel jest." But didn't you see the earlier ad we printed, addressed "To the Gentlemen at Bermuda," in which we encouraged them.[12] There was nothing personal there. We started out wishing them success and saying that this is an historical opportunity to save lives. We didn't start out with a negative attitude.

W: No, but afterward you condemned what they did.

K: Well, it certainly should have been condemned. Like I told Mrs. Roosevelt, I don't think we could have condemned it sharply enough. I mean it was an outrage.

W: Let me get back then to the basic question of the techniques you used to build support. Now you've been talking about how you approached the Congress—

K: The technique was very simple, we didn't know we had a technique, you know. It's like a guy who paints and then after he paints for thirty years, he discovers he had a technique. What we did is—you walk into a congressman, and you outline the cause to him, and either because of humanitarian reasons, or because he didn't see who would be against it, he joined. Once he joined, it doesn't become that easy to get him to quit. And some of them, especially, became really involved.

W: That was pretty much hit or miss, as you would go through the list and some would respond?

K: Right. Once we got a few, one led to another. We'd organize special functions.

W: And, as you were saying earlier, if you had a contact in a Cabinet department at a lower level, you'd follow that up, and that would lead somewhere else.

K: Right, that's right.

W: Were all of your small inner circle carrying on this effort?

K: No. Washington was my—

W: Did you do almost all this footwork yourself?

K: No. We had Americans helping. We had volunteers. We had paid people. We had a staff. In Washington in the very beginning I had a man who was a former [congregational] rabbi, Baruch Rabinowitz, who was quite effective.* He used to be a rabbi in Hagerstown, Maryland. Then his wife got killed in a car accident, he was shook up, and he quit being a rabbi. He came and worked with us.

---

*Baruch Rabinowitz (1914–) is the descendant of a distinguished line of Hasidic rabbis beginning with the founder of Hasidism, the Baal Shem Tov. While studying for rabbinical ordination at the Rabbi Isaac Elchanan Theological Seminary (the forerunner of Yeshiva University) in New York City in the 1930s, he became a follower of Vladimir Ze'ev Jabotinsky and was active in the American wing of Jabotinsky's Revisionist Zionist movement. Rabinowitz served as rabbi of Congregation B'nai Abraham in Hagerstown, Maryland, from 1937 until the death of his wife in an automobile accident in 1940, following which he left the pulpit to work full-time as the Bergson group's chief lobbyist in Washington, D.C. After the war, Rabinowitz immigrated to Israel, where he presently resides.

W: These people worked for the same low pay that you people did?

K: A little better, but low.

W: But still very substandard; in other words it's a case of dedication to what you were doing.

K: Yes. Oh, yes. And some were volunteers, various people that we would bring in. But very few of the core group of Palestinian Jews came to Washington regularly except myself.

They were in New York. They were in Chicago. They were in Philadelphia. All trying to organize branches. They did organizational work more than I did. Also because we felt that Washington would be more responsive to Americans—get a feeling that there is a popular movement behind it, not only an ideal, not only a humanitarian thing, there was backing from a grass roots movement. And once we started getting people, some of them got very involved, and the others came along because of their leadership.

Say a man like Senator Thomas was a very much admired man in the Senate. He was a professor of political science. He was a very religious man, he was a real Mormon, a real practicing religious man. And he was very much looked up to. And the fact that he stood, and Johnson stood, and Gillette, made a small but very strong core. We had a big mortality rate, so to say, of people who joined from the outside. If they became subject to pressure to quit, many more of them quit than in Congress. Because by the time the pressure started in Congress—if it was a matter of only three congressmen, probably two would have quit. But by the time it started we had a hundred and fifty, and it worked the other way. They said, "Who else is quitting? Who from this list is quitting?" They didn't want to part from the pack. And there weren't enough quitting. They never succeeded in organizing, say, thirty to quit at once. Here and there one congressman would. From the whole list of senators, Truman was the only one who quit. And this was our worst period, when this Lucas thing happened.

I think this was the main incentive—we offered them an opportunity they didn't have before. Gillette and I became very friendly, and sometimes he really said, "I'm grateful to you for giving me the opportunity to be in this thing." It's very peculiar, but that's how it was.

He wanted to do something. There was no other opportunity. After all, this was an issue that was around. You couldn't be a senator, let's say, and not be aware of this thing. And they did not get a genuine opportunity to participate till we gave them this opportunity. And the same thing happened with the intellectuals to a large degree.

You know, let's take Ben Hecht. How did we come to Ben Hecht? There was a paper called *PM*. One day I was reading *PM* and I saw he writes columns. I liked his columns. I didn't then know that he was an important writer. He wrote an article in which he was poking fun at some assimilationist Jews—a very sharp article. He was talking about all these Jews who hide under the carpet—hide their Jewishness and this and that. And Ben Hecht wasn't a so-called Jewish Jew, you know. But he was different. I read this and I liked the article. And he got very strongly attacked. So then he wrote an article called "My Tribe Is Israel," explaining his positive attitude toward being a Jew. And why, because of this, he permits himself to attack what he thinks is wrong—what he called "yellow-bellied crawling Jews." That's what he called them.

And I sat down and wrote him a little note with a compliment on his article, saying we liked it very much, saying we were from Palestine, and this and that. We want to meet him. I said I'll take the liberty to call you for an appointment. And I did, and he set a time at the "21" Club. It is true the way he tells it in *A Child of the Century*. He has a beautiful opening there. If you didn't read it, read just the opening.*
The way he describes how he got involved, and it is all true except the

---

*"I offer my evidence neither as Jew nor propagandist but as an honest writer who was walking down the street one day when he bumped into history. I had no notion on that April day in 1941 that any such collision was taking place. All that was evident was that I was buying drinks for a pair of male strangers in the Twenty One Club. One was a tall, sunburned fellow in a sort of naval uniform. He was Captain Jeremiah Helpern, who had recently created a Hebrew Navy for the nonexisting Hebrew Republic of Palestine. The navy had consisted of a one training ship that had run aground in the Mediterranean a few months before and been put out of service. Captain "Irma" Helpern had come to the U.S. in search of some Maecenas to buy him a new navy. My other companion was a man in his thirties, of medium height, with a small blonde mustache, an English accent and a voice inclined to squeak under excitement. He was Peter Bergson of Warsaw, London and Jerusalem." (*A Child of the Century*, 516.)

part that we were hungry—physically hungry. That was also true, but not on that day. You know, a writer fuses things.

We talked, and he became intrigued with what we had to say—never heard of the Irgun, never heard of any of it. And we spoke to him about the idea of a Jewish army. And he became very interested.

Charlie MacArthur,[13] who was Hecht's close friend, and they wrote many things together, later on used to pester the hell out of me. Because, he says, "Ben was never with any cause more than six weeks. And I was waiting for the six weeks to pass," he says, "and you son of a bitch, it's now *five years*. How did you do it?" And he kept on pestering me. He didn't understand how come this man stayed with this thing from 1940 till 1948. It was the only time in his life he was involved in something on that continuous a basis. It also—obviously he was emotionally involved because he wrote two plays, one book, and a lot of other things about it. It affected his whole personality, you know.

I think the reason was that we spoke a language that these people understood, even though we had accents, that we were more attuned to the time without realizing it. And, also, that what we asked them to do, nobody else ever asked them to do. I mean, nobody came to Ben Hecht and said to write an ad, write something. He was a writer. I mean, you know what he could do—write a pageant. Let's do something theatrical.

MAX LERNER RECALLS:[14]

The group around Peter Bergson was a quite fascinating group. This was the first time that any group of Jews really made use of the state of the art in publicity, in public relations. There was a touch of genius about Bergson, but a touch of genius, I think, lay in his being a master of publicity or what we later came to call the art of public relations. He seemed to have grown up with this capacity, perhaps with his mother's milk, I don't know, but he was so good at it. . . . I am sure Ben Hecht recognized that element of publicity genius in Bergson. They were a remarkable duo. What they produced in the way of newspaper ads, in the way of Madison Square Garden extravaganzas, in the way of controversy and so on, was a publicist's dream. And for that reason, I think, I was lucky to be able to find a group like that to work with.

I think Ben Hecht's talent lay in his capacity to dramatize whatever it was that he touched. He could make a breakfast egg seem theatrical. . . . And by some merciful gift of history, Ben Hecht's talents became available for a cause like ours.

W: You didn't have difficulty getting people like Moss Hart, and Billy Rose and—?[15]

K: We had a very strong division of arts, as we called it—writers, artists— and it was a very beehive of activity. They did an awful lot. Marlon Brando, for instance, who was not a Jew—he was of Italian origin—he worked with us for a couple of years. He appeared in our pageant, the second one. In 1946, we did a play, it wasn't a pageant, it was a beautiful play that Ben Hecht did called *A Flag Is Born*. And it was Brando's second big chance on Broadway, really. He had appeared before, but not in as good a part as this because the other play folded.

WILL ROGERS, JR., RECALLS:[16]

I might not have ever become fully active if it had not been for Ben Hecht. Because Peter Bergson spoke, he sometimes spoke in a way that complicated things. But when Ben Hecht was connected with it, I knew that this was a group that was going to actually rescue Jews. And that is what I was interested in. . . . I wanted to be associated with Ben Hecht. I didn't want to be associated with these Jewish groups running around in Philadelphia and Boston and worrying about their meetings and all that stuff. But Ben Hecht was a literary man out of Hollywood. He was a great guy. I thought it was wonderful. Oh good, I can go down and meet Ben Hecht. That's one of the things I liked. [There was a] report that he got his Academy Award statuette and he used it as a doorknob. And so I admired him even more when I read about that. . . .

He wrote the best ads. He wrote simple, direct, declarative sentences that went straight to the point. I think the Ben Hecht ads did more than any other single event to stimulate Americans that wanted to save Jews, to take action.

MAX LERNER RECALLS:[17]

One of the things that used be said about Peter Bergson was that he used people like Ben Hecht and Will Rogers, Jr., and people like me. It's possible, but I didn't care whether I was being used or not. I was using him as well as he was using me. I was using him as a lever, some kind of leverage in order to make my small energies more effective than they would otherwise be. And if in the process he was using me—why, God bless him. That was all to the good. We were using each other, but the critical question was for what purposes. And these purposes really were the dominant things. . . . What counted for me was my chance to work with any group. I didn't care what group, any group in which in my small way I could be somewhat effective in saving as many Jews as possible.

W: Now, you have this great mass of signatures, that is, I don't know how many hundreds of people ultimately signed your "Proclamation on the Moral Rights."[18]

K: A few thousand. About five thousand, eventually. We didn't publish all of them.

W: Well, most of these people couldn't have been approached individually. Did you send mailings out, and they just signed the declaration and sent it back in, and it was no more than that kind of support? They were interested, willing to lend their name, and that was the end of it.

K: By mail, sure. In that period, Americans were responsive to causes, and there was little fear around. If you approached somebody with something that seemed to be right and just, he would join. Most of these people signed. Some of them were spoken to. Some of them— you see, what was done is that many of the signatures were gotten, not by us, but by somebody who was spoken to. There wasn't one mailing, there were various mailings. So that if we wanted to get people in the University of Massachusetts, we'll speak to you, if we run into you. If you agreed, then we would ask you, under your stationery, to send out a letter to all the professors there saying I'm enclosing a declaration which I signed and I believe this is a worthy cause, and this and that, in your own words. And I'm writing to ask you, will you join with the others and myself and sign this thing. That's how most of the signatures were gotten, by getting, in each category, somebody to do a small mailing. Sometimes people did a letter and gave us the stationery, and we had it typed and sent it back to them. Sometimes they did it themselves. It took a long time. It was a massive effort.

W: You must have been constantly making these lists, trying to get a good list together.

K: Merlin was working. The chief of operations was Merlin. He was a remarkably effective man.

Another thing I should have mentioned to you, it is very important, is the religious aspect of this thing. To many of these people, to Senator Thomas, for instance, this was a religious thing, very much so. I mean he felt a kind of moral-religious duty to do this. And to many people this came back to the basic, what van Paassen used to call the Judaic-Christian civilization. Which had a very great meaning to many of these people.

W: You just don't associate this with politicians much.

K: No. But it was there. I remember when Merlin first met George Maurice Morris, a Washington lawyer who backed us loyally. Morris was a conservative Republican and was president of the American Bar Association. And at one point I told Merlin that Morris was working for us and had even once tried to write an ad and wanted me to put a thing from the New Testament on top of the ad.

So, once there was a meeting in New York, and George Maurice Morris came up, and afterward he and Merlin and I went somewhere for coffee. And finally Merlin and I got home and Merlin says, "You know he barely makes it under the line of being an anti-Semite. How do you get a guy like *this* to work?" I said, "I don't know. Here he is." He was a very important lawyer, a senior partner in a firm, president of the bar association, very social. You couldn't pick up a social column in a paper—and I used to read them because it was mixed with diplomatic things—Ambassador So-and-so and Mrs. Pumpamaduke had a dinner and among the guests were the George Maurice Morrises, and this and that, and what Mrs. Morris wore. And where does *he* come into this thing to save Jews? And to withstand pressure. No sooner was he with us than he got letters that he shouldn't be there, and phone calls. And he got involved, he stayed involved. There was some basic decency about these people.

The quote he wanted to put on top of the ad was: "Lord, if thou hadst been here, my brother would not have died." (John: 11:21 and 11:32). I thought it was a very nice quote. Though this ad led to some trouble with some of the Orthodox guys around. With them that's like converting. What do you mean? You run an ad with a quotation from the New Testament? Emergency Committee to Save the Jewish People of Europe and a quote from—but we did it, and with pleasure. I didn't see anything wrong with it at all, though this ad never materialized. So the religious aspect played a role, not overtly, but I'm sure it was there. I'm sure it was there.

WYMAN: Did you get a substantial amount of non-Jewish support?[19]

MERLIN: Names, we got. Figureheads. The names were mostly non-Jewish, because we aimed at non-Jewish. We aimed at the members of the Supreme Court, we aimed at members of the Cabinet. We aimed at labor leaders. The non-Jewish labor leaders were for us; the Jewish labor leaders against us. The rank and file—of the 750,000 people who sent in contributions in amounts from $1 to $5,000—these people, I would estimate, that of each hundred contributions maybe one or two or three were from non-Jews. I don't know. I can't prove it.

But on the other hand, adverse reactions from Christians, from non-Jews, were practically nil. We used to get hundreds of letters every day. There were a few—perhaps through the years, one hundred—letters by cranks, anti-Semites and so on.

On the other hand, we always had some expressions of sympathy. For instance, the FBI. One morning, quite early, around five minutes past nine, my secretary came in and said, "Two gentlemen want to talk with you." They identified themselves as from the FBI. They are accountants. They came to see our books. So I said, of course. They said we need a room and we will use it for seven weeks. And actually they moved in; the first few days there were three guys. Then there were two guys. And they worked from 9 till 4:30 every day. I told our bookkeeper to cooperate and to give them everything they want. And they became a part, a feature of the office. Every day they came in, like everybody else. So after several weeks, many weeks—and they changed some teams—but the original two were still there, and one of them came in and said that he appreciates greatly our cooperation with them, that of course he cannot tell us what his report will be, but in order to make clear his feelings, he took out some money and he said this is our contribution, but it has to be anonymous, he said. And second, you have to write it in your books.

KOOK: The Internal Revenue Service also examined the Emergency Committee. Do you remember when the Internal Revenue people came? They also made a contribution.

W: Did the Emergency Committee attempt to collaborate with other American ethnic groups, such as American Poles, American-Czech groups, people of national backgrounds who were also being oppressed by the Nazis? You did it with the Hungarians.[20]

K: We did it with the Hungarians. In the Emergency Committee, we did a very definite thing with the Hungarians, both with the clergy and with a couple of committees that they had. I don't remember there being any Polish committee, or us being aware of a Polish committee.

W: Well, there are dozens of Polish-American organizations—

K: Yes, but that's a different thing. The Poles, while one shouldn't generalize, and I don't want to make a generalization, but the feeling about the Poles on this issue was a very touchy thing, because there were many stories circulating at the time about the Poles being willing accomplices with the Germans.

We worked with Indians, later on. We helped them an awful lot because we were a lot stronger than they were in Congress. We always tried to find—we worked with the Koreans, we worked with Syngman

Rhee.[21] It was government-in-exile, you know. We even gave him a little money.

And we did work with the governments, with the embassies. When we did the pageant "We Will Never Die," in Washington, I did quite a lot of maneuvering, because these damn ambassadors—we couldn't get anyone to take a first step. We wanted them to sponsor it—which they did, finally. The invitation read "under the auspices of the ambassadors of occupied Europe." I went to the Polish ambassador, to the Czechs. With the Poles, there was this professor, who was their representative to the League of Nations before this [Jan] Ciechanowski, the ambassador to the United States. And I said, "Look, Poland is the graveyard of the Jews, you have to take the initiative in this." And he said, "No, in the diplomatic corps we have to go to the dean of the diplomatic corps, who is the oldest one, who is the Belgian ambassador." So I went to the Belgian ambassador and he says, "No, the Polish ambassador," and this and that.

And finally, I decided to play a trick, and I made two appointments with them around half an hour within each other. I don't remember which one I saw first. I think that I saw the Belgian ambassador first because he was nearer. And I saw him, and I said, "Your Excellency, I am happy to tell you that the Polish ambassador accepted your point, and he has agreed to be one of the sponsors." And he says, "Oh, well, in this case I agree with you." Then I ran to the Polish ambassador and told him that the Belgian agreed, see. Then we had a crisis with them because of the French, because we insisted on having the representative of the French Committee of National Liberation. And they wouldn't have him, because they said he's not an ambassador. And we finally pushed that through, and the French were very appreciative. We worked closely with the Free French, from the beginning.

Generally speaking, maybe we overlooked—we probably overlooked a lot of things—I don't recall any activities on an ethnic basis, of Poles joining with us, even though we had a Congressman Dingell, who was one of our better congressmen, who was of Polish origin.[22]

W: If you were trying to build public pressure, mass public pressure—

K: There were a couple of other congressmen who had either big ethnic constituencies, or were themselves first-generation Americans who were still sensitive to the subject. Probably it was a mistake, we probably could have gotten wider support. Besides the Poles, there were many other groups. There were a lot of other groups.

W: Taft, who was conservative, supported the rescue bill.* And Gillette and several of the other people were not what you'd call real New Dealers. They weren't people that Roosevelt could count on to go down the line, like Wagner. You had a real mix. Guys like Ickes, who were supported by the liberals, and guys on the right, such as Wiley from Wisconsin[23]—

K: Wiley was on the right, Langer was on the right. Thomas of Utah and Johnson of Colorado were middle-of-the-roaders. What we really did, after we became a little bit more sophisticated, is that we ignored Wagner. We did exactly the reverse, you see. I mean, first we went to Wagner, naturally. And then we sort of ignored him. We did—I played the same game with Celler.† He and I became fairly friendly over the years; Manny Celler was a sort of all-Jewish congressman. To Celler I used to say, "Look, you're a Democrat and a Jew from New York, a life-long Zionist. We are delighted that you didn't yield to pressure and you stayed with the Emergency Committee." He wasn't active in the Committee, because we weren't interested, because the Zionists had him in their hip pocket. He would make statements on Palestine every day

---

*Robert Taft (1889–1953), Republican of Ohio, served in the Senate from 1939 to 1953. A prominent member of the Senate Foreign Relations Committee, Taft cosponsored the Gillette-Rogers rescue resolution, and was the lead sponsor of the Taft-Wright-Compton resolution of 1944–45, which endorsed Jewish statehood and ignited a conflict between the Roosevelt administration, Congress, and the American Jewish community. Although Taft was not associated with the Bergson group, his intercession with the British government resulted in the release of Eri Jabotinsky from detention in Palestine, making it possible for him to join his Bergson group colleagues in the United States in 1942.

†Emanuel Celler (1888–1981), Democrat of New York, served twenty-five consecutive terms in the House of Representatives, from 1923 through 1973. He appeared on one of the panels of experts at Bergson's July 1943 Emergency Conference to Save the Jewish People of Europe.

of the week, every time the [Zionist leadership] wanted him to. You know, for him to say something, it didn't mean much.

In the Zionist effort to fight us, or to curb us, they stopped at nothing. This congressman Samuel Dickstein,* he was bad news. He was bad news. And he was head of the Immigration Committee. One day, I get an invitation from Dickstein, whom I barely knew, to come at a certain hour to meet with a group of Jewish congressmen. About 5:00 or 6:00 in the afternoon in Dickstein's committee office. I come in. It looked like an inquisition. There was one of those machines with a stenographer. Dickstein; Congressman Sabath,[24] who was the dean of the House, the oldest congressman alive, from Chicago—he was a very old man, didn't know what was going on anymore; Klein, who was a very young congressman from Brooklyn.[25] It was just his first term. Celler, and one other guy I don't remember. Five of them there were—five or six: Dickstein, Celler, Klein, Sabath, and two more. Six.

The spokesman was Dickstein. And he started talking this and that, and he simply—to boil it down very simply, you know, he more or less said, "You either behave, or we'll deport you." He didn't say it in so many words, but he couldn't have been more explicit. And he was chairman of the committee, and he stressed it a few times, and he said, "This is all on the record, and this is this, and one shouldn't mistake democracy with lawlessness, and don't feel that you can just come to this country without—on a temporary visitor's visa and do whatever you wish, and this and that and so forth." And I don't remember ever being so harsh with people. Honest to God, I'd pay anything for this record, but it's stupid to even hope that it exists, you know, because they probably destroyed it that evening. 'Cause Celler wound

---

*Samuel Dickstein (1885–1954), Democrat of New York, served eleven consecutive terms in the House of Representatives, from 1923 through 1945. He chaired the House Committee on Immigration and Naturalization from 1931 to 1945. Although he endorsed the Committee for a Jewish Army in its earliest phase, served on one of the panels of experts at Bergson's July 1943 Emergency Conference to Save the Jewish People of Europe, and his name appeared on some of the Bergson newspaper advertisements, relations between Dickstein and the Bergson group later soured.

up inviting me to dinner. I mean, I thought they were crucifying me, I thought I'd never get out of this building.

W: You didn't have relationships with any of these people at this time?

K: Yes, I did! I'd met Celler several times without any real contact, you know. You know, a politician—

W: Was Bloom there?

K: No, Bloom wasn't there. He was sympathetic and cautious, sort of neutral, you know. He said, "Look, generally I'd join, you know. I mean, I think you're all right, but occasionally you boys—" Let's say he was acting more or less like you were playing devil's advocate before. He'd say, "Now, boys, you did this wrong." And he was trying to calm down the Zionists. He was really better than I thought. I thought he was a grouchy man, but there was no conflict between us.

This meeting with the six Jewish Congressmen was after the Bermuda blowup—the thing with Lucas and all that. It wasn't Bloom. It wasn't Bloom, it was the Zionists. That was a politicianist thing. It was. That was a real Mafia kind of stuff. And, I just blew my stack, you know. And I talk too much as you know, and I did then, too. Except that I was much younger and much more volatile then. And this guy was the only non-Jew there, the one taking the record; you know he's never heard such stuff. I told them, "How American is it that six Jewish congressmen sit here?" You know, this kind of stuff started coming out. "I mean, are you really acting now as Americans, or as Jews, or is there a conflict between the two? What are you doing here? In what capacity are you talking to me, Mr. Dickstein? In what capacity are you blackmailing me?" I used terrible words. And the reason I remember is that I said, "If you think that a little bit of jail and a little deportation is going to mean anything to me at a time when thousands of people are getting killed a day," I said, "you've got the wrong man." And Dickstein—it was terrible.

There was a real scrap, real scrap. Then Celler sort of made peace. There was no peace, you see, because Dickstein I never saw again. I had no use for him. He was trying to do a hatchet thing, you know. And why he decided to do it in the presence of the others, I don't know. He could have done it in his office, but apparently he thought it smart.

They didn't anticipate such a reaction. Celler said, "You misunderstood, he didn't mean it, and this and that and there, and now let's talk. And it's a terrible thing that Jews fight, and after all, we are here because, you know. We have nothing against you." And, you know, stuff like that, playing it the other way. And he meant it, Celler. He meant it. He was a little shook up the way it came out. I remember he wound up, he says, "Young man, I want you to have dinner with me." And I tried to get out of it 'cause I was angry. And I didn't want to fight with him because he was really all right. He was there, and demonstrated it: First he kept quiet, so I attacked all of them, and then he started talking, and then the thing sort of broke off with nothing. And he and I went and had dinner at the Mayflower, where he was living at the time, Celler, you know. Ah, that was a terrible thing. A real awful thing.

CHAPTER

4

The Opposition

Although Kook's rescue campaign attracted widespread support in the Jewish community at large, many leaders of established Jewish organizations strongly opposed and intentionally obstructed his activities. In this chapter, Kook discusses the reasons for the Jewish leadership's opposition and reflects upon instances in which some of his supporters were persuaded to sever their ties with him. Kook also recalls how President Roosevelt, in agreement with his Jewish advisers, was unwilling to allow him or his supporters to present their case to him. Kook describes how he attempted to influence the president through First Lady Eleanor Roosevelt. As in previous chapters, events discussed by Kook are also briefly seen from the perspectives of Will Rogers, Jr., Max Lerner, and Samuel Merlin.

Kook: There could have been no reason why we [and the Jewish leaders] shouldn't work together.[1] There were a lot of very able people there. But we couldn't get them to budge. We couldn't get them to budge.

The fact is that after all [compared with] their potential for doing things, we were a very small thing. We became a big thing because they did so little. But their potential was so vast by comparison, with what they could have done, with the resources that they had. You have to remember that most of the time we spent most of our efforts getting the few dollars to do what we were doing.

WYMAN: Do you remember specific instances that we haven't already discussed, where you tried to approach them with the proposition that you work together on rescue?

K: Yes. But they wouldn't talk to us. It isn't this, you see. The best time to approach them was when they came to us, because then, at least, they acknowledged we were something—we had some sort of bargaining point. Other times, you called them, they wouldn't come to the phone. Gillette—this is much later, by the way, it's not on this issue—Gillette became president of the American League for a Free Palestine after the war. He was a very important senator, a very important politician in these days, with great national standing. He had stood up to Roosevelt on the packing of the Court, and he won. He did a tremendous act of self-sacrifice in becoming president of the American League for a Free Palestine. He could have gotten jobs paying four or five times that amount, and much more prestigious. And what did he need it for? He did it as a matter of conscience, you know.

And he thought—he knew about all our problems with the Jews— he received enough Jewish delegations to try to pressure him, and got enough letters—but he figured that if he will become president of the American League for a Free Palestine, then he will be able to get the Jews to work together. And this apparently played a much bigger role in his decision than I imagined. If he had told me this, I would have cooled him a little on it. But he figured that if he, Senator Gillette, is going to write a letter to all these big Jewish leaders, and he is president of the American League, and he will suggest a joint action, that he'll get a response. He wrote them a letter, and most of them didn't even answer it. The man was heartbroken.

W: The Jewish leaders' whole approach to their contact with American society had been, "Don't be unconventional. Don't make a splash. Do it fairly quietly. We might have a boycott or a mass meeting. But to go beyond that to any loud, shrill kind of thing, such as some of these ads, would be provocative."

K: Yes. But they didn't even do a lot of behind-the-scene things. They didn't.

W: My point is that your style of operation—

K: Alienated them. Possible.

W: It was foreign to their whole way of acting. It made them shudder.

K: Maybe this is the reason why they paid no attention to our efforts to do something together. It's possible. Whatever contacts we had with some individuals who were—there were some guys who were sympathizing with us, there was a man called Rudolph Sonneborn who worked on the Committee for a Jewish Army and then moved to work with them.[2] We remained sort of friendly, personally, and I would keep in touch with him in this, and I used to push him.

Later on I pushed him to do this big illegal immigration Haganah* got involved in after the war. He was the big guy in this bricha† thing they write books about, and I pushed him into it. I said, "You guys should do it, we don't have the money." And I told him, "Look, we did illegal immigration before the war because the people could finance it. Now the Jews are paupers, don't have the money that it costs them, the costs are much higher. We don't have this kind of money." Later on we managed to raise enough money from [our 1946 Broadway play] *A Flag Is Born* to buy a boat and call it the *Ben Hecht* and bring in one boat. Because it cost a blasted fortune. We couldn't raise the money. Actually, we brought in two boats. The *Ben Hecht* and the *Altalena* later, and we had two little boats that were sabotaged and burned, I don't know by whom, in Italy.

W: At this point do you think that your Irgunist connection had anything to do with the Jewish leaders' attitude toward you, toward your group?

---

*The underground militia of the Labor Zionists in Palestine.

†*Bricha*, the Hebrew term for 'escape' or 'flight', refers to the movement that organized the mass migration of Holocaust survivors from eastern Europe to Displaced Persons (DP) camps and other locations in southern and western Europe, during the late 1940s, in preparation for their emigration to Palestine. The presence of hundreds of thousands of Jewish refugees in the DP camps, clamoring for permission to settle in Palestine, contributed to international pressure on Great Britain to withdraw from Palestine.

K: Possible. Yes. On the question of extermination again, I would say that the crux of it really is that they treated it routinely. It was another pogrom, like—they had a kind of fatalism about it, which prevented them from seeing the magnitude of the horror. And they acted normally. And we didn't succeed. I felt a terrible sense of frustration. Once, I thought I broke through in that meeting in Proskauer's home. But it wasn't, it wasn't real. We didn't succeed to convey to them what we conveyed to other people. And this is what it was. I don't know, it isn't a question of they didn't believe, because there was no debate about it, they knew what was going on. But, they didn't act!

[In August 1943], there was an American Jewish Conference in New York City organized to come up with a unified Jewish position on postwar Palestine. But not on the saving of the Jews.* In the middle of the extermination!

I went there with great expectations, as part of the audience. I had thought: "At long last, the Jews are going to get together and do something for rescue." I remember being flabbergasted to find that I was wrong. I went to the opening session and I was sick! I walked out. I was sick at the whole thing, because I had been sure that this was a

---

*In an effort to achieve unity among American Jewish organizations on the question of implementing Jewish rights in Palestine after the war, B'nai B'rith president Henry Monsky convened the first American Jewish Conference in 1943. Following local elections in various Jewish communities in June, the conference opened in New York City on August 29. All Jewish organizations were permitted to take part in the elections, except for the Revisionist Zionists and two Jewish Communist groups. One faction of prominent Zionists, led by Stephen Wise, sought to soften the conference's stand on Jewish statehood, in deference to pressure from State Department officials and the American Jewish Committee, which was anti-Zionist. But a groundswell of pressure from the delegates, coupled with a fiery speech by Abba Hillel Silver, resulted in the overwhelming passage of a strongly pro-Zionist resolution, prompting the AJCommittee's withdrawal from the conference.

The issue of rescue was added to the conference agenda just before the gathering began, and did not play any major role in the conference proceedings. As historian Isaac Neustadt-Noy has remarked, "The paradox of the AJConference, was that the very drive for its establishment originated in an atmosphere of emergency expressing the psychological impact of the Holocaust. However, feelings of helplessness, and fear that Jewish unity would be considered damaging to the war effort, channeled most of the Conference's energy to the postwar period."[3]

conference on saving Jews. And I was even playing around with the idea of making some sort of a dramatic statement, of saying even though we weren't invited, and we are not a Jewish organization, so we will help, try to do *something*. I sat there completely flabbergasted. They started talking as if nothing was happening. And I didn't go anymore. I left. I didn't even stay till the end of the session.

W: I wonder if age was a factor. They were much more set in their ways, in their channels. They had their workaday approach to their positions. And it would have taken a lot to shift them out of that. Whereas you people, not having settled into any groove, were ready to try all kinds of things.

K: Yes. Also perhaps there's another thing, maybe it's going too far from the field. In those days the Jewish leadership continued to have the pattern, long since given up, that was brought over from East Europe, where the leaders were volunteers. That's to say, the prominent businessman, the prominent lawyer, the prominent industrialist; usually people with money; not the prominent professor, not the intellectual, not the prominent writer. Proskauer was a rich lawyer, Shulman was a rich lawyer, Monsky was a rich lawyer. Three lawyers, but all very wealthy lawyers. Then there was Rabbi Wise and Rabbi Silver. And the second rank of leadership were businesspeople. Now beneath them—they were all busy with their own careers, their own lives. And to them this was like a charity activity. It was an extracurricular activity to which they gave a certain part. If they worked thirty hours a month on these issues, it was a lot.

W: Well, along with their other activities. This was only one of many activities, fit in—

K: No, but they were working with their business things. I would say that with a guy like Proskauer, if he gave the American Jewish Committee an average of two hours a day, it was a lot.

W: But the executive secretaries of these committees—

K: Yes, but executive secretaries weren't important enough in those days because Jews had contempt for people who worked for Jews professionally.

W: You were working sixteen or more hours a day, and seven days a week on this thing. Which they were not able to do, psychologically or oth-

erwise. They had families, they had friends, they had social functions
to attend, that had become part of their way of life.

K: And their own businesses.

W: Szamuel Zygielbojm, a Jewish member of the Polish government-in-
exile who committed suicide in London in 1943 to protest the world's
abandonment of the Jews, had, just before his death, met with a
courier from the Warsaw Ghetto. The courier said that when he asked
the leaders of the Warsaw Jewish underground what message he
should bring to Jewish leaders in the Free World, they said: "Jewish
leaders abroad won't be interested. At eleven in the morning you will
begin telling them about the anguish of the Jews in Poland, but at 1
P.M. they will ask you to halt the narrative so they can have lunch. That
is a difference which cannot be bridged. They will go on lunching at
the regular hour at their favorite restaurant."[4]*

K: Yes. Their routine life, yes.

---

*The lack of urgency among many American Jewish leaders during this period is evident
from a number of episodes. For example, Frederick A. Lazin has noted that in the spring
of 1939—during the same period as the crisis over the refugee ship SS *St. Louis*—the
American Jewish Committee could not hold meetings of its leadership on Sundays
"because in the spring so many of the members went to the country for weekends."
(Frederick A. Lazin, "The Response of the American Jewish Committee to the Crisis of
German Jewry, 1933–1939," *American Jewish History* 68 [March 1979], 304.) Palestine
Labor Zionist leader David Ben-Gurion, visiting New York City in the summer of 1942,
complained to a colleague that it was impossible to arrange a meeting of Zionist leaders on
a Friday afternoon because "even with Rommel nearing Alexandria, everybody left for the
country for the week-end." (Ben-Gurion to Shertok, July 8, 1942, S25/1458, Central Zionist Archives, Jerusalem.) Dr. Nahum Goldmann of the World Jewish Congress, who met
with a State Department official on July 14, 1943, to discuss plans to rescue Jewish
refugees in Rumania and France, remarked at the end of the meeting that he "was leaving
on his vacation at the end of the week," so any further discussion of this critical rescue plan
would have to be handled by one of his deputies. (Memo of conversation between Dr.
Nahum Goldmann and Bernard Meltzer, Acting Chief of the Division of Foreign Funds
Control, State Department, July 14, 1943, State Department 840.48 Refugees/4063,
National Archives.)

Emanuel Neumann, a senior staff member of the Zionist Organization of America, who
was negotiating the terms for Abba Hillel Silver to become cochairman of the American
Zionist Emergency Council in 1943, recalls in his memoirs how "Silver went to Maine with
his family for their summer vacation, while I was left in New York, entrusted with the delicate and difficult task of working out the tricky details of the future management of the

K: The Zionist leaders thought that we were disrupting the Zionist cause, and this was on the rescue issue. You know, during the days of the Army Committee, we were not respectable, our style was jarring to them. And they thought that someplace, you know, it isn't good form for Jews to behave this way. It didn't fit. We were also foreigners—we were acknowledged foreigners, and they thought this was in bad taste.

During the rescue campaign, they thought that the whole content of our activity was damaging the Zionist cause. They thought that we were taking away the brunt of the pressure that had to be brought on Congress, on the administration, to pressure the British to open the gates of Palestine. The main pressure was to open the gates—they thought we were taking it away. The British could have bought them off then with 25,000 immigration permission certificates. They would have been quiet.

I once had a debate with Rabbi Wise. He turns to me and he says, quoting the Bible, and he says, "*Mi samcha,* who appointed you?"[5] The literal translation is: "Who put you in charge?" In other words, "Who is your constituency? Who appointed you? In whose name do you speak? We are the recognized leaders." When he said that we are endangering American Jewry, you see. So, when it came my turn, I said, "Rabbi Wise, you said, 'Whom do we represent?'" I said, "We represent the conscience of the Hebrew nation. We represent ourselves. You are an American clergyman and a member of the Democratic Party. Just as Rabbi Silver is an American clergyman and a member of the Republican Party.[6] And I want to solemnly declare here—" you know, also being a little dramatic to his dramatizing, I speak off-the-cuff, by the way, I never prepare speeches. So, I said, "that on the day on which

---

Council between these two formidable principals, [Stephen] Wise and Silver." (Emanuel Neumann, *In The Arena* [New York, 1976], 189.) The following year, Silver spoke similarly of Wise. When the scheduling of a meeting between American Zionist leaders and Secretary of State Stettinius was delayed because Wise was vacationing at Lake Placid in upstate New York, Silver complained: "The Zionist Movement in these critical war times must conform with the lecture schedule and the vacation schedule of Dr. Wise." (Silver to Neumann, August 22, 1944, A123/315, Central Zionist Archives, Jerusalem.)

one square yard of Palestine will be free, I shall be there as a citizen, and abide by the decision of whoever will be the government of the Hebrew people—of the Hebrew Republic—or of the Free Palestine." Whatever words I used then, I don't remember. "Whereas you will then continue to be an American clergyman, member of the Democratic Party."

And I saw that this thing shook him a little. So, like all people who have to make hundreds of speeches, this theme crept up in various other talks in which the question of authority between us and the Jewish Agency came up. And I said, "We are an emergency thing. We were born out of an emergency, speaking by the power of our own conscience, hoping that we represent a consensus of the need of the Hebrew people. Whereas these people are leaders of a community of a different nation, and intend to remain there." And Rabbi Wise wasn't going to go out and say that when Palestine will be free, he will move there.

WILL ROGERS, JR., RECALLS:[7]

When it was known that I was becoming a member of the Bergson group, then there was a terrific amount of pressure from all sorts of areas. I went back to Beverly Hills and I remember meeting with Rabbi Stephen S. Wise in a synagogue. I had never been in a synagogue before. I didn't know quite what a synagogue was. And I put on that little funny hat and all the stuff and went down there. He took me aside and he said, "Now, young man. I knew your father very well. Now you are getting confused, you are getting mixed up with the wrong type of people. Let me tell you and steer you clear when you come on the Jewish problem, or want to meet the right people, the responsible people." He put the heat on me very, very heavy, but very, very suave, very indirect. He was quite the diplomat. He didn't say, "If you do get mixed up with them, you are not going to be reelected." He wasn't that direct, but he certainly made every pressure that he could, and where he knew it would be effective. I greatly admired and respected him. And he used that, and he used our association and my father's association with him as a means of trying to convince me to stop being connected with the Bergson outfit.

He said I was killing myself with the Jewish community. But I didn't care because after all, I was not going to be reelected to Congress. I was going off to the army. And I knew that I was right. I knew that these people had to be saved and we, the rescue committee, was a good committee. And while he was lambasting Peter Bergson, I knew that that wasn't true. He just didn't know that I was unreachable on this particular issue, because I felt so keenly and so deeply that we had to have this rescue effort.

The threat that establishment Jewry felt toward the Bergson outfit was that here were a bunch of upstarts, raising money, raising Cain. Getting readership and getting notice. Effective notice. And taking it away from the Jewish organizations. I think that they felt that Bergson was stealing their thunder.

Having the name Will Rogers, Jr., by the way, did give me a certain importance. Especially when it came to the rescue of the Jews. Because my father was supposed to represent the best of America, his name was as American as America itself, and things of that kind. And I carried a little bit of that with me, yes. I recognized that it was a big boost to the committee which was regarded by some as radicals, as a bunch of outsiders, and they were un-American. Well, they found it very difficult to attack me as being un-American and I think it was a big advantage to the organization.

W: One of the questions that was thrown at the Emergency Committee was about financial irresponsibility.[8] It was claimed that you people were taking in all this money and who knows what you were doing with it, and your reply was that there were quarterly financial statements that were openly available.

K: To try and attach to us financial charges is a mean, criminal offense. Not only immoral, it's criminal, because anyone can check the whole record of our functioning and existence.

For instance, the guys at the War Refugee Board became quite friendly with us. There was a situation where if you got a government permit to send money from here to Switzerland, there was a rate differential, which constituted about—if you send a thousand dollars, you made $300. With the permit, you send $1,000 to Switzerland and you got so many Swiss francs at an official rate of exchange. With the francs you got back $1,300—at the same bank. So, now, a couple of the guys at the War Refugee Board called me in and said, "Look, you're struggling all the time for money. These businessmen, we keep on giving them licenses and they're just kiting the money. We know what they're doing. They take a million dollars, or half a million dollars, and they get the license—they borrow it. They send it there, they pay back the million dollars, and you see? The Swiss are going to shut this thing off because all these other people are using it. Why don't you ask for a permit? Never say that we told you about it."*

It was absolutely legal. So we submitted the request, and they gave us a license for a quarter of a million dollars. And then I ran around like a chicken without a head to borrow it. We didn't have a quarter of a million dollars. To borrow a quarter of a million dollars, we finally did it. It was the first time that we managed to send a little bit of money to the Irgun in Palestine, who were breathing heavy on our necks all the time to send them money, 'cause they really didn't care that much about what we were doing, 'cause they were choking there, and we didn't have any money here. We said, "Look, if we don't pay for what we are doing, we can't live here at all." We sent them some money, and we had some money, it was our biggest financial income.

At one point, as part of all this fighting and these attacks on us, the Internal Revenue swooped down on us. I don't remember in what year, probably in '44. And they sat in the offices in New York, I don't know, for two or three weeks—maybe half a dozen guys, because this was an effort to knock us out, you know, like they use the Internal Revenue to convict gangsters. They figured they'll catch us in something here. We were tax-exempt, and they'd probably find that we did something. What happened is—two things happened. One is that the guys who worked there, when they finished, made a contribution between them. This is a fact. They scratched together—every one of them gave a few dollars, and they said there's

*As it happened, the Treasury Department officials who directed the work of the War Refugee Board were also connected with the Treasury's Foreign Funds Control unit, the agency responsible for issuing permits for the transmission of funds abroad.

never been an organization like this. And digging through all these documents, they became convinced. They were mostly non-Jews, they were mixed, Jews and non-Jews. All of them, without exception, pitched in and gave a contribution to the guy who was our comptroller, a fellow called Maurie Rifkin.[9]

He was comptroller, running the money, a very fine man. Because there could have been some hanky-panky. We were working under great pressure.

W: But Mrs. Frances Gunther was always on your ad as the treasurer.[10]

K: Yeah, we just used her name. With her, we could have stolen all the money. She had blind faith in us. No, the man who really ran it was Rifkin. Then when things got bigger, he had an assistant. I wouldn't vouch that here and there a few dollars didn't disappear, because it was a large organization. But we were the only Jewish organization that liquidated itself. I don't think—I don't want to slur anybody—there was any organization that was run in a more considerate way financially than this thing was run.

There's another thing. I got a letter as a result of this examination, personally, from the Treasury, from the Internal Revenue Service, assessing me ninety-some dollars on insufficient taxes. And I hit the ceiling. I wrote them a bitter letter, of three pages or something, of denunciation, that this was a political thing, and so forth, and so forth. And a very nice man called me, called me up, and said, "I would like to meet you, Mr. Bergson, [I'm from] Internal Revenue." And I came there, and really he gave me a lesson, you know, because I didn't really have much experience—we were working like dogs—you know, a good sense sort of thing. And he says, "Why are you so angry? Why did you write us such an angry letter?" So I said, I mean, we were getting—we started with $25 a week—at the end, as chairman of the Hebrew Committee, I got $75 a week. And then we had expenses, see, so we were getting $15 a week expenses—$25 salary and $15 expenses.

W: This was in the Emergency Committee?

K: Yeah. In the days of the Committee for a Jewish Army and the Emergency Committee. What did I do? We had—Merlin and I lived in a one-room apartment. Most of the eating was at public or semipublic functions, in most cases. Occasionally we had time to buy a bag of groceries and go home and have a quiet meal. It was hard to get some money to buy a suit. One guy *shlepped* me once in Philadelphia and forced me to take three suits from his factory, so I was done with suits. Forced me to wear nice suits, though I didn't like it. I wore them because I couldn't afford to buy another one.

Anyway, the Internal Revenue Service guy says to me, "You should take this letter of the Treasury and frame it and hang it on your wall. There isn't a man in Washington who wouldn't regard this as a citation, that over a period of three years or something, you have underpaid ninety-some dollars in taxes." And he explained to me what it was. And they were right, by the way, and I paid it. He showed me the law. You see, to save effort we made a flat thing of $15 a week for expenses. And the law says that any fixed amount for expenses is regarded as compensation. You can submit, you submit a voucher that would come in one week to $14.75 and the next week to $17.45, and the other week to $12 or something. But, as long as you didn't itemize—and we got $25 salary, $15 expenses—and they simply ruled, not ruled, the law was it's all salary. As this was so little, it didn't make that much of a difference, because together it was $40 a week. So I paid the thing. But this was after a very careful examination, you know, and what they were looking for was exactly to find out whether we used any expense money for personal things.

W: I get the impression that some of your strongest backing came from Orthodox Jewry. And especially the few Jewish leaders who supported the Emergency Committee tended to come from the Orthodox—

K: The leaders? Yes. Rabbi [Eliezer] Silver was the head.[11]

W: And Wolf Gold[12] gave you a little support, at least in the rabbis' pilgrimage in Washington—he was part of that.

K: Only then. Or maybe in a couple of very little—Rabbi Gold, very little. The pilgrimage, yes.

W: Is this a correct assessment, that what support you did receive from important Jewish circles tended to come from the Orthodox?

K: Well, I would say—there's something to it. We had a separate, what we called a Jewish section [called the National Jewish Council]. We had some Jewish journalists and we had a few people—by Jewish, I mean Yiddish-speaking people. And also, it was a purely Jewish outfit because to the Orthodox people, this business of a nonsectarian organization didn't—they didn't feel comfortable in it. So we had a separate thing. Our whole approach, from the beginning, from the Committee for a Jewish Army, from the American Friends for a Jewish Palestine, was a nonsectarian approach.

W: Did you realize it was essential to involve non-Jews—you couldn't expect 5 million Jewish Americans to swing anything politically, without the help of non-Jews . . . ?

K: Frankly, we weren't that smart. Our whole feeling was, from the very beginning, was that we are a national liberation movement, and we thought that we will appeal to the American people, and we deserve their support. Why should Americans help Ireland and not us? We were a good cause. Because somewhere we were freed of this feeling that Jews are hated. We felt that Jews are hated, that there is anti-Semitism, and there are also other people. And I still feel so.

Maybe I'm influenced as I'm thinking now, by the fact that during very critical years we were victimized by so many Jews—many places—[in] some little town some guy would get a letter or something, or write us a letter and join—some prominent non-Jew in the community. And all hell would break loose, where all the Jews have jumped on his back. Our files are full with letters from people confused and apologetically withdrawing, saying, "Look, we don't want to get involved in any internal Jewish fight."

W: Let me get back to this question about support from the Orthodox wing of American Jewry. The Union of Orthodox Rabbis tended to back you up. The pilgrimage where you brought about four hundred Orthodox rabbis to Washington—this has to indicate Orthodox support for what you were doing. You couldn't have got fifty Reform rabbis down there, I don't think.

K: There were a couple. And we had this rabbi who helped during the rescue campaign, who came from Harrisburg. Bookstaber.[13] He was

Reform. But very few. Rabbi Louis Newman for a while supported us.[14] He was Reform. But then he was a sort of a follower of Jabotinsky, and then he—under pressure from his congregation—backed away.

W: Why do you think you had more of an appeal to these Orthodox than you did to the others?

K: I think they were a little more courageous.

W: Do you think that it had anything to do with the fact that you were the nephew of the Chief Rabbi [of Palestine]?[15]

K: No. I don't think it hurt, though. It wasn't on that level. It may have helped psychologically. Our march of rabbis—we just decided there should be a march of rabbis in Washington. We talked to the [mainstream Jewish] leaders and they said no. We thought that the rabbis are people, they are Jews like any other Jews. And we thought if we called the masses of the Jews to come despite the leaders, we would get some of the rabbis to come, the rank-and-file rabbis, maybe the younger ones.

What turned out was that [at first] we got no rabbis and we were getting panicky. We didn't want to call it off. We were going to do what we did in Madison Square Garden. In "We Will Never Die," we had a scene with rabbis. To average people, a Jew with a beard, carrying a holy scroll, is a rabbi. We wanted to have real rabbis, but we couldn't get any. Then somebody went to a home for the aged and gave them a little donation. And fifty old men—for walking on at Madison Square Garden—we had a mass scene of old Jews parading with the scrolls. [In the end, in the Washington march of rabbis, the Union of Orthodox Rabbis and the Union of Grand Rabbis did help. Hundreds of genuine rabbis participated.]

W: Did your rapport with the Orthodox have something to do with your ability to get along with the Yiddish press, which spoke to that community?[16]

K: We didn't get along very well with the Yiddish press. The majority of them attacked us. I don't think so. I think that Orthodox rabbis were simply more responsive, more—more Jewish, in a sense. They were more sensitive to the issue, and less affected by the environment.

W: What about the Vaad Hahatzala?*

K: We worked very closely with them. They worked very well. But they concentrated mostly on physical rescue, you know, like ransom, like taking out a specific number of people. They operated on the old Jewish theological concept of "He who saves one soul, saves the whole world."[17] They were not as politically attuned, in other words they weren't—they had a sympathy to what we were doing, but they believed that what was more important was concrete things such as bringing out a few Jews from Hungary. Not that we were against it. We helped them, and they helped us.

W: What about the accusations that you misrepresented things, in some of the advertisements. This is the question that Senator Lucas brought up in the Senate, when he charged that you had given the impression that all the senators whose names appeared on the "Bermuda Was a 'Cruel Mockery'" advertisement had agreed with the full text of the ad. Wasn't there a little bit of sleight of hand in that?†

K: Well, take a good look at the ads, and I don't think it would look like it, if you look at the full size of it.

W: Sometimes your opponents gave the example of when you had the ad saying "70,000 Jews for sale at $50 each."[18] Some people felt that you indicated there that you had a rescue apparatus in operation that actu-

---

*The Vaad Hahatzala, or Emergency Committee for War-Torn Yeshivoth, was established in 1939 by the Agudat ha-Rabbanim, an association of Orthodox rabbis in the United States. Its purpose was to raise funds to assist Polish rabbis and their students who had fled the Nazi invasion of Poland and were living as refugees in Lithuania. The Vaad gradually evolved into a full-time rescue agency that both provided material assistance to European Jewish refugees and sought to find haven for them in various countries, including the United States. The Vaad's activities also included attempts to bribe Nazi officials to suspend deportations of Jews to the death camps; lobbying U.S. officials to bomb the railroads leading to Auschwitz; and organizing hundreds of rabbis to take part in the Bergson group's October 1943 march on Washington. For a detailed account of the Vaad's history, see Efraim Zuroff, *The Response of Orthodox Jewry in the United States to the Holocaust: The Activities of the Vaad ha-Hatzala Rescue Committee, 1939–1945* (New York, 2000).

†The question was discussed in Chapter 3, pp. 82–86.

ally could bring them out for $50. Which at that time certainly was not true.

K: Nowhere! Nowhere, could you get such an impression from that ad. Only a malicious person could charge it. You know, you as a scientist may want to be very careful and say, "Well, you couldn't say that it was impossible to get such an impression," but certainly the average reader wouldn't get such an impression. Not for a headline that says "Guaranteed Human Beings," you know. I mean, who on earth would take such a statement in its face value—in its literal face?

W: Let me quote you from another ad, the one about "My Uncle Abraham Reports"; and this is at the end, where that coupon is, to send in: "This committee is asking the American people for a half million dollars with which it hopes and believes results can be secured effecting the rescue of the 4,000,000 martyred Jews in Europe."[19] Now, you see, technically speaking, you're not saying that this money is going to go to rescue operations. But it can certainly give that impression, that you are carrying on rescue.

K: Obviously, the intent was not to create an erroneous impression. We didn't sit there and very carefully word it so that people would think there is a way [to save Jews], because if there was a way we would be talking about it. We didn't say we have secret ways of saving individual Jews. We called the whole campaign "The Emergency Committee to Save the Jewish People of Europe." Obviously we thought this ought to be done by the government. The main thrust was—every one of those ads said, "Write to your Congressman, write to this, do this," you know.

I did have a great deal to do [with the ads] personally, so the accusation, if it is an accusation, should be addressed to me because we had professional people advising us and helping us and doing a great deal of the job, advertising people, but I had a certain feel for it and had a great deal of influence. I didn't determine it, many of the ads were done without my even knowing them, but generally I don't back away by saying I didn't do it. To the contrary. I don't think that, fairly, anybody with a modicum of goodwill could say that this was designed to mislead. I think it's vicious.

I think that people, in a time like that, who took—and it bothered me a great deal then and it still bothers me now—who took the trouble to question this. Of what importance is it, I mean, of what importance is it? We tried to raise some money, you know. When we said we were trying to raise half a million dollars, obviously we didn't hope to get half a million dollars. If you hoped to get half a million, you would say two million. 'Cause you never get your aim. You are trying to get people to send you five dollars instead of one. By mentioning a more respectable figure, you think that you will get a bigger amount. We were choking.

The sad part was that we had to devote a big part of our effort to raise the money. Because we tried to do both jobs at the same, you know, run an ad which does some good and also raises money at the same time. You couldn't raise money. You had to sit in Washington. You had to run around seeing people. You had to do a lot of PR work, which is quite costly. No matter how many volunteers you have, it still costs money.

W: You made yourself vulnerable if you put forward an ad that made it possible for that charge to be made. If the ad was ambiguous in any way, these people were going to seize on it.

K: I don't see anything wrong with this statement there, I don't see anything wrong.

W: Well, it says we need to raise a half million dollars so that "results can be secured effecting the rescue—" It doesn't say "by publicizing." It does just give the impression that—

K: No. But it doesn't say—it says "results can be secured effecting the rescue." Why, the whole campaign was a campaign to pressure the government to move. I mean, after all what is the whole ad? The ad is about Roosevelt.

W: Don't you think you put yourself in a position where you were vulnerable?

K: You forget the punch of the ad. The punch of the ad—

W: Your opposition isn't even going to look at the punch of the ad.

K: To hell with the opposition!

W: There's the chink in your armor.

K: We didn't care about them. We did not, we did not consider the opposition. I don't say that we ignored them completely, we are human beings; it probably affected us somewhat. But we tried not to be affected as much as possible, and we did what we thought would get the most results in the cause.

Why this was a unique ad, one of its kind. When you take the whole text, which is obviously a political drive at Roosevelt, you know—two thirds of the ad was the thing about "My Uncle Abraham." And there's no relation here to saying "Help save another Abraham."

W: I have to say that this particular ad is an unusual case. I've looked at many of these ads, and I've looked at every one in terms of "Do the opposition's charges hold up?" And this example is the one strong case I could find. In many, if not most, cases it specifically says on the coupon in the ad, "We need more money to publicize this further."

K: I read a long memorandum that was prepared by some—probably astute public relations people, PR people for one of the major Jewish organizations. It was entitled "The Machinations" or "The Shenanigans" or something, or "The Bergson Group and Its Shenanigans"—I don't know what it's called. A vicious analysis; careful, clever, analyzing—and they really say there that since we couldn't make any headway with the Jewish Army Committee, we then seized upon the opportunity for establishing the Emergency Committee. How debased can a person be? I'm not speaking with anger. I'm just speaking now, after the fact. I mean, here is a situation in which thousands of people a day are being murdered. No question about it, many thousands. And here come a few people who scream. And here come other people who say, "They are cheats. They are liars. They really don't care. They're just using it." I mean, what kind of a rotten person thinks of that?

W: They could have genuinely felt that. They were very suspicious of you. You were doing things in a very unusual way for them. You rocked their boat terrifically.

K: No. It takes a callous, insensitive human being to accuse somebody of exploiting the extermination of the Jews just because they wanted to have a cause. To me, it's beyond forgiving.

W: But look, for example, at the Greek shipowners we were speaking about earlier, who grossly inflated the rates that escaping Jews had to pay them. Weren't the Greek shipowners trying to make money on the tragedy of the Jews? There were a lot of people who did try to make personal gain out of it.

K: Right, right. I don't try to say that they were noble people, but I don't— I say that they're not as debased as the other people, who came out and said that the Emergency Committee didn't really care about the Jews being killed, they're just *using* the fact that they're being killed. I think it takes a depraved person to make a charge like this, to poke fun and say that when the cause of the dying Jews of Europe didn't seem to be profitable enough, Bergson invented another committee.

MAX LERNER RECALLS:[20]

In all my dealings with Peter Bergson I was aware of a kind of dark cloud that hung over. It was a dark cloud that made many Jews of goodwill, those who wanted to help their brothers and sisters, think that Bergson was the wrong person to use for those purposes. And when I tried to ask why he was wrong, the answer that came back was always ideological. . . . Yes, he's a Zionist, but the wrong kind of Zionist. The right kind is Chaim Weizmann. The right kind is Stephen Wise. The right kind is not Jabotinsky. . . .

I had never been very close to these ideological splits . . . so that when they told me about Jabotinsky and the rest . . . I said in return, "Who do you think I am? Do you think that I want to give up for purposes of ideological partisanship the humanity of my people and their survival?" How dwarfish! How petty all of that loomed in perspective when you set it against the greater thing that was happening.

And my mind kept coming back constantly to a figure of speech about the Holocaust. The more I got to understand what the Holocaust meant, the Final Solution, I saw it as a deep red gash across the living body of history. Everything on one side was what had been, everything on the other side was what was now. It became for me the greatest historical event of my life. And that was what was involved, not ideology—when people talked about Bergson.

My friends thought, "Well, this is like Max; Max goes in with these crazy radical, quixotic ideas." I had a reputation as pretty leftist for a while, pretty radical. In my writings. But the same people who criticized me for being too leftist, as soon as they found me lining up with someone like the Berg-son group, which was afterward pretty far right from their standpoint, then they criticized me for that, too. Of course they tried to exert pressure in every possible way, in correspondence, in conversation, in all kinds of ways.

W: Why did Max Lerner leave the Emergency Committee?[21] The people in the War Refugee Board had the idea that you sent out telegrams under his name without consulting him. That was their opinion.

K: God, no!

W: Why did he quit?

K: Max Lerner was enrolled by me to participate in the Emergency Con-ference, in which he did an excellent job. He was then a columnist for *PM*, in which he wrote an article called "What About the Jews, FDR?"[22] And then, directly after the Emergency Conference, he became one of the cochairmen [of the Emergency Committee]. And sometime later he called me up on the telephone, and he said that he was going—reluctantly—that he was going to have to quit. If we did something, he certainly, since he quit, he certainly would have been glad to have an excuse. And nowhere will you find that he used some-thing [as an excuse]. He called me up on the phone and he said, "I'm sending you a letter of resignation." He just sent a letter that said that he's resigning. And he said I want to explain to you personally that I do not want to take sides in a sort of—he didn't say parochial, I don't remember the word he used—inside organizational Jewish fight. "It doesn't interest me," he said.*

To which I got angry, and I said, "What about the Jews, Max Lerner?" And he blew his stack, and he says, "Peter, no matter how highly I think of you—and you know what I think of you—I'm not going to permit you or anybody to preach to me about my morality. It has nothing to do with what I feel about the Jews. It has to do with this and that, and I cannot be a part of Jewish organizational strife." Well,

---

*Lerner, who had been associated earlier with the Committee for a Jewish Army, resigned from the Emergency Committee in November 1943, unquestionably as a result of extreme pressure from opponents of Bergson.

he should have known better. We don't try to produce organizational strife. I mean, we didn't pick fights with anybody. We weren't an organization trying to unseat another organization. I mean, he spoke as if there was an American Jewish Congress and we organized an American Jewish Assembly to compete with them. And he knew; we used him like other people to try and talk to these people. He tried to get some of them to come to the Emergency Conference, and he couldn't. But apparently they got to him, and I don't know how, or with what pressure, and he quit.

W: You think this was Zionist pressure again?

K: No doubt about it. No doubt about it. He said so. He said he doesn't want to be a part of an internal thing. And the reason I remember this is because the more intelligent a person was, the more articulate, and also the closer a man was to the Jewish scene—I used to call him sometimes, and his father would answer the phone, he spoke with a thick Yiddish accent—well, when a non-Jew wrote to us that he joined for humanitarian reasons, but he doesn't want to be involved in an internal Jewish fight, it was hard to get mad at him. But with Lerner I got mad, because Lerner should have known better and should have cared more.

Believe me, I didn't even remember Dean Alfange left us.[23] If you were to ask me, "Did Dean Alfange stick out till the end?" I would have said, "Yes." It didn't impress me. You know, as a fairly minor politician, I mean, what the hell, you know. He was with us for a couple of years. But Max Lerner hurt. Not that he was so important, it hurt because he was one of us, you know. He was a guy who I thought felt like I did. And he worked, and he worked very well. He worked very well. He was good. He was a professor at the time, and he was very good at organizing, you know. During the conference he was the central figure because, you know, he was young then, relatively. No, he was young. Older than we were, but young. And a very vigorous guy, and very eloquent, you know, and he was just an up-and-coming star. And it hurt that he quit. Because we were looking for—he was a good writer, you know, and he had standing. And the reasoning! That was it!

I didn't see him for years. I felt very uncomfortable. I used to write him.

W: He didn't given you any excuse other than this?

K: No. He didn't want to be in an inside Jewish fight.

W: What about the resignation of Pierre van Paassen?

K: I liked old Pierre, you know. I have nothing bad against van Paassen, not now that he's dead, not before. As a matter of fact, he joined a new committee of mine in 1955. In 1955, I formed a committee called The Committee to Save the Middle East from Communism, after Nasser made his deal with the Czechs for $100 million worth of arms, and I saw what was coming in the Middle East and the Zionists didn't. And I quit my business then, and I formed the committee. And eventually the Israeli government forced me to get out of it. It's a separate story. But I then went to van Paassen, and he joined!

W: In van Paassen's letter of resignation, which was published in Kenneth Leslie's *Protestant* magazine[24] in April 1944 and reprinted by the American Jewish Conference, he wrote "that the people who are the leadership of these various organizations are four or five young men who were sent to the United States as a Palestine delegation by a small political group in the Holy Land known as the Irgun Zvai Leumi," and he mentions the National Jewish Council, the American League for a Free Palestine, the Emergency Committee, and the Committee for a Jewish Army.

K: The Leslie group was a Communist-front outfit. The real fight, the real fight really started later, after the Hebrew Committee began in May 1944. That's when they became vicious.

W: Isn't what van Paassen wrote essentially true?

K: One word isn't true—the word "small political organization."

W: Well, what could he say, a military organization?

K: Well, I mean, political denotes a Zionist faction, which it wasn't. The Irgun was a revolutionary outfit that claimed national interest. What he wrote was misleading. Of course you can say, "What is national interest?" Every party says they represent the whole nation, you know. But still there's a difference between a political faction and an underground revolutionary group that says "We speak in the name of the conscience of the nation." But otherwise it's exact. It's correct.

W: You don't deny the Irgun connection.

K: We were the Irgun delegation. No question about it.

W: That hurt you in this country, though.

K: Sure, it did! It hampered our work. But later on it helped. By the time it helped, [Zionist leaders] had started working on the Irgun [to persuade the Irgun leaders in Palestine] to deny that we were Irgun. Zionists claimed that "It's not true that Bergson represents the Irgun"! By 1947, when the Irgun became much more popular. And they said, "Bergson is a fraud because he doesn't represent the Irgun," you see. But the historical fact is that in 1939, there came a delegation of the Irgun [to the United States]. In 1940, I came here as the senior man of the Irgun abroad to take responsibility. Anyplace I said I was not a member of the Irgun, I was lying, because if I did, I would have been deported or God knows what, you know.

W: I have articles which quote you as saying, "Yes, I used to be in the Irgun, but if you're out of Palestine, ipso facto, you can't be in the Irgun."

K: Well, sure. Weaseling. It's also 100 percent true that we didn't do a single thing in this country except what we did publicly. We didn't do anything illegal. [After the war,] there were a couple of attempts, done without my knowledge, to try and smuggle some arms.[25] And I blew my top. We did not do, as a matter of principle, any underground activities in the United States.

W: Some of your opponents claimed that the Irgun was fascistic. The way fascistic was defined by the North American Newspaper Alliance was that it involved blind obedience to superiors. Were you bound fully to obey the command of the superior?

K: An underground organization which is organized in a military fashion obeys officers. The United States Army isn't fascistic, even though a sergeant takes an order from a lieutenant and a lieutenant takes an order from a captain, you know, and the captain from the colonel. Jabotinsky was called a fascist because he was a leader type. Mussolini was a leader type who had followers, Hitler was a leader type. Jabotinsky had a lot of what they call charisma, I mean, he had a lot of personal magnetism and he was—and that made him a "fascist," because he had blind followers, you see. Not in the military sense, but people were willing to follow him blindly. And also because Jabotinsky was a very effective opponent and they wanted to fight him. And they based it on the fact that Betar, the revisionist youth movement, way before the Nazis, had brown shirts. Then came the Nazis and took brown shirts. You see, they say, "Well, you're not only fascist, you're Nazis." By the way, after the Nazis took brown shirts, the Revisionists finally changed it to blue shirts, because they got tired of the argument and it became repugnant to them, no matter if they did it first.

Then Jabotinsky came and he defined the aim of Zionism as the establishment of what he called the Jewish state. And then he said that until such time, social internal problems should be delayed. That the nation should be united to achieve the statehood aim and the debates between free enterprise, capitalism, socialism, should be delayed until afterward. His opponents said, "This is fascist." If these guys are poor and they're underpaid and they're exploited, we want to improve their condition today. We don't want to wait until the Messiah builds a Jewish state.

W: It was a question of priorities.

K: Right. This was a legitimate difference of opinion. A base of a legitimate difference of opinion. Now, Jabotinsky was a kind of a genius in many fields. By the way, he was a great orator, he was a great writer. He translated Edgar Allan Poe into Hebrew and improved him, you know, he was also a poet. He was an extraordinary man.

We were even attacked as "fascists" because we approached William Randolph Hearst several times. He wrote an editorial about saving the Jews in all his papers—front-page editorial—he used to write them on the front page. And this got these guys—boy, did they go after us, you know, the whole [pro-Communist] fellow-traveling crowd, you know. Hearst was the, the—I mean, Nixon isn't as hated today as Hearst was then. What right did we have to decide who should save the Jews? For God's sake, we would go to anybody. I mean, would we need a rabbi to say, "Save the Jews"? We were delighted that we got Hearst to say "Save the Jews."

MAX LERNER RECALLS:[26]

One of the turning points for me in this whole question of the Jews in Europe came when I was teaching at Williams College. I was the only Jew on the faculty, and considered quite a radical Jew. And I was writing about the Nazis and about the treatment of the Jews, but of course I didn't know the full extent to which that had gone and one day I got a telephone call and it was from a man called Peter Bergson and he explained to me who he was and he said that he and a group had come from [Mandatory Palestine] to try to organize an effort to rescue the Jews of Europe. And that they were indeed in dire danger. Would I help? And without any question I said of course I would. How could there be any question? These were my brothers and sisters, these were my father's family and my mother's family. Of course I would help, I would do anything to help.

And then I found out from a number of my friends that Peter Bergson was a very dubious character indeed, that he was not a liberal, that he came from the Jabotinsky group, that he was a "Jabotinsky fascist," and that I should have nothing to do with him. And my answer to that was quite simple: Anyone that wants to help my brothers and sisters in Europe, really help them to get out, that's the man I want to work with. I don't care what party he belongs to.

W: Were there others who accused you of having rightist connections?[27]

K: Many of the so-called liberals didn't like it, but they were more reasonable about it. *PM* was needling us around. Also for the same reason. What was annoying is that I had a long discussion with Lerner. You see, the Lerner thing hurt, because Lerner became like a colleague, you know. He was an intellectual, and he had the kind of a personality, the kind of a mind that you connected [with], and then you connected on an issue like this, you know. I mean, the issue was there, the emergency was there, and on top of it you personally connect.

Do you know that Lerner and Herbert Hoover spoke on the same radio program? And Herbert Hoover was no darling of *PM*, you know. And it took a couple of hours' discussion, and Lerner agreed. I said to him, "Look, we have asked Hoover, and I hope he agrees, and I've managed through some people I know to get an appointment with him, and I think it's going to be terribly important to get him."

W: You saw Hoover yourself?

K: I saw Hoover, and I got him.[28]

W: Did he come to the Emergency Conference?

K: No, but he addressed the conference by radio. We had a national broadcast in which Lerner, Hoover, and myself participated. And at this time the biggest thing was a coast-to-coast broadcast on a network, you know, either Columbia, or National, or Mutual—and we had one—I think—CBS, I think it was. And we got a half hour or fifteen minutes. And we got Lerner, while he was on *PM,* at the closing session of the conference, there was a broadcast with Lerner and Hearst, who was a cochairman of the conference. And Lerner agreed, because I said, "For God's sake, if you want to mobilize American public opinion, these people are American public opinion." The thing that you were concerned with, in a deeper sense—that America, the administration, would not take any action, because it's not a popular cause—obviously we were attuned to. And we tried to get as wide a segment of the American people as possible behind it, in order to be able to get some political action. Obviously.

W: Let me quote something else from van Paassen's letter of resignation that was published in Leslie's *Protestant* magazine. "The Committee to Save the Jewish People of Europe," by which he means the Emergency Committee, "has been abandoned by many liberals and is today almost homogeneously made up of reactionaries on the one hand, and on the other hand of well meaning persons who are distressed over the woes of Israel, but do not know the background, origin, ambitions, and real objectives of the Committee's parent body, namely the Irgun, and its ultimate objectives." Now is there anything in this? Did you lose liberal support because of bringing in conservatives?

K: Some. Exaggerated, though. This is a propaganda line—the only people we lost on this ground were liberals who were fellow-travelers [of the Communists]. Lerner, who was a non-fellow-traveler liberal, quit because of the Jewish thing. Alfange left because of Zionist pressure, it is obvious in this clipping, because they keep on yelling, "Free Palestine! Free Palestine!" Which was our committee—the American League for a Free Palestine. But they wanted to say that they are not quitting because of this. I mean, they wanted to make sure that they're holding up Zionism. Alfange says, "I'm not a Jew, but I'm a lifelong Zionist."[29]

W: Let me get into another of van Paassen's charges: "They refused to collaborate with established Jewish and non-Jewish bodies. Like the Irgun in Palestine, they wanted to play, and did play, a lone hand. The real reasons for my resignation were always carefully hidden, or totally misrepresented by the directors of the Committee for a Jewish Army, so that many people to this day are, and remain, under the false impression that I am still an active supporter of the Committee or of one or more of its various offshoots. This illusion was furthered a good deal by the reproduction in the Irgunist periodical, *The Answer,* of articles and statements from my pen which had appeared elsewhere, but which were presented in that publication as original material. I never had any connection with *The Answer,* and I stopped the sale of my recent book by its editors." Is there anything to that?

K: No. It's a propaganda piece. If van Paassen articles appeared in *The Answer* after he quit, I don't know. It can be checked, though. I doubt whether they would put in an article that was printed someplace else and make it look as if it appeared there after van Paassen resigned. It just doesn't sound reasonable.

W: The impression one gets from *The Answer* was that he quit for reasons of health. That was your attempt to cover up?

K: Yeah. We did not want—you see, even now it's embarrassing for me. I mean, this expression "fellow-traveler" is not one that I use with relish, because words have a stamp, you know.

W: Are you saying you'd just as soon have gotten rid of him, you were as glad to see him go as he was to leave?

K: No! Because we thought he was a victim. That's why I said I make peace with him despite this. And he at one point attacked the Zionists.

Van Paassen is all right. He's a very weak man. He's a peculiar man. You know we used his signature an awful lot, and Joe Brainin[30] used to sign van Paassen, and that's what we used. We used replicas of it, you know. And one day van Paassen was in the office, and the young woman in the office asked him to sign a fairly important letter. She thought it would be a good occasion, you know, to have him sign it. Then she came and said, "We can't use it because it doesn't look like van Paassen's signature."

Joe Brainin was his business manager, and his manager, and he really had incredible influence on him. And finally they had an outing, Brainin and van Paassen. Shortly thereafter, after this, van Paassen and Brainin and Leslie split. Van Paassen, apparently, got a little wiser to what was going on, and he split—way before the McCarthy period—a couple of years later,'45 maybe, or '46.

By that time there was an effort to deport me. When it appeared in the paper that I was arrested, a little later van Paassen wrote a letter to the [New York] Post on his own initiative, we weren't in touch with him. He called the Zionist leaders "stool pigeons" and "indicateurs de police."[31] And he said that he had resigned from Bergson's committees because of differences of opinion. But this is one thing. It's legitimate to attack difference of opinion, but I want to protest these attacks and personal assassinations.

And, you see, as I remember it, van Paassen's resignation—you see, we regarded it as an inevitable step due to his relationship with Joe Brainin and [Kenneth Leslie]. There was no bitterness. We thought it was possible he didn't even write [his letter of resignation], didn't even sign it. I mean, this guy controlled him completely, he really did, you know. There were no hard feelings there. Not by me, and not by him.

W: With Lerner, there was this sort of sad departure—

K: Lerner? Yeah, because, you see, Lerner—first of all, the Committee for a Jewish Army wasn't anywhere as important and as raw emotionally as the Emergency Committee. Even van Paassen quit like Lerner. And secondly, van Paassen was a helluva nice and confused guy, you know. He was a former preacher, you know. He was funny. He kept on telling us somebody tried to shoot at him, and things like this. He was the kind of a guy you couldn't attribute malice to. The most you can say, you say, "He's weak."

W: Now, as for Dean Alfange, he quit the Emergency Committee at the second Emergency Conference, which was in August 1944. And the reason he gave was that he didn't approve of its political affiliations. Was that the Irgun issue again?

K: Probably. But the Emergency Committee didn't have any political affiliations. That's the Hebrew Committee, I guess.

W: It must be that he associated the Emergency Committee with the Hebrew Committee, which was set up in May 1944. This is August 1944. Do you think Alfange had an eye to the Jewish vote?

K: Alfange was a candidate for governor, and he ran for something and got a surprisingly large vote even though he didn't win—one of those protest votes. He is the first one who got a sizable vote as a liberal and he made a factor out of the Liberal Party.

W: Do you feel that Alfange felt the pressure from the Zionists in this?

K: Absolutely.

W: He hung on, though, for quite a long time, didn't he?

K: Yeah. The story speaks for itself.

Lisa Sergio I remember now, and it's a pity [that she left us].[32] She was a nice Italian lady, she was not of Italian origin, she was actually Italian, but she'd been in this country for a number of years, and she was a very popular commentator at that time.

W: What happened to her?

K: Same pressure. And I don't know, I remember that we were sort of betwixt a little why she gave in, but it was some reason, some reason she did.

Actually, Alfange requested that he not be reappointed cochairman of the Emergency Committee. He didn't even officially resign. He did it as a politician; he didn't want to hurt us too much, either.

W: He would never say why, he just said political differences?

K: Yeah, but when you read what he says, "While I fully agree with the humanitarian purpose of the Emergency Committee, I don't approve of its political affiliation. Though I am a Christian, I've been a lifelong Zionist, and a firm believer in the political aims of Zionism."[33]

At this time, the Zionists thought we were hurting the Zionist cause. It was very funny, by the way. The whole thing was that the accusations ran parallel during this period. You get two lines of attack: One says, "These people are Irgunists or the most rabid Revisionists." But the Revisionists were Zionists, the Revisionists were the most extreme Zionists. So, on the one hand they say we are too extreme Zionists, we belong to the Irgun, the Irgun is the most extreme wing of the Revisionists. And on the other hand, they are saying that we hurt the Zionist cause, that the work of the Emergency Committee ignores Palestine and ignores the need of Jewish immigration to Palestine. All at the same time!

Wise was very vain. There's a joke that Leonard Lyons printed about him, I don't know if he invented it, or somebody invented it, but he says that when Wise met with Freud, Wise said he's glad to meet the most important Jew in America. And Freud said, "No, if anybody deserves this title, it's you," and Wise replied, "No, no, no—it's you, Dr. Freud." And Freud said, "One 'no' would have been enough." [laughter] It's probably not a true story, but it gives the point, gives the character.[34]

The only real sort of personal chat, not business conversation, because there was no friendly relationship, was in San Franciso in 1945. It was during the founding of the United Nations, and I headed the Hebrew Committee delegation there. Wise was there for the Jewish Agency. We stayed at the same hotel and used to run into each other in the lobby. One Saturday morning, I ran into him, and he says, "Would you like to come? I am delivering a guest sermon at such and such synagogue. Would you like to come and hear my sermon?" He wanted me to come with him. He says, "And I'll introduce you to the congregation." He's buttering me up. And I didn't want to go. But I didn't want to insult him, either. So I said to him, "You know, Rabbi, it might sound strange to you, but—" And he says, "I have a car waiting." Well, I am a boy from Jerusalem, the idea of a rabbi driving on the Sabbath, you know—it's a capital sin to ride in a car on the Sabbath. I myself do ride, you know, but still I needed an excuse, so I said, "Look, the synagogue to me is connected with Orthodox Judaism—my father was a rabbi, as you know," I said to him, "and I couldn't write to my father that I went with you to the synagogue, and I couldn't lie to him and say that we walked to the synagogue. We'll be riding, and I don't think it goes together with my upbringing to ride on the Sabbath." And he swallowed that.

And there was another guy, a Zionist leader named Louis Lipsky, who was there.[35] So once the three of us were sitting and it was sort of like a lull in the fight, so to say. The war was just over, the Germans surrendered, I felt great relief. Otherwise, probably I wouldn't have been sitting there, chatting with them. I don't know why they were nice to me all of a sudden. But they were nice to me. And Lipsky says, "You know, really, the trouble with you is that you run too fast. We also run, we have our machinery and we are all the time on the move. Not at your pace, but we are on the move. And you treat us as if we are standing still. We are not standing still. We are moving in our way and you are moving fast in your way. If you could somehow run together with us, you'd probably influence us. You should find a way." They were sweet-talking me all over the place. I think that was the last time I ever saw Wise.

WYMAN: Did policy orders come to American Zionists from the Jewish Agency [regarding the Bergson group]?[36]

MERLIN: The American organizations had cabled time and again to the Jewish Agency asking them to give them orders to condemn us, to come out against us. I don't want to get into polemics about jealousies, about prestige, about status. Their main motivation was that in order to achieve any results, the Jews have to be united. Through unity there is strength. If there is dissidence, this weakens the Jewish position generally. So this was a very important point, to them.

W: No matter what the objective was?

M: Regardless of what the objective was, because they believed that their objectives are more or less the same as ours. And they believed that we are hindering, we are handicapping, them by the very fact that the governments, or powerful groups, or powerful individuals will become confused and disheartened at the fact that there is disunity among the

Jews themselves. They were afraid that people will say, "Well, how can we help you if you cannot bring your own house into order?" This is one motivation.

Second, and this is much more important, people think in certain categories, they have a certain mold of thought. And it takes time to adjust to new conditions. For decades they were thinking in categories of elite, in the sense that Palestine will be rebuilt by the young, the courageous, the dedicated. And their ideology was that in order to enable this elite of the youth, the best, to come to Palestine and to build a new life of social justice, it would be worthwhile to overlook and even to sacrifice the others. But at that time, before Hitler, to sacrifice the others didn't mean to deliver them to death. Though, strangely enough, they spoke as if they were aware that they are being delivered to death. For instance, Weizmann, the president of the Zionist organization, had it laid before the Peel Commission and, at the Zionist Congress before the war, he said, very proudly, "I told the Peel Commission that we want only to save the youth, the remnant. And all the others," he says, "are dust upon the wheels of history, and the cruel winds will disperse them to all the corners of the world."

Authors' Note: During his testimony before the Peel Commission, the British Royal Commission investigating the causes of Palestinian Arab rioting in 1936, Weizmann was asked if the Zionist movement sought to "bring six million Jews to Palestine." He replied in the negative and added: "The old ones will pass; they will bear their fate, or they will not. They were dust, economic and moral dust in a cruel world. . . . Only a branch will survive." ("Twentieth Zionist Congress—August 3–17, 1937: Dr. Weizmann's Review," New Judea 13 [August–September 1937], 215.) Weizmann made similar statements over the years; for example, he once wrote that if large numbers of Jews were forced to leave eastern Europe, "we shall have all the miserable refugees who will be driven out of Poland, Galicia, Rumania, etc., at the doors of Palestine. We shall be swamped in Palestine and shall never be able to set up a community worth having there." (Weizmann to Steed, November 30, 1918, The Letters and Papers of Chaim Weizmann [New Brunswick, NJ, 1980], Vol. 9, No. 45, 50.)

Such remarks reflected at once a pessimistic forecast regarding Pales-
tine's economic absorptive abilities and a decidedly conservative approach
to the building of the Jewish national home, an assumption that it could
be achieved only very gradually and only by a certain type of immigrant.
Hence Weizmann supported the immigration policy of the Labor Zion-
ist–dominated Jewish Agency, known as "selective immigration," accord-
ing to which priority was given to those would-be immigrants who were
young, physically fit, and associated with socialist-Zionist parties—those
whom Agency chairman David Ben-Gurion characterized as "the most
appropriate ones for aliya [immigration]." Jabotinsky and the Revisionists,
by contrast, rejected selectivity, called for immediate mass evacuation of
European Jews to Palestine, and initiated a program of unauthorized
immigration. (Abraham J. Edelheit, The Yishuv in the Shadow of the
Holocaust: Zionist Politics and Rescue Aliya, 1933–1939 *[Boulder,*
CO, 1996], 16, 60, 64–66, 169–70.)

K: It is all a question of priorities and a sense of proportion.[37] I don't say
that we were infallible. We probably made many mistakes. But I say
that in the main thrust we reacted to the massacre as the kind of an
emergency that it was, to any degree that a human being could react.
My anger, which is not diminishing but getting bigger, as the years go
by, was that I am still totally perplexed as to how it was possible *not* to
react—the way the Jewish leaders didn't react. And I believed then
and I believe now that these were people who belonged to something
else. They didn't have any real identity; because I don't think that they
would have not reacted in this way if the pogrom was in New Jersey. I
think they would have reacted. But because it was *there,* they didn't
react.

The effort that we had to waste defending ourselves and losing
people—we spent so much effort in getting a convert, in getting somebody to help, to give a few dollars to organize something to get some
money, because the scope of activity depended on the budget we
could generate. And we had very few prominent, wealthy people with
us. We had many prominent *political* people; but they didn't give us
any money. The money had to come from Jews, and from some

wealthy non-Jews who were not in the habit. There was no precedent of non-Jews giving money to Jewish causes, because they were never asked. They used to be flabbergasted when we talked to them. Sometimes people thought there was some religious indiscretion here, as if we were a church or something. So our financial problems all this period were hampering and most exasperating.

You wanted to do things and you couldn't because you didn't have the money, and you didn't have the time because you *had* to allocate so much time to fund-raising and to people who had no other meaning except raising some money. And *there* was the constant—that's where they fought us most. You would see this on the level of personal relations. You organize a meeting in somebody's home and, put under pressure, they would call it off the last day. It happened by the dozens. By the hundreds, I would say. It was a part of our daily life.

MERLIN: Jewish leaders identified themselves with Roosevelt and Churchill and everyone who said that nothing serious can be done during the war to rescue the Jews.[38] They agreed that one could do nothing significant. They themselves said, how are you going to save so many people. You know what it means to save *one* person. They said, since it's impossible to do anything on an adequate scale during the war, one has to concentrate upon creating the best and most favorable conditions for the postwar period. And *we* said, the Jews who are being exterminated on such a scale cannot wait for postwar conditions. The situation can arrive when there will be no more Jews to enjoy those beautiful conditions for which you are fighting with so much passion.

One has to look upon this controversy not only from the point of view of jealousy or whatnot, but also from the point of view of certain attitudes, a philosophy of viewing things. In many respects they were very sincere. There was an honest difference. Even when they called us all the names under the sun; they called us imposters and embezzlers and whatever. At the same time, they actually believed that what is more important than anything else is unity. They actually believed that dissent is a crime, because the only hope that the Jews had for advancing Jewish interests—whatever the interests were—depended first of all on unity, discipline. They believed that without unity, without discipline, everything is lost. And, therefore, they considered our activities as a crime, as undermining Jewish power, Jewish interests, because they thought the first priority, transcending everything—they were metaphysical about it—first of all unity—unity and discipline. Where's your mandate? By whose authority are you—?

Of course it's silly, because they themselves didn't have any authority. The only authority they had was that, in the Palestine Mandate, it is written that there will be a Jewish agency to collaborate with the British. This is exactly what we said they are doing: They are an agency to collaborate with the British, and that's all there is to it. They didn't have anything else. At that time, the Zionists were a minority among American Jews. In the course of the very few years that we worked here, we got contributions from almost 750,000 people. And the Zionist organizations never had such a number of contributors. We were not competing with them for leadership or whatnot, because we were always ad hoc organizations. We always had a specific purpose. And once we achieved our purpose, we dissolved the organization—actually we are the only group in Jewish public life that ever liquidated themselves voluntarily.

W: If they had done their job, and you had done your job—if they hadn't taken their time and energy to try to counter what you were doing—then maybe something more effective could have been accomplished.[39]

K: First of all, they succeeded in keeping us away from Roosevelt.

MAX LERNER RECALLS:[40]

I am quite sure that the people around Roosevelt, including the Jews, including Rabbi Stephen Wise, who was a friend of mine and a close friend—I am sure that they were part of the effort not to treat [news of the genocide] in too dramatic a fashion. Rabbi Wise was a disappointment to me because we had worked closely together and I had great affection for him and trust in him but the way in which he reacted to the Peter Bergson group, the way in which he reacted to my membership in it, and the way in which he failed to pressure the president, to whom he was so close—this disappointed me bitterly.

K: Without sounding cocky, there was a certain drive that we generated in those days that did get us some pretty important people.[41] Now who can tell whether a character like Roosevelt, who came out and said he learned more in five minutes from Ibn Saud than from all the things together*—you remember this?—maybe he would've learned something from talking with us. Maybe by some hook, I mean, certainly it couldn't have hurt. The worst that would've happened, he would have talked to me for ten minutes and ushered me out. And actually, there were three or four times where appointments were on the verge of being set up. And apparently we did get to him through the propaganda, because he was impressed with it, on several occasions. And David Niles,[42] whom I had met with several times, and who appreciated what we were doing, but he was a politician, he was a link with the mainstream Jews, and they pressured him, they pressured him not to do it. Rosenman† I couldn't get to. Rosenman to me is the most guilty of the bunch.

---

*In the course of his address to a joint session of Congress on March 1, 1945, Roosevelt referred to his meeting with Saudi Arabian King Ibn Saud aboard the USS *Quincy* off the coast of Egypt on February 14, 1945. Roosevelt told Congress: "I learned more about the whole problem of Arabia—the Moslems—the Jewish problem—by talking to Ibn Saud for five minutes than I could have learned in the exchange of two or three dozen letters."[43]

†Samuel Rosenman (1896–1973), an attorney who was appointed justice of the New York State Supreme Court, served as one of President Roosevelt's senior speechwriters as well as his closest adviser on Jewish affairs. A prominent member of the American Jewish Committee, Rosenman often counseled FDR to ignore requests from Jewish organizations for steps such as increasing refugee immigration to the United States, pressing Britain on its Palestine policy, or taking measures to rescue Jews from Hitler. It was Rosenman who persuaded Roosevelt to refrain from meeting representatives of the four hundred rabbis whom the Bergson group brought to Washington in October 1943.[44]

W: He had the most influence on Roosevelt of any Jew. On Jewish matters, Roosevelt would turn to him and say, "What do I do now?" Because Roosevelt never had time or energy to understand the factions within the Jewish community.

K: Sure, I know. I know. And Rosenman was the worst guy of the lot. Not in terms that he was evil. But in terms that he had all these shortcomings somewhere put together. In a guy who was least suspected of [not being fully an] American. He should have felt more liberated than the others.

W: What about Mrs. Roosevelt's reaction?

K: The first time I got to her was through Helen Gahagan Douglas, who was a congresswoman from California.[45] She, you know, was moved by the situation, and I—as I used to, I always asked: Help, you know, sort of, what can you do for us, and this and that, and I said, "Can you get us through to see people?" and so forth, and she said, "I think I can get you to Mrs. Roosevelt." I said, "That would be wonderful." And she did. And she arranged the first appointment, and then this contact was established, and Mrs. Roosevelt was interested. Sometimes you didn't get anyplace. I don't say she became very involved, which she wasn't. But she didn't remain completely aloof, either. And I frankly talked to her, the fact that we did not succeed to get to the president personally.

W: You never did?

K: No.

W: None of your group ever did?

K: No.

W: Not even your senators or congressmen were able to get to him on this issue?

K: Not specifically, not specifically. They were—they saw him, but they weren't close enough that they could go on this issue to him. We tried to, we tried to engineer this, and this didn't work, either.

W: But do you—how many times would you think you saw Mrs. Roosevelt?

K: In the White House, I think about three or four, that's all. Three or four times.

W: She wasn't able to do anything specific?

K: Not very much.

W: She tried to approach him?

K: Well, from what I read later, I don't know how effective she was with him. I mean, I didn't know it at the time, you know, all the stories that came out later about their relationship. But she did tell me, "I spoke to the president about this," and I presume it was correct.

Authors' Note: In at least one instance, Eleanor Roosevelt did pass along to the president a letter that Bergson sent her, obviously for that purpose. It called for a special governmental rescue agency and outlined a few specific rescue proposals. Enclosed with it was a two-page copy of the "Recommendations of the Emergency Conference." This took place shortly after the Emergency Conference was held and immediately following a meeting between Mrs. Roosevelt and Bergson. The president expressed no interest, however. He returned the items to his wife's secretary a few days later, along with a one-sentence note: "I do not think this needs an answer at this time."[46]

EMANUEL CELLER RECALLS:[47]

I had gone to complain to Roosevelt about the rotten ships that they had used to [smuggle] some of the Jews to Palestine, in violation of the White Paper. . . . They were in rotten ships, and some of the ships sunk in Haifa harbor, creating a tremendous catastrophe. I went to Roosevelt, representing a number of welfare organizations that wanted to open up Palestine. And I tried to urge him to come to the conclusion that the White Paper should be amended. And he then said, "Listen to me. Stop making waves. I have an arrangement with Churchill that surreptitiously was going to allow Jews to enter Palestine without hindrance as to number, so that your views will be satisfied." I was very happy to hear that. But there wasn't a bit of truth to that ploy. He simply used that to stop me from, as he put it, "making waves." Now that indicated that Roosevelt, although he may have desired to help the Jews, didn't raise a finger to help the Jews.

K: The Jewish advisers to Roosevelt prevented me from seeing the president.[48]

But I saw Mrs. Roosevelt several times in the White House, after we brought the pageant "We Will Never Die," which was a very effective, tremendous piece of propaganda. We did it in Madison Square Garden twice and we brought it to Constitution Hall in Washington to an invited audience, which included hundreds of congressmen and senators, four Supreme Court justices, Mrs. Roosevelt, most of the diplomatic corps, 90 percent of it, maybe more even, except that the British Embassy didn't come and Roosevelt didn't come.

Then I saw her several times at the White House and she used to tell us—we used her to get to the president. The president was reading our ads. And in one case, she said this story—we did an ad called "My Uncle Abraham Reports," which Ben Hecht wrote, which was a fairy tale about Jewish ghosts meeting and discussing how come a great man like Roosevelt doesn't do something to save them, survivors, the little children. So then they send a ghost as a delegate. It was his Uncle Abraham who was chosen as a delegate. The story ends that he sits on the windowsill of the White House, but he left his notebook behind. In other words, he has nothing to report. And she said that the president said that this is hitting below the belt. And I told her that I am very happy to hear that he is reading it and that it affects him.

She and I spoke to Jews on a joint broadcast on the radio. Mrs. Roosevelt, former President Hoover, and I did a joint thing. I spoke in Yiddish, and they spoke in English, and it was translated and transmitted to Europe by the Office of War Information. So I said to her, what we are doing, what you are doing, if I felt that it didn't save some people, I probably would go insane. I don't think I had much success with her, but it was better than nothing.[49]

After the war, I became sort of friendly with Elliott Roosevelt[50] and his then-wife, Faye Emerson. He wanted to volunteer to sail in to Palestine with a boatload of Jewish refugees from Europe, you see, to break the British blockade of Palestine. And we thought it would be quite a thing, even though, even though he was no longer the son of the president. But he was still Elliott Roosevelt, a general in the United States Army, on reserve. And the son of the former president. And he said—we said, "We'll do it." That was before we did the

SS *Ben Hecht*. We were working on the SS *Ben Hecht*. So it was in late 1946.

And we had the money, and we said, "Look, we are going to buy—we are looking around for a boat. We'll buy a boat and you sail it in, see? With people." And we thought it would be a cinch, would be very easy to do, you know, because he's a yachtsman, and he could do it from the south of France someplace. Very unsuspecting. You see, the British, the reason they caught those boats was that they had such effective navy units. They always knew when they left. You know, because boats are easy to spot, and they had their people in the various ports, see. So they followed these things. But this kind of a ship, we figured it could really sail into Haifa, make a world sensation.

And then he says, "I want to discuss it with my mother." And I told him that I have had the privilege of meeting your mother and she did this and that and so forth. But I don't think she's going to let you do this. If you want to do it, don't ask her. If you ask her, you won't do it. She wouldn't let him. So then when he told me she wouldn't let him, I went to see her. To try to tell her that, if it's from the point of view of a mother worrying about her son, I can only tell her that I don't think that it was dangerous, that even poor Jewish refugees who came without anybody—you know, the British didn't kill anybody, you know, the British were fighting clean. Which was true. Maybe some, a couple of guys were beaten up, on a couple of occasions when they tried to push them back to Europe, the survivors. But basically when the people didn't resist and they went, say, to Cyprus, they didn't shoot on those boats, you know, they didn't use any violence. And certainly they wouldn't do it to Elliott Roosevelt. And if it was political, I wanted to argue with her about it, but I couldn't convince her.

CHAPTER

5

The Rescue Resolution

The climax of Kook's rescue campaign came with the introduction, in late 1943, of a congressional resolution urging the creation of a U.S. government agency to rescue Jews from Hitler. In this chapter, Kook describes how both the State Department and some Jewish leaders worked to undermine the resolution. Congressman Will Rogers, Jr., recalls his own key role in the battle over the resolution, and Congressman Emanuel Celler criticizes the responses of his congressional colleague Sol Bloom to the rescue issue.

MERLIN: [American Zionist leaders] were unhappy with the Gillette-Rogers rescue resolution for two reasons.[1] One was, it was our resolution. This was enough. Second, and perhaps this was even more important to them, that this resolution didn't mention Palestine. When Stephen Wise testified before Sol Bloom's [House Foreign Affairs] Committee, he said it is a fine resolution except it doesn't go far enough. It is inadequate and it doesn't go far enough because it doesn't specify that the only practical solution to the save the Jewish people of Europe was to open the gates of Palestine and to do away with the British White Paper.*[2]

WILL ROGERS, JR., RECALLS:[3]

After I got to know Peter Bergson fairly well, and after we sat down to work out parts of the resolution, I was even more impressed by him because he came from Palestine, his whole life was bound up with Palestine, and yet he was willing to forget the Palestine issue completely in order to save Jewish lives. He went after the main point, and I thought that was a really good judgment. He was awfully good on that. And I admired him very much for doing that. . . .

I knew as well as Rabbi Wise knew that putting Palestine in [the rescue resolution] was just going to kill it. It was a method, a means, which he used to try and kill this resolution. He did not openly oppose it. He really couldn't. There was no way, nobody can openly oppose trying to be a humanitarian. But they just wanted to wiggle around and sabotage and change the wording or do something else.†

MERLIN: Now what was our attitude?[4] We were interested mainly in two things. First of all, for the first time to pin down the American government to speak out clearly that what we are talking about is the Jewish tragedy, the Jewish disaster, per se. Because until then, every time one spoke in anonymous terms—persecuted people, refugees, whatever it is—for us it was, in order to tackle the problem, a condition sine qua non was that the problem has to be defined as such. And therefore we formulated—or tried to help formulate it in the sense that one needs to face the problem in its realistic terms and scope. Namely, that it has to do with the Jewish people, per se, as such. And second, the bureaucracy is so rami-

---

*At his appearance before the House Foreign Affairs Committee, Wise, in addition to speaking, distributed a written statement. In it, he criticized the resolution as "inadequate" and "offering little hope that a constructive and affirmative program will be undertaken."

†For Senator Guy Gillette's views on Stephen Wise's position regarding the rescue resolution, see Gillette's letter of August 1944 in the Appendix, page 223.

fied, the government, especially the United States government, has so many departments, there are so many agencies, there are so many secretaries in the Cabinet, that it became practically impossible—it became futile—to do something because it was impossible to pin down one address—where to go and what to do.

We wanted one institution, one authority. We wanted a board or a commission created for one specific purpose. This is to deal with the problem of the Jews in Europe.

WYMAN: You felt that by keeping it that simple you'd have a better chance of getting it through.

M: Not only, no, no, no, no. Not only is it that we had a better chance to get it through, because the moment you specify things you immediately create adversaries for specific things. There again you disperse. We actually wanted to simplify the thing in order to bring about the best possible achievement, which was a special agency to deal with the Jewish problem.

WILL ROGERS, JR., RECALLS:[5]

I was no hero. At the time that I introduced the resolution, it was just a normal resolution—it was what I thought a normal person should do in Congress. And I was very glad that I could participate in it with Senator Gillette. Only later did I realize that it was rather unusual for a freshman congressman to come in against official Jewry and against the Democratic Party, to have introduced and stuck with this resolution.

I was very independent. When anybody comes to Congress, the first thing they want to do is be reelected and the first thing they are doing is working on their reelection. Well, I knew that I was not going to be reelected—I was going into the army. And so I was quite free, and the pressures that were brought on me by the Jewish [organizations] and by the administration and by the State Department, they didn't mean a thing to me. They couldn't touch me, and that was the unique position that I had. . . .

I just did what anybody would have done. I was not concerned with the outcome so much as I was with making a statement and that somebody makes a statement and that my country makes a statement. I did very much want the United States—as a country and as a nation—to protest and to stand for the rescue of these people when it could be done. . . .

[The resolution meant] taking on my commander in chief. And that worried me more than anything else. . . . I did not feel comfortable in opposing President Roosevelt. I was a New Dealer right down to the bricks and I believed in him very, very strongly. . . . It was difficult to have to come against your own party and your own leader in which you believe so strongly. But I thought that he was very wrong on this point. I thought that he should have interested himself immediately [in the rescue issue] and made stirring declarations and set up a committee or a group that could save these people when he knew they were being killed en masse. I thought it was more important that the Jews be saved than that the Democratic Party be saved.

KOOK: Wise arranged the hearings.[6] I was angry at having the hearings. The hearings were a stall. There was no purpose for these hearings. This was not the type of resolution that required hearings. It wasn't a law. They didn't do it to help us. Bloom did it against us.

Bloom's idea was to use the hearings to discredit the resolution and discredit the Emergency Committee.[7] And if he was sold a bill of goods that we are fighting him politically, then he thought it was very important. He was not a bright guy at all, by the way. This was a small potato guy who got where he was merely by seniority, by being in a safe Democratic district and getting elected every year. He was a weasling kind of guy. Generally. He wasn't an impressive fellow on any score.

EMANUEL CELLER RECALLS:[8]

Sol Bloom was one of those who always hung on the coattails of the State Department. He always wanted to curry favor with the State Department. He liked to attend the state dinners and he liked the diplomacy that the State Department could accord him. He had a daughter of whom he was very proud, and the daughter attended these sumptuous dinners at the State Department. And the State Department was always stroking Bloom the right way, never against his fur. And the result was that Bloom became more or less a sycophant of the State Department. When he went to Bermuda, he may have had pretty good intentions that he was going to do something worthwhile, but he came back empty-handed. He did nothing. He may have tried, but he was a weakling. He was not the strong man we thought he was, and he didn't help with reference to rescuing the refugees.

W: On the first day of the hearings, in Herbert Moore's testimony,[9] he keeps saying, "This never should have hearings anyway," which is what you said—that it's an open-and-shut case, it's obvious on the merits of it, and so it should just be put through.[10]

K: This is the kind of resolution that should have gone to the House [floor]. What we thought when we introduced it was that this will go to the House and Senate and pass both committees. Our strategy was to have it pass both committees as a gesture. And then, once it passed the committees, and it gets some respectability, stage a very impressive debate for a couple of hours in Congress. And have it pass.

You know, you get a couple of hours from the Speaker, you know, planned, and then you get one man in charge. Rogers, in the House, would have been in charge, as a leading sponsor of the resolution; and he yields, you know, to so-and-so and so-and-so and arranges a list of twenty or thirty guys. That's the way it was supposed to be done. We have had many such things in Congress, by the way. In which we had one or two debates going on with somebody who talks some time and then yields it to a lot of people. We had it a few times. And then, have it come up for a vote and then get it by unanimous consent or something like this. But it didn't work.

Authors' Note: Contrary to Bloom's insistence on committee hearings in the House, and his use of those hearings to try to undermine the rescue resolution, the Senate Foreign Relations Committee required no hearings. It unanimously approved the resolution on December 20, 1943, and it was scheduled to go to the floor of the Senate in January. Senator Guy Gillette, the resolution's chief sponsor in the Senate and a leading member of the Foreign Relations Committee, forecast Senate passage "without a dissenting vote."

Gillette, who was a dedicated friend of Zionism, candidly discussed the obstruction that he encountered from Zionist leaders:

"These people used every effort, every means at their disposal, to block the resolution. . . . [They] tried to defeat it by offering an amendment, insisting on an amendment to it that would raise the question, the controversial question of Zionism or anti-Zionism, . . . or anything that might stop and block the action that we were seeking."

Gillette also disclosed a comment made by one of his colleages the day the Senate Foreign Relations Committee was to vote on the measure:

"I wish these damned Jews would make up their minds what they want. I could not get inside the committee room without being buttonholed out here in the corridor by representatives who said that the Jewish people of America did not want the passage of this resolution."[11]

W: Well, you know Bloom was looking for any opening he could find to discredit you and your group. I'll give you an example where he thought he could. He pressed this when you testified at the hearings. It is about a fund-raising telegram the Emergency Committee sent to a list of its members on November 13, a week before the hearings began.[12]

The telegram said this resolution will "enable our office Washington, London, Palestine, England, Turkey to continue work on larger scale." Which implies that there's big-scale work going on in those places, which there wasn't, not at that time.

K: Yeah, we had one guy in Turkey.

W: You had one guy in jail in Palestine. Ben-Eliezer.[13] That's your headquarters in Palestine, that's the jail. [Laughter.] Your headquarters in England is one guy running around making a Jewish army—

K: On November 13, he wasn't in jail yet.

W: Well, he wasn't doing much rescue in Palestine.

K: No, he wasn't. But we had one man in Turkey who was working for us and for the [Orthodox] rabbis, a man called Klarman.[14] I'm not saying it in defense for this.

This is appeal stuff. This is an exuberant fund-raising letter. Very definitely. I claim no defense. It also says that the main task is to mobilize public opinion. It says it pretty openly. But obviously the offices in Turkey aren't mobilizing public opinion. It doesn't say what they do, but—I don't think it's effective, either, by the way. I think the telegram would be more effective without it. It distracts from the main issue, the fact that the rescue resolutions were introduced. They should be concentrated on. In terms of effectiveness.

W: It uses the phrase "to force passage resolution"—

K: Fund-raising. The only defense you can claim for this is poverty. You know, we needed money. Obviously. It was written by a hungry guy.

W: Well, Bloom grabbed the phrase "to force passage." The idea is, these guys are ramming it through. So he says, "What the hell's this all about? You're going to *force* us to act?" Every congressman immediately bristles. Anybody, nobody forces us to do anything. That's the kind of thing he was doing.

K: This is about, you know, as damaging a document against us as I've seen. In all these years.

W: The telegram that's yours, you mean.

K: Yeah. It's pretty stupid, you know? Have you seen anything that stupid amongst our stuff? The first time you show me something that really embarrasses me. You don't have to say "forced passage," you know. You can say, "achieve speedy passage," which says the same thing. This is disrespectful of the Congress. You don't say "to force passage." And then a mistake to say London and England, which is sloppy work.

W: But you don't know what the picture there is. You ultimately come up with a few, with a few—what Bloom maintains, that the idea of the resolution was for effect. Not to get an agency. He makes this charge. That it was publicity—

K: Publicity stunt, yeah, garbage.

W: Not stunt, but an effort.

K: Garbage. Because the notion of getting a government agency was advanced months before. And we were working on the idea of the resolution. The most concrete recommendation that came out of the Emergency Conference was the special government agency. And this had been done on many occasions, the idea of a special agency was advocated. I mean, it is true that the resolution was not a law, which the president must do it or veto it—this wasn't this kind of a thing.

W: It was advisory.

K: But it was a part of the pressure on the executive, which means on the president, to do it. But it's serious pressure, not a flighty thing.

W: Bloom actually doesn't come out openly against the bill at any point. So you feel that he tried to stifle it, that everything he did was trying to block it—

K: Oh, of course. I mean, he was trying to discredit the people behind it. It was obvious that the Emergency Committee was behind it. It wasn't a situation of ghostwriting. Congressmen openly said that they are doing this as part of a committee of which they are members, as part of a public effort. He was trying to discredit the organization which was sponsoring it. So obviously he was against the bill.

W: Now, [New York Post publisher Ted] Thackrey[15] sent Bloom a telegram that said why he's for it, and why don't you support it? And Bloom sends back a telegram which says, I agree with your telegram, that is, I support it. And Thackrey prints this in the paper. What do you make of that?

K: Well [laughing], Bloom's a politician. The New York Post is very important for him. He didn't support the bill, obviously, because he pigeonholed it. The record proves that he didn't support the bill, there's no question about that.*

W: In the hearings, there's a lot of evasive talk in there—some of the Republicans said, "You know, if we pass this, this is going to imply that the administration wasn't doing everything right." And Bloom says, "No, it doesn't really mean that"—something to that effect, and then another says, "Well, if everything's being done already, then why do we bother with this? Let's throw it out." But Bloom didn't want to say no—

K: Yeah, politics.

---

*After the first three days of hearings, a columnist in the New York Yiddish-language *Forward* wrote: "It is truly difficult to understand why it is such a life and death matter for Congressman Bloom to dig up arguments against the resolution."[16]

W: In February, a couple of months afterward, and after the War Refugee Board has been set up—this is a letter to Bloom from Bloom's secretary in New York: "Now that Mr. Merlin says so emphatically that their main idea is to make peace with you, Mr. [Abe] Engelman (who's another of his advisors in New York) asked me to tell you that he is of the opinion that possibly it would be a good idea for you to make the appointment with Mr. Bergson, and that you have one or two of your secretaries present. . . . Merlin stated that Mr. Bergson wanted to see the Congressman in order to tell him that they did not have anything against him. Under the circumstances, possibly it would be a good idea for you to see Mr. Bergson."[17]

K: Well, he did. Yeah. I saw him, and I assured him that we had nothing against him, that it's a pity we haven't met and that we attacked the Bermuda Conference—you know, I showed him the ad where we praised the Bermuda Conference, where we encouraged them in the beginning. And I said that unfortunately the Bermuda Conference was a very tragic thing and it's a pity we were there, and so forth. But this is nothing personal against you. And so forth and so forth. And completely disabused him of the rumor that we had possibly planned to run somebody as a candidate against him. I mean, we felt that there was nothing to be gained by having Bloom as an enemy and everything to be gained by pacifying him, except some loss of prestige, which I couldn't care a damn about. I didn't mind to go and eat crow with Bloom. I mean, what difference does it make to me? So I went and I did it and I think it did some good. Certainly it didn't hurt.

The way things developed, there was too much tension. You cannot go to a guy who smears you. If I have to save myself, I—if you would have read the nastiness with which he treated me in the committee hearing. That it was quite a step to take an initiative to go and talk to him and say, "Look—" Because he should have done the reverse. If we were conventional politicos or Jewish so-called leaders, or whatever—which we weren't—I was concerned that Bloom's animosity might hurt the cause someplace.

That's when he told me this thing about what a good Jew he is, you know, that he doesn't smoke a cigar on the Sabbath, for the Jews, he doesn't smoke a cigar. He tells everybody proudly, "I'm a Jew. That's what I do for the Jewish people." He thought this was important, you know.

W: The State Department was opposing or questioning the rescue bill, and saying, really, that we already have an agency doing this—this Intergovernmental Committee* and the State Department. Breckin-ridge Long said that.

K: The Intergovernmental Committee was a hoax and a fraud. Anyway, the magnitude of the slaughter wasn't anything that a charitable organization would handle. Only a government could handle it. You had a government using all its power to do the murder. Only another government could oppose it.

One of the things that I used very often and persistently, which was also on the maj—I remember walking around Washington with this guy, Nahum Goldmann,† who was one of the biggest Zionist leaders then. And he told me, he tried to dissuade me from having the resolution introduced. And he said it won't pass and it will just hurt the Zionist cause. And I said, "Look, if we only slow down, if we put monkey wrenches into the German piece of machinery—they have established a death piece of machinery—if we can't stop it, if we can't get the governments to fight it, if we only slow it, you see, if we put monkey wrenches there and we slow it down, instead of 10,000 a day they'll kill 2,000 a day. That'll make a hell of a difference, won't it?" I mean 8,000 a day, we save. Just by doing whatever—I mean people are

---

*The Intergovernmental Committee was established at the 1938 international refugee conference held in Evian, France. At the Bermuda Conference, the Intergovernmental Committee's work was supposed to be revived, but in fact, throughout its existence, it never accomplished much to alleviate the refugee crisis.

†Nahum Goldmann (1894–1982), a German-born Zionist, cofounded the World Jewish Congress with Stephen Wise in 1936. Fleeing war-torn Europe for the United States in 1940, Goldmann became the Jewish Agency's representative in Washington, and remained a fixture in the U.S. Jewish establishment for decades to follow. A harsh critic of the Bergson group, Goldmann privately urged Roosevelt administration officials in 1944 to either draft Bergson or deport him.[18]

thinking, they'll do something, you know. And it will have some effect somewhere to slow this thing down.

W: Was Breckinridge Long anti-Semitic?*

K: I don't know. He was hostile. Why, I don't know.

W: He was hostile to you, of course, because you were too active.

K: No, he wasn't only hostile to us. He was hostile to the issue. For any person to have said that there was an existing machinery to save the Jews was either criminal or just outright stupid. He couldn't have been that dense, because he fooled us pretty well. He was sabotaging us with great dexterity. He was outmaneuvering us.

W: You think he was insensitive to the killing of the Jews?

K: Totally, totally, totally, for God's sake. I mean, you couldn't make a dent. The whole organization functioned really as an emergency committee. You know, many committees are called "emergency," but when you go in, there's no emergency. This thing functioned like an emergency. Bloom didn't believe it's an emergency, but he got a feeling of emergency. Because we were screaming so much. Bloom didn't mean it in terms of the word; he meant that the pressure on him was, you know, there's a fire going on. You couldn't get it across to Long—I didn't meet him so many times, maybe four or five times in all, I think, and not always alone. Once he sat in the meeting with Hull. And maybe four more times. I remember the feeling of getting absolutely nowhere in terms of conveying the human urgency of it.

You know, I didn't want to talk as we were talking to Adolf Berle, who used to talk about the Committee for a Jewish Army, and then I used to try to calm myself. I would tell myself, "Look, it means a lot more to you than to him—it has to, you know, it's not that important to

*Long testified at length at a closed session of Bloom's committee. In his effort subtly to persuade the committee that the State Department was already doing everything that could be done to help the refugees, he presented important misleading information; particularly, grossly inflated statistics as to the number of refugees who had been taken into the United States since 1933. Because many committee members believed and were greatly impressed by Long's deceitful testimony, the rescue resolution suffered a significant setback in the House committee. Two weeks afterward, Long's testimony was made public and immediately set off a major controversy that redounded strongly against Long.[19]

him. Now, don't press. If you press too hard, you won't get anywhere."
I used to try and copy these guys' style, to talk more relaxed, to seem
more relaxed, and with Breckinridge Long, I couldn't. I tried very hard.
I said, "You cannot discuss this like we would discuss the Jewish army
with Adolf Berle," which, by the way, worked with Berle, because
some contact was established. Because we didn't say that we'll save
the war effort. We spoke in practical terms, said we might get as many
as 200,000 men. Maybe it's a little exaggerated, so if we have 100,000
it's also good. It's a respectable number and it's helpful. You know, we
undersold. On *this* thing, you couldn't undersell. And you couldn't get
a sense of emergency.

I tried to go back to Berle [on the rescue issue], and he said it's out
of his hands. That it was moved over to Long, who was another assistant
secretary—they were the same rank. I didn't get far. I didn't get far at all.

W: How involved was [Secretary of the Interior] Harold Ickes?*

K: He was just a man, I would say, with a conscience. What happened
with Ickes is what should have happened with most people in this
thing, but it didn't. Ickes, I would say, was a normal, good human
being. I mean, he was way above normal in intelligence. We got to him
through Assistant Secretary Oscar Chapman[20] and Solicitor-General
Fowler Harper.[21] What happened is that the minute they sort of forced
the door open and he listened to us—he had a normal human reaction, and he couldn't say no. And from that point on, everything the
Zionists did against us, involving him, worked in the opposite direction. They sort of threw him more into our camp than he was really—
he became a little more, more in it, because he resented the pressure.

---

*Harold L. Ickes (1874–1952), Franklin Roosevelt's Secretary of the Interior, took an early
interest in the Jewish refugee problem and during the late 1930s tried, unsuccessfully, to
interest FDR in the idea of permitting refugees to settle in the Virgin Islands and Alaska.
Ickes served as honorary chairman of Bergson's July 1943 Emergency Conference to Save
the Jewish People of Europe and as honorary chairman of the Washington, D.C., chapter of
the Emergency Committee to Save the Jewish People of Europe. In 1945, he successfully
lobbied within the administration to permit the 834 European Jewish refugees remaining
at the Oswego camp in upstate New York to leave the camp and integrate into American
society.

He resented the pressure, it didn't work. Wise wrote him a letter, pressuring him to quit the Emergency Committee.* And Ickes wrote a nasty letter back.

K: [Reading from a November 24, 1943, news report in the Yiddish-language *Jewish Morning Journal* about the hearings]: It says[22] that Bloom tried to prove that the previous resolution which was passed through Congress about the European Jews† was stronger than the present one. And Bergson said the previous resolution was only an expression of sympathy, while this present resolution is looking for action. Mr. Bloom insisted on defending the present policy of the government about Jews, indicating there is no need for new action. He maintains that it is necessary to have $2,000 for every Jew that might be saved. To save two million at $2,000 apiece, you need a few billion dollars. He wanted to show it was financially impossible.‡ Congressman [Andrew] Schiffler [Republican—West Virginia] pointed out that the money problem was irrelevant when one is dealing with human lives. Bergson said there is a difference between persecution and extermination; the Jews of Europe, if they are not saved, will be totally exterminated. This is what we are trying to clarify before the Committee and the American people.

WILL ROGERS, JR., RECALLS:[25]

I greatly admired and respected the old man [Sol Bloom]. He had been a vaudevillian. He had been around New York theater when my father had

---

*For the text of the letter from Wise to Ickes, see the Appendix, page 221.

†In March 1943, both houses of Congress unanimously approved a resolution, sponsored by Senate majority leader Alben W. Barkley, deploring "the mass murder of Jewish men, women, and children" and asserting that those responsible should "be held accountable and punished," but making no reference to rescue action.[23]

‡Bloom restricted the actual discussion about the number of refugees to be rescued to 100,000, thereby indicating a total cost of $200 million. The Emergency Committee and its supporters, however, spoke of the need to rescue approximately 2 million, entailing a much larger cost.[24]

been around New York theater. . . . We were very friendly, and he would often break into song. I liked him very, very much. But when I began to go over to the Bergson group, this friendly attitude changed almost immediately. He said, "What are you doing over there? This is going to wreck your career." Well, I didn't worry about that very much, but he said, "This is not the people you should be associated with." And then he just cut off all communication with me. [Before that,] we used to sit and talk or be friendly or say hello or how's the weather, but he just cut it off completely. Totally. And that was about the strongest opposition I guess he could make at the time. Again, it didn't mean a damn to me. I would like to have been friends with him, but he had no political pressure on me and neither did Rabbi Wise and neither, on this particular matter, neither did President Roosevelt.

W: Dorothy Detzer,[26] a Washington lobbyist for the Women's International League for Peace and Freedom, was interested in the rescue resolution, and she was clearly of the opinion that if Roosevelt had not established the War Refugee Board, this legislation would have been passed.[27]

K: Oh, sure. It would have passed in the Senate, it would have passed in the Senate right there.*

W: The House?

K: The House, I don't know, because you cannot bring up a bill without a chairman. There's no way to take it out of the committee under the rules. If it was passed in the Senate, it would have constituted pressure on Bloom to do something in the House. He couldn't have sat there doing nothing. He would have had either to turn it down in the committee and then it has to come to the floor, which could override

---

*When the Senate Foreign Relations Committee considered the rescue resolution, its members unanimously approved it. Their formal message to the Senate, Senate Report No. 625, penetrated to the heart of the issue:

> The problem is immediate. The problem is essentially a
> humanitarian one. It is not a Jewish problem alone. It is
> a Christian problem and a problem for enlightened
> civilization. . . . We have talked; we have sympathized;
> we have expressed our horror; the time to act is long past due.[28]

the committee, or he had to approve it—he couldn't have, even though it's not a law, it doesn't go through a conference.

A concurrent resolution, as far as I remember—I sort of knew the rules then—if you have a *bill*, it has to go to a joint conference. If you have a situation like this, or one house acted and the other didn't, or there's a difference, it goes to conference. A concurrent resolution really doesn't have to. But if I recall it correctly, something would have happened in the House if it was voted in the Senate. This way, it couldn't have continued, where it sits in the House committee. But you couldn't do anything to force it out of committee, short of passing it through the Senate.

W: Well, her feeling was that it had the votes in the House, once it got to the House floor.

K: Oh, no doubt about it.

Authors' Note: Treasury Department officials, closely watching the fight over the rescue resolution, observed at its most critical point (mid-January 1944) that "Bloom is having to do everything he can possibly do to keep that resolution from being reported out of the House Foreign [Affairs] Committee." Bloom "feels it would be a problem to have the full debate both on the floors of the Senate and the House, because he doesn't think he could hold the resolution in the House Committee, and it would also be a direct attack on the Administration, including the President, for having failed to act."[29]

WILL ROGERS, JR., RECALLS:[30]

The major achievement of the Bergson group was making things so hot for the administration that they could no longer do nothing. There had to be some action. Whether it was going to be the resolution that I and Senator Gillette introduced or something else, they had to move. And so they did set up the War Refugee Board. And that was due to the actions of the Bergson committee.

6

The War Refugee Board

In this chapter, Kook recalls his initial elation over—and then gradual disenchantment with—the War Refugee Board, the government agency created by President Roosevelt to help rescue Jews from the Nazis. Kook describes the obstacles that impeded the WRB, and his feeling of being in a "race against death," a race neither he nor the underpowered and poorly funded WRB was capable of winning.

WYMAN: You have indicated that the War Refugee Board hadn't been anything like what the hopes for it were.[1]

KOOK: Right. In the general frustrating frenzy, I would say, of activity that we had, one thing was clear all the time, and the purpose of the whole activity was this thing. And this is that only governmental action can save a serious portion of the intended victims. And that's why, even today, thirty years later, I get annoyed when they say, "How many Jews did you save?" Because we didn't work— not that it's not important—but our whole preoccupation was not on trying to go over and save five hundred people. Five hundred lives are an awful lot of things, and I'm not sneering at it. But our whole concept, our whole activity, as you see, was aiming at one thing. There was a powerful government [Germany] using all its resources. By the time we learned about it, it's killed 2 million people. A method of destruction of such a scope had to be counteracted by another big force. Individuals and charitable organizations couldn't do much. Not that they shouldn't be doing, they should be swarming there, saving whatever they can.

But we weren't that. When we started yelling—that's what we started doing, really, at first. That's all we did. We yelled out, you see. But then, I started thinking constantly what could be done. And the one really basic idea that occurred to me was to convince the government it's their job. It's impossible there should be a federal power commission, and a federal interstate trade commission—and we said, "Like this, there should be a save-the-Jews commission." And I used to use these comparisons, you see. There ought to be an agency, an agency of the government where people come in the morning.

I remember telling [World Jewish Congress President] Nahum Goldmann that if there'll be an office of three rooms, and three good Americans will come there in the morning to work. And they will know that their job for their government is to do what they can to save the Jews, and if they are government officials, they have the whole resources of the government behind them. I don't know what they have even. I mean, I'm not that much of an expert on what the government of the United States has—there's an OSS [Office of Strategic Services], the forerunner of the CIA, there's the army, there's the State Department—all sorts of things going on. So that the whole pressure was in this line. Wherever I got a real response—if I spoke to a person and he had some sort of an interest—then the conversation went over from the general thing of saving the Jews, to try and develop more specific things.

By the time I met with the people who were later the staff of the War Refugee Board, which was a week or so before—a couple of weeks, I think—before the War Refugee Board was established, and it was known it's going to be established, and they were already working. With them, all the conversations practically, much sooner than you would believe possible, were not ques-

tions here and there, "What do you think of Ira Hirschmann," or
"What do you think of this or that?" All the conversations
were—and they between them had this attitude. They had this
attitude. I mean, these guys wanted to do a major job.

The very day after the Board was established, or maybe before,
DuBois* comes out—a funny-looking, very tiny little fellow, very
short, shorter than me, very husky, like this, and didn't look like
the brainy guy that he is. And he's very brainy. You know, he looked
an anti-intellectual sort of type. And he's a lawyer with a very good
mind. And they were talking something. I said to them, "I was
thinking yesterday," and this and that, and they talk, and then they
tell me that they've pinpointed—I believe it was 70-some million
or 60-some million—but to me, it sounded a very impressive sum
of money, certainly in those days. And I remember being elated at
the scope in which they were thinking. At the beginning, you see,
they were thinking, "How are we going to finance this?" in terms
of government regulations and budgets—exactly the things I was
pushing for. And we were completely on line, onstream on this—
identical. They understood that this was the job. The job is how to
use the government machinery. Later on, they always said, "Look,
anything we do, we begin by saying, 'Will it go through the State
Department or won't it? What are the chances?' If we can't do this,
we've got to do something else, and it'll go through State." And we
were talking all the time.

Our proposal to threaten to use poison gas against the Nazis
if the mass murder continued—that would have been a national
policy of major magnitude.[2] If this would have been tried, it
might have stopped the massacre right there and then. It would

---

*Josiah E. DuBois, Jr. (1913–1983), a senior aide to Treasury Secretary Henry Morgenthau,
was actively involved in the investigation of the State Department's obstruction of rescue
efforts, leading to the establishment of the War Refugee Board. There is some evidence that
Morgenthau agreed to press Roosevelt to create a rescue agency in part because DuBois
threatened that if he did not do so, he, DuBois, would resign from the Treasury, call a press
conference in Washington, and rip the lid off the entire State Department refugee scandal.
DuBois became a leading official in the War Refugee Board and, after the war, he was
appointed deputy chief counsel for the prosecution of Nazi war criminals at Nuremberg.

have returned to a pogrom of various proportions, a little more so. The major extermination effort, however, could have been stopped, in my opinion, if there would have been a governmental decision to stop it. To intervene. Not to stop, to intervene. We failed. The War Refugee Board started out—the words of the resolution were that there should be a government agency to save the Jewish people of Europe. The War Refugee Board, as it turned out, was an effective, large-scale charitable effort to save some Jews of Europe. It never really got started. The biggest despair I had was *after* the War Refugee Board was formed—not immediately after—when it was formed I had a sense of elation. But a few months later, I was just worn out. I was beat. There was a sense of losing. A sense of failure.

We expected the War Refugee Board to start sitting in conferences with General Marshall over at his people in the War Department. We expected it to pick up suggestions. The one suggestion that came out of the Jewish leadership that had merit was the suggestion to bomb the railroads and the gas chambers.*

---

*In addition to the Emergency Committee to Save the Jewish People of Europe, the idea of the Allies bombing the death camps or the railways leading to them (or taking some other military action against the camps) was advocated by the American Jewish Conference (a coalition of all leading U.S. Jewish organizations); Nahum Goldmann, president of the World Jewish Congress, as well as the WJC's representatives in London and Geneva; the Labor Zionists of America; the American Orthodox group Agudath Israel; the U.S. Orthodox rescue group Vaad Hahatzala; the executive director of the War Refugee Board, John Pehle, as well as his deputy, Benjamin Akzin, and the Board's London representative, James Mann; the Czech Goverment-in-Exile; the Polish Government-in-Exile; Slovak Jewish leaders Gisi Fleischmann and Rabbi Michael Weissmandel; Czech Jewish leader Ernest Frischer; the editors of the Jewish Telegraphic Agency, the Independent Jewish Press Service, *Jewish Forum* magazine, and *Congress Monthly,* official journal of the American Jewish Congress; and columnists for the Yiddish daily *Jewish Morning Journal,* and *Opinion* magazine.

Many senior officials of the Jewish Agency lobbied Allied representatives on behalf of the idea of bombing the camps, including Chaim Weizmann, president of the World Zionist Organization–Jewish Agency; Moshe Shertok, chief of the Jewish Agency's Political Department; the chairman of the Agency's Rescue Committee, Yitzhak Gruenbaum; the Agency's Geneva representatives, Richard Lichtheim and Chaim Pozner; its Budapest representative, Moshe Krausz; its Istanbul representative, Chaim Barlas; and Agency chairman David Ben-Gurion's deputy, Eliahu Epstein.[3]

Our suggestion to threaten to use poison gas, as a warning—I mean, if Roosevelt, Churchill, and Stalin would have come out with such a warning to the Germans. But they didn't. When you think about it now, it's still bloodcurdling, as to why a statement like this wasn't made.

The heartbreaking thing about it was that the crowd at the War Refugee Board, which fed Morgenthau what to do—not only the heart was on the right track, they grasped this, they understood it. They understood it before and they went in with this spirit. They didn't go in with the [idea that they would be an agency to facilitate] the work of the private aid organizations. They did not go in with this idea. They went in with a political task. They saw in this a governmental—you see, they saw themselves as a government, a war agency, War Refugee Board, you know.

My recollections of those days of the War Refugee Board are that it was like a train that jumped the tracks. It didn't jump, it slowly got off, it didn't turn over.

W: Are you saying that the War Refugee Board deteriorated from a broad governmental approach to one of facilitating a series of smaller projects—

K: It did, yes! Absolutely.

W: I would agree that a lot of the work that was done under their aegis was done by the several private aid organizations, separately. For instance, the Joint Distribution Committee,* the Vaad Hahatzala, and so forth. With their own money.

K: Right.

W: But with cooperation from the War Refugee Board, which tried to facilitate, and to help with the communications, and—

K: That was really the major thing the board did. If you look back, that's most of the work. The concept of the War Refugee Board—forgive

---

*The American Jewish Joint Distribution Committee, established in 1914, is the premier Jewish organization for the distribution of relief funds to beleaguered Jewish communities around the world.

me—in the concept, this thing should have been 3 percent and the other [larger] things 97 percent.

These [War Refugee Board] guys knew it wasn't the War Refugee Board that they'd hoped it was going to be. The thing was much smaller. It's a complicated subject to explain because it deteriorated into a charitable organization. Now, charitable organizations are very good. But that was not the issue at the time. [Though it is true that] in the field of charity they did much more than was being done before, by far.

You know, you had the three senior departments of the U.S. government committed to this thing, and you had nothing at the same time. It became a very complicated way in which—with good or with bad intentions, I don't know, probably mostly with good—just complexities of the thing or lack of knowledge on our part. The thing just didn't work. Even with Pehle* and DuBois and Luxford.[4] They were very busy with all sorts of things and it was very hard to come and tell them, "Look, this is nonsense." I mean, I never had a fight with them. I should have.

W: Didn't you raise this issue with them, about how they were going off the track?

K: Sure I did.

W: How did they react?

K: They were struggling, and it happened gradually—it was like getting a small dose of poison. It wasn't dramatic, and so there was never a confrontation. And I feel terrible about it, because if at least I [had] walked in some, one day there and [said], "Damn it, you guys are really not doing what you're supposed to do, you're operating on this principle that the road to hell is paved with good intentions. Your intentions are wonderful, but you're going to hell." I didn't say that.

W: But you did point the problem out?

K: Oh, yeah; they used to point it out themselves. Especially DuBois. They used to have a sign, this was a sign meaning "Bull!" I didn't know

---

*John Pehle (1914–), a senior aide to Treasury Secretary Henry Morgenthau, was actively involved in the investigation of the State Department's obstruction of rescue efforts, leading to the establishment of the War Refugee Board, and subsequently was appointed the Board's first executive director.

that—they taught me this. When somebody was talking, they used to go like this and signal—[holds up hand with index finger and pinkie up and two middle fingers bent down, then partially hides it behind his ear, as if leaning upon it]. The first time I learned it was when I went down to one of those meetings with Morgenthau. DuBois was doing this to Pehle—somebody was talking to Morgenthau. They were doing it in all sorts of places. When that other person wasn't supposed to know—they were signaling to each other.

During this period, I had really close relations, which started fading out because I was getting nowhere with them, and they couldn't do it. But I had close relations with Pehle and Luxford, and especially DuBois. They had a permanent fight whatever they wanted to do. They always sat and they planned strategy—how to get things through the State Department. They spent most of the time when I was there—they always tried to maneuver how to get things past the State Department. Because while it was accepted in the War Refugee Board that, where the Secretary of State was senior to Morgenthau, that Morgenthau is sort of the driving spirit of it, and that the staff is in the Treasury. It was because of Morgenthau's personal involvement, really. Because this should have been work which involved the State Department, not the Treasury. At the same time, the State Department never abdicated its official role in this thing.

Two months after the War Refugee Board was founded—not that John Pehle didn't want to see me—but he couldn't avoid seeing ten, fifteen delegations a day. I would come in there and he says, "My God,"—he couldn't. He was a young man who suddenly started being quoted in the papers and articles were written about him and all this, and he was being pressured. He had to learn. Is Judge Proskauer important? Must he see him or must he not? They said he must see him. There were endless guys like this. And the minute the War Refugee Board was formed, the family all became lions. You see, all these mice, who didn't have an idea of what to do, suddenly started running. And also physically these people—it's hard for me to explain to you what happened, except that this thing just got off the track. It got off the track.

W: The War Refugee Board did pursue the bombing idea. Pehle did try to do something about that. They were stopped, by John McCloy[5] and the War Department, who said they couldn't do it. In fact, they were running bombing missions right up there. Four times they bombed Auschwitz. Not the camp; the adjoining manufacturing areas. At the same time that the War Department insisted that the plan was not practical, that it would require diversion of a large amount of air power that was essential to decisive war operations elsewhere.

K: We failed. We—meaning all of us who worked on it—I don't mean the Emergency Committee as such; it includes the War Refugee Board. We failed in getting across to the government of the United States—where we concentrated most of the effort. After all, we didn't concentrate on convincing the government of Great Britain. The French weren't a factor, to speak of. So, actually the whole effort was to convince the government of the United States, the people, the five hundred or whatever it is, who make up the policy-making thing of the government. To convince them that this is an important war task that they have to engage in. We failed. This is the truth. Because if we would have done that—we came close, we came close. We came close. We were outmaneuvered by politicians, really. Not by sinister politicians who had a master plan. But each time, say, when we wanted the effect of a congressional bill, Roosevelt wanted to blunt it by doing without a congressional bill. And we—either out of weakness, or—I must admit that then when we were told it, I thought it's a victory. Because we thought the creation of the thing is important.

W: You didn't have any thought at all of continuing with the rescue bill.

K: No, no. It wouldn't have made any sense. We wouldn't say, this is the wrong agency, because we thought it was the right agency because we had the guys on the inside who were good. These guys were good. I mean, it's a heartbreaking story.

If you read the childlike euphoria that my wife was writing about John Pehle, this is the atmosphere of victory that was around. We thought, you know—see, it's childlike euphoria, I mean, she was in a state of euphoria when she wrote it. Because we thought that these people were going to save millions of people. And they acted like it and they would have. And somehow we got worn out, like water on a rock. By inability to overcome the various counterforces which all worked against us.

W: You think perhaps that by the time—once the board had got underway during that hopeful period at the beginning—that maybe you people sort of had a letdown, figuring, "Thank God, we've done it"—you've exhausted yourselves for a year and a half of this steady work, and sort of slackened off at that point.

K: We had that for a while, and then we didn't. We had a sense of victory, and then despair. That was the case, at least with me. During the euphoric period after the War Refugee Board was born, we thought that now, you know, not only *we* get up in the morning worrying about the Jews, but there's a government agency worrying about them. The War Refugee Board gave us a relief, like water to the thirsty—and we wanted to believe it, one of the reasons that I said before I felt very bad for not having tried harder to change it. Maybe I would have felt better if I got into a fight with them. But I didn't. But the reason is also that you want to believe. Same as that thing we talked about, of the Jews not wanting to believe there's a massacre to begin with. Or me not wanting to believe. And later on you wanted or hoped that the War Refugee Board is going to do it. So you don't see things as clear—they seem clear later. I saw it after a while, but not as early as I should have seen it.

On the issue of the extermination of the Jews and our rescue work with the Emergency Committee, the latter part, out of fatigue and out of a kind of despair, because the Jews were being killed—it wasn't any more 4 million to save. We started off [in December 1942] by saying a memorial to 2 million dead Jews, save the others, while the figures were changing like in a race, so many killed and so many to go. You didn't really know if there were still Jews there, you hoped there were. You hoped there were, but it was a sense of losing, a sense of failure.

W: Hopelessness.

K: Yeah. And mostly because these guys were good. My feeling is that if it was a separate agency with the right people, it could have been done. John Pehle fundamentally was a good guy but a bureaucrat. And he fell into this thing because he was used to working. Shoveling papers like this. And this very concept meant failure to the thing from the beginning. If you had a William Allen White* on it, *he* would have had access to Roosevelt because he would have been independent. And *he* would have raised hell!†

It's painful, it's painful. On this thing it hurts like hell. Because we came close to having achieved something. If the United States government, assuming that Roosevelt comes to the Cabinet and says, "I've determined that we are going to do whatever we can to try and stop"—that, if such a decision would have been made, that the majority of the people would have been saved. This is my feeling, I still feel so. Large numbers, a sizable percentage. It's hard to talk in numbers, because you begin feeling like—but a substantial percentage—say if the Germans have massacred 100 percent of what they massacred, it would have been 50, or 30, or 60, and when you translate this into human beings and numbers it becomes horrifying.

And to me, the villain in this picture—if I have to choose one man—I mean, I take the Jewish leadership as a group—the guy whom I've cursed, and you know, I'm not a bitter man generally—is [Samuel] Rosenman. Somehow I have a feeling that he was the quintessence of the general Jewish position on this. The man with the most influence.

If he would have had the healthy attitude of saying, "Mr. President," or "Franklin"—or whatever he called him—and he said, "Look, I was born a Jew, my name is Samuel"—or whatever it is—"I cannot be your adviser on Jewish things. I can be your speechwriter. Please don't rely upon me in Jewish matters." But he didn't. He functioned as a Jew all the time.

---

*William Allen White (1868–1944), the Pulitzer Prize–winning editor of the *Emporia* (Kansas) *Gazette,* was one of America's most prominent newspapermen from the early 1900s until his death. In addition to his career in journalism, White in 1939 founded the Committee to Defend America by Aiding the Allies, which he chaired until early 1941. White was a member of Bergson's Committee for a Jewish Army, and endorsed the Emergency Conference to Save the Jewish People of Europe.

†An additional problem hampered the effectiveness of the War Refugee Board late in 1944. Secretary Morgenthau, in line with widespread expectations that the war was nearly over, recommended to Pehle that he assume the helm at the Treasury Department's Procurement Division, the unit responsible for disposing of surplus military property. Once Pehle took the position, late in November 1944, he was able to work for the War Refugee Board only part-time.[6]

W: What were your efforts in 1944 involving the Apostolic Delegate in Washington [Archbishop Amleto Cicognani]?

K: Well, I don't recall the dates or the details, but amongst the innumerable appeals we made to all sorts of people in positions of power and influence, I remember sending off some letters and appeals to the Papal Nuncio—whatever the title is—in Washington. It was sort of like the ambassador of the Vatican. I also met with him at least twice, at least on two occasions. I'm not even sure whether it was the same person twice. I don't remember. What I do remember was that there was a polite brush-off. No encouragement at all. Nothing in a practical sense. We tried to ask some concrete things. It wasn't just a general appeal for help, you know, saying do what you can. We did design a couple of concrete things. But we didn't get anyplace. He said he'll transfer it further to the Pope, but—nothing.

Authors' Note: As noted in Chapter 1, the Bergson group established the Hebrew Committee of National Liberation in May 1944 as the government-in-exile for the Jewish state (yet to be established) in Palestine. Declaring the HCNL the authentic representative of Palestine Jewry and those stateless European Jews hoping to immigrate to the Holy Land, Bergson directly challenged the authority of the World Zionist Organization and the Jewish Agency, which considered themselves the sole legitimate representatives of the Palestine Jewish community. The result was a barrage of vehement attacks by the American Zionist leadership, and by non-Zionist Jewish leaders as well, which forced Bergson to divert considerable energy to responding to his critics. The critics also denounced the HCNL's assertions that Jewish identity should be redefined, with Jews in Palestine and stateless European Jews to be described as "Hebrews," and with the word "Jews" to refer to American and other Diaspora Jews in strictly religious (rather than ethnic or nationalistic) terms.

W: Why did you decide in May 1944 to establish the Hebrew Committee of National Liberation? And what impact did the controversy that followed have on your efforts to rescue Jews?

K: In a way, maybe the years of Zionist attacks on us found their mark.

You know, this is a thought that never occurred to me until this minute. Because if you take a little Jewish fellow born in Russia, going through pogroms, raised as a Zionist, becoming a member of the Haganah, going through all this, and then being accused of betraying the national cause. Now I wash it off very easy, and then it didn't bother me because I was busy screaming, "Help! Save the Jews!" You know, but somewhere it probably found its mark. How long can you live in emergency? I would say that the weariness was another factor. A desire to do something else. It blended in, because the Hebrew Committee, in the beginning, all of the activities—with the exception of establishing the concept of the Hebrew nation—all were on rescue.

W: The rescue aspect could have been done through the Emergency Committee—

K: Yes, yes, but we wanted to add this dimension to it.

W: Was there anything unique about the Hebrew Committee that was of value to rescue?

K: Yes. The definition of the nation. Genocide. We felt that the major reason why nobody did anything was the confusion—that the Germans are killing their own Jews and it's none of our business. Fundamentally, the Jews were nationals of other nations, and not an entity which other people could interfere on. We felt that pointing out that this is a separate nation may help. We failed, because you don't put across such a concept that easily. But we felt it will help in crystallizing the thing.

W: One might draw the conclusion that your establishment of the Hebrew Committee hurt your rescue effort. It heated up your conflicts with the American Jewish leadership to a very high level of intensity.* It had to divert your energy and their energy. It had to tie up your time and energy and money and detract from other things you might have been doing.

---

*Animosities reached a point where Stephen Wise told John Pehle of the War Refugee Board that he seriously believed the Bergson group might kill him. Ansel Luxford of the WRB told a small group of top WRB officials who were meeting with Henry Morgenthau: "You can talk about Wise. [But] I think the feeling is so strong in this issue that I wouldn't be surprised to see Bergson killed. I wouldn't."[7]

K: We didn't think the reaction would be as violent as it was, I must admit. We didn't know the attacks would be that ferocious. We thought it would get a little mudslinging and so forth, and we'd continue doing our job as we did before. And we considered that. We did not think it'll—all the energy. There was a time there in which all the Jewish leaders seemed to do nothing else but fight us. Fighting us was their main preoccupation. It was unbelievable, what was going on there. You can see it in the minutes of every meeting of theirs.

We didn't foresee this. We foresaw a mudslinging campaign, and we thought it would be rather short. I can't deny that, along with the Hebrew Committee's positive impact on rescue, there was also the negative aspect: It opened the way for the various Jewish groups to attack both the Hebrew Committee and the Emergency Committee. I'm very sorry to say that there's no question about it. Post facto, now.

There were other dimensions, though. I mean, the thrust of the Hebrew nation concept, while we failed to put it across in a major way, we did achieve some results here and there. For instance, we started working with the various embassies of occupied Europe. And we were getting a response from them on this thing. With them, I mean, it took exactly fifteen minutes to sell this to the Polish ambassador. They loved the concept. First of all, it fit with their personal feelings and upbringing that the Jews were aliens. Number two, it relieved them from some feelings of guilt about their citizens being killed. Now the Germans weren't killing Polish Jews, they were killing Hebrews. And we had our own reasons why we wanted to say, they're killing Hebrew citizens, not Polish citizens. So, here and there it probably helped some places. It confused some people, but it clarified for some people.

I cannot possibly deny that as things turned out, it hindered the work of the Emergency Committee, it hindered it too much. Achieving any successes—I don't know—but it hindered the work of the Emergency Committee. This is a hard admission for me to make. But I don't think that it was entirely without compensation.

W: In terms of rescue?

K: Yes. It wasn't completely just negative. Maybe we made an error of judgment. We tried to add a dimension on the rescue thing. And when we went into it, we didn't know if it was going to be effective or not. The Hebrew Committee, in a sense, was two things at the same time. It was an expression of hope and an act of desperation.

W: Ira Hirschmann,* who was a member of the Emergency Committee, became the War Refugee Board's representative in Turkey.† When you went in to see Breckinridge Long, in the months after the Emergency Conference, you took Hirschmann with you a couple of times. How did that work out?

K: Yeah. We selected Hirschmann as one of our proposed delegation to Turkey. You know, we finally cut—Long was pressuring us—we wanted to send three, four people. Long says, "There's no place, and this and that," and we finally cut it down to two people—Hirschmann and Eri Jabotinsky.‡ And this was approved. And then he said that first they'll have a place for one, and then the other one. Then, apparently—some of the stuff I'm telling you I discovered afterward— apparently there was a relationship developed between Hirschmann and Breckinridge Long before that.

W: After you took him in, but before he went?

K: Yes. You know, when we were talking, Hirschmann told me, and I sort

---

*Ira Hirschmann (1901–1989), a business executive, held senior positions with Lord & Taylor, Saks Fifth Avenue, and Bloomingdale's. He was also a close associate of New York City Mayor Fiorello LaGuardia. He served as a vice president of the Emergency Committee to Save the Jewish People of Europe.

†The War Refugee Board stationed representatives in Turkey, Switzerland, Sweden, North Africa, Italy, and Portugal.

‡Eri Jabotinsky (1910–1969) was the only child of Vladimir Ze'ev Jabotinsky, founder of Revisionist Zionism. Active in the Irgun Zvai Leumi's effort to organize unauthorized immigration from Europe to Palestine, Jabotinsky was jailed by the British in 1940 for his role in organizing the voyage of the refugee ship *Sakarya*. He was released in 1942 due to the intervention of U.S. Senator Robert Taft (R-OH), and traveled to the United States to work full-time for the Bergson group. In early 1944, Bergson sent Jabotinsky to Istanbul to facilitate rescue activities. The British, accusing Jabotinsky of links to the Irgun, asked the Turkish authorities to expel him. In April 1944, he was placed on a Palestine-bound train, and arrested by the British, who detained him in the Acre prison for one year and then released him without charges.

of took it naively, Hirschmann says, "You know I met with Breckinridge Long, he came to New York, I invited him to my home." I thought it's very good. Breckinridge Long was anything but friendly, and I thought it's very good if he could develop some personal relations. Later on I started thinking what this personal relationship meant. It was working the other way. It wasn't that Hirschmann was converting Long, but Long was converting Hirschmann.

Hirschmann was too small a guy for the job. I mean, he had too much consideration for his personal status socially, for his possible business benefits. He was a guy who made a fairly, for him, big jump into being vice president of Bloomingdale's. He thought this was sitting on top of the world, you know. And suddenly, he became an international political figure, through this little thing he did with us. He was with us only a couple of months. I asked him to join because we didn't suffer from any surplus of people of any kind of standing in the community. So we took him and he was just a guy who didn't live up to the occasion, no more than the other Jewish leaders—not that he was a Jewish leader. They didn't live up to the occasion. They were more concerned with their routines. And so was he. It was more important for him to have dinner with [Laurence] Steinhardt [the U.S. ambassador to Turkey], you know.

And he got caught in a double fix. On the one hand, the snobbery and the allure of the State Department, the aura of the State Department—government, administration, Secretary of State. On the other hand, the Jewish Agency, which were also important people. Chaim Weizmann was a big name, and there were all these Jewish Agency guys there in Turkey. And, between the two—and he had a good justification, he says, "I'm now not Emergency Committee really. I've finished my job with the Emergency Committee. I'm War Refugee Board." And he did what he thought was the best under the circumstances, which I think was very poor. That's about all there is to it. I mean, if Ira Hirschmann would have come to the War Refugee Board on his own, without me knowing him, I would have nothing against him. I'm a peculiar guy this way, you know. Like van Paassen—I have no rancor against van Paassen. I understood what made him work and it wasn't that sensitive. Lerner, you won't find one bad word from Lerner on us, on us or me, not one word. And yet I'm angry at him till now.

W: Because he disappointed you?

K: No! Because what did he quit? What kind of a cause did he quit and for what reason? And after what he said, you know. I'm disappointed in him.

And the same thing Hirschmann. I kept on running into him in New York, and each time he says, "Let's have lunch." And I didn't say, "Look, you son of a bitch, don't bother me." I said, "Fine, thank you," and I never met him—I didn't want to. What's the point in telling him, "Look, you didn't live up to my expectations, or to what you should have done"? Or, "You had the opportunity to do big things and save hundreds of thousands of people, and you didn't." He did his best, which was very small in a big situation. He didn't live up to the emergency. That's what it amounts to.

He was one of the least effective people in the War Refugee Board, whereas his job should have been to upgrade the War Refugee Board, and he did the reverse. Because, after all, he came to the War Refugee Board through the Emergency Committee, and he should have been—he should have seen himself as an Emergency Committee man there trying to push the whole scope of what we wanted. Maybe if I would have been there, I couldn't have done it, either. But he didn't try.

W: I thought I saw that Hirschmann had broken with the Emergency Committee by late 1943, before he went to Turkey.

K: Even after he was in Turkey, Hirschmann never broke with the Committee. When he came back after he was in Turkey as an emissary of the War Refugee Board, he came back and appeared at one of our meetings and said, "I owe you a report, not officially, but morally," and this and that and so forth. He never broke with the Committee.

Later on, you see, what happened is that Hirschmann felt that we are angry at him because of his disagreements with Eri Jabotinsky. And then the British arrested Jabotinsky. And Jabotinsky said that Hirschmann could have prevented it, and he didn't. He never accused Hirschmann of having a hand in his arrest. But he said that Hirschmann could have like this [a snap of the fingers], by picking up a phone and telling the Jewish Agency guys that he won't tolerate it, that Jabotinsky wouldn't have been arrested, and he refused to do it. And Hirschmann felt that we are angry at him, which was true. And the contact was just lost. We felt there wasn't much point writing to Hirschmann in Ankara when he's so much under the influence of all the things—I mean, he was doing what he was doing and that was it, you know. We just felt he was a War Refugee Board man, and that's it.

W: What about William O'Dwyer,[8] who succeeded Pehle as War Refugee Board director in January 1945?

K: He didn't grasp it, he was not—he didn't grasp the problem. By that time he talked in terms of, "Look, we did this, we did that."

W: Getting food into the camps at the very end of the war—that was the main thing he did, he got food into the camps—

K: Talking of things like this, and it was futile to try and tell him, "Look, this is not a job." And that was that. I can't even remember what I came to see him about. I came to see him, first of all, to be there. And there was—he knew to what extent I was involved in this, and this and that, he gave me compliments. And then I always had the feeling he was sitting there as a political stepping-stone, which is exactly what it was.

W: One story is that Roosevelt put him in there so that he would add the Jewish vote to the Irish vote in New York to become mayor. It seems that Roosevelt was grooming him for the mayorship of New York.

K: Possible, yeah.

W: And he had the Irish vote; this would give him the Jewish vote. He had been doing relief work in Italy, so he had the Italian vote. How do you lose in New York with the Irish, Italian, and Jewish vote?

K: With all this baloney, I remember years later when I was in Cuba on business I ran into O'Dwyer, who by then was ambassador to Spain, or ex-ambassador to Spain, whatever he was—and he was sitting getting drunk at the National Hotel in Cuba, feeding me drinks and telling me, "Do I remember?" telling people, you know, "This is the great man who did so much for the Jews," and "I was on the War Refugee Board," and I stayed there about just three minutes. I didn't want to make a row—I disappeared, I just got up and left, politely, you know, without anyone noticing. But I couldn't stomach it in the middle of drinking daiquiris.

K: You know, it dawns on me now, sitting here and thinking very hard about my behavior in those days—that DuBois, Pehle, and the others, and myself didn't want to believe we were off the track. I remember realizing it, but not as early as I should have. And by the time I started talking a little bit—first of all, I never raised a fuss, so I'm in a sense as guilty as I'm accusing the Jewish leaders of. But I didn't realize it—I realized it, but I don't know, I was worn out. There must have been the sin of—putting it in theological terms—the sin, not of pride, but of the desperate desire to feel that you've succeeded and you did something. The clouded judgment. For a while, for long, for a couple of months, maybe, there was this feeling of achievement that continued. Now we have a War Refugee Board that's doing the job.

Because in later years, when people talk to me—not now, but twenty years ago—and say, "Oh, Peter Bergson, he's responsible practically single-handed for creating the War Refugee Board." I say, "Who the hell is the War Refugee Board?" This is my reaction, you see. The reason it's so painful is because I have a frustrating sense of failure there.

CHAPTER
7

Epilogue

When the war ended, Kook threw himself into the struggle to help bring about the creation of the State of Israel. In this chapter, he recalls how his energies were diverted by his fight to avoid deportation from the United States, a step that some of his opponents had been urging the government to undertake. But Kook could not escape intra-Jewish conflicts even after he left America's shores. He describes how he arrived in Israel in 1948 amidst clashes between rival Jewish forces, and, because of his ties to the Irgun Zvai Leumi militia, ended up in prison. At the conclusion of the interview, Kook looks back with profound sadness on his bitter experiences, and reflects on the lessons to be learned.

KOOK: My wife worked in Europe.[1] When the war was over, she went to Europe to work on what we called the repatriation. I couldn't get a visa, I was trapped in the United States because my British passport, Palestinian passport, expired—the British wouldn't renew it. I had no documents. So the State Department wanted me to declare myself stateless and then they'll give me a traveling document. And I wouldn't. I said, "I'm not stateless, I'm a Palestinian."

But before that, they had wanted to deport me, and I was under arrest and this thing wasn't settled for some time. Meanwhile, there was a [senior Justice Department official] called [James P.] McGranery[2] who we knew. He was an Irish guy from Pennsylvania, had been one of our congressmen. And we were fairly strong in Pennsylvania. Senator [Hugh] Scott from Pennsylvania[3] was one of our men. He was chairman of the American League for a Free Palestine in Pennsylvania and of the Emergency Committee. And he was like Andy Somers—practically next to Somers, he was. And so we were strong in Pennsylvania—this comes from the technique of the Temperance League people. We simply went to McGranery and he got my file, and he told this guy—I wasn't there—but he told this guy, Joe Sharfsin,[4] who was one of our guys who knew him well—McGranery knew me—he took the thing, he says, "Look, you see this drawer? You start worrying when I stop running this office. As long as I'm here, I'm 'studying' these files."

Nothing happened. Then the immigration thing got divided into two—the State Department and the Immigration Service.* It took time. Joe Sharfsin started working on this thing with me. We finally hit on an idea—his idea. And I went to the British Embassy and gave them my passport. I said, "I want to prolong my passport"—all the time I hadn't gone because I knew they wouldn't prolong my passport. I was on the wanted list. There was a price on my head, you know.

WYMAN: For illegal activity in Palestine?

K: Yeah, I am on the wanted list of the Irgun since 1937. They knew who I was, I mean, they knew the name Hillel Kook, and all this was to them very terrible stuff, and they would be delighted to get rid of me.

So the idea was that I should go to the British Embassy. Ask, naively, for a renewal of the passport. Sharfsin says, "What will happen then, they'll take it away because there's some sort of an international custom that if the passport had expired, they don't let you keep it. You will show them the passport, and they will say, 'This passport expired.' You'll say, 'Please prolong it.' And they'll take it and won't give it back to you." He says, "Then you ask them for a receipt. Then the receipt will

*The Immigration and Naturalization Service was a division of the Department of Justice.

say that they have the passport," he says. Then he has an idea what we'll do in the State Department. So we did that in stages.

I went to the British Embassy. The official there took the passport, he wouldn't give it back to me. He says, "Oh, this is invalid. It's no use to you. We're not allowed to give it to you." And he says, "I have to cable Jerusalem." And he cabled them. Then I came back. After a week, I called him up, and I said, "Could I come and see you for a couple of minutes?" And he said, "Yes." And I said, "Look. Now I have nothing. Before I had an expired passport. I have nothing, I mean, I'm a person without any identity." If I dropped dead in the street, they would have a problem identifying who I am. I have no legal document attesting who I am. So he says, "Yeah, it's a problem." And I said, "Could you give me, write me a letter saying—addressed to me saying, my passport—that I was the holder of passport number so-and-so, which expired, and that you cannot prolong it, so at least I'll have that." And he fell into the trap and wrote me a letter.

Then my lawyer went to the State Department and we cooked up the following things. I made—you see, a stateless person used to make an affidavit that said, "I, John Doe, attest and swear that I am stateless." And after that it said, name, color of hair—like on a passport—personal description. And this affidavit of statelessness was notarized by the Secretary of State of the United States and it became a traveling document, in place of a passport. It was an affidavit, really. That's what the State Department wanted me to do, but I didn't. Instead, we designed a kind of a cross-breed, in which mine said, "I, Hillel Kook, depose and swear that I am a citizen of Palestine and that my passport number so-and-so is in the hands of the British Embassy and I cannot obtain it." And I had a document to prove it, see? Color of hair, color of whatever. Now, this was, at last then, a political victory.*

W: There were efforts to deport you from the beginning—

K: But they never were able to do it. In May 1945, it reached the point in

*Kook successfully used this affidavit, in lieu of a passport, on his trips abroad after he was finally legally admitted to the United States as a permanent resident in December 1946. (Permanent residency did not include eligibility for a U.S. passport; American citizenship was needed for that.)[5]

which the Department of Justice, the Immigration Service of the Department of Justice, started a formal deportation procedure.

During the war, they had encouraged everybody [who was here on a visitor's visa] to go to Canada and [obtain a permanent U.S. visa and] come back again, to become a permanent resident.* I tried to do it then, and they rejected me because I answered the question "Do I want to be an American citizen?" wrong. When I appeared before the immigration board, before all the real troubles, I *thought* it was political. It became clear to us that it was, in 1945 when they were trying to deport me. Because we used connections then to take a look in the file, you see. Sharfsin looked at the files that day. It said Hillel Kook, alias Peter H. Birgson with an "i"—I saw it—B-i-r-g-s-o-n—Birgson, alias Peter H. Bergson. So I tell the guy, "Look, at least one favor do me. It's been enough time. I am also known as, you know, I have an alias. *One.* Obviously Birgson is a misspelling for Bergson. I mean, I never appeared as the name of Birgson." I assure you, he says, "It can't be done." Each document had three names on it. Alias Birgson, alias Bergson.

So in 1942 or 1943, we went as a routine, you know, when you went to renew your visitor's visa they told you, "Don't renew your visa. File an application for permanent resident for immigration." So we filed. Everybody did. I filed, and then started along this long procedure. And then you were invited before a board of the Immigration Service. They ask you all sorts of questions. And one question was, "Do you wish to become an American citizen?" To which I answered with a speech about how nice it was, but I couldn't because I'm fighting for the freedom of my own country. This disqualified me technically.

But as long as the war was on, they had a regulation [that the visitors' visas would be repeatedly renewed]. If I said I didn't want to be a permanent resident, they wouldn't have deported me while the war was on. And they didn't. Nobody. There are people who claimed neutrality— Swiss, or Palestinians. And they let them stay till the war ended. After the war they started kicking them out. Well, I was in this category.

---

*Kook was in the United States on a visitor's visa from the time of his arrival in July 1940 until the deportation issue was settled in December 1946.

W: This is why in 1945 they began, they told you to get out by November 1?

K: They wouldn't have done it if it wasn't for the pressure of people like Lucas and the Zionists, you know. They would have called me again and said, "File another application. Do something." But somebody instigated this and I left myself open. It was probably Lucas. I think it started two or three years before, it was in the works. You see, Lucas thought he would find something obnoxious about me which would enable them—deporting for trafficking in drugs. You know, deported for being a pig. But since he didn't find anything, and since the law was that any law-abiding, decent foreigner could stay until after the war, they had to wait until after the war. But the procedure was started. Then immediately after the war they went after me.

One day I came back from a speaking trip, and I found a notice in the office saying, "Please call Mr. So-and-so at the Immigration." So I called him. And he said that he would like me to come by there and see him. And I said, "In connection with what?" And he said, "In connection with your status." So I came there. I walked in, I said, "I'm Mr. Kook." He said, "I'm Mr. So-and-so." And he gets up, and he says, "Under Section so-and-so of the law I hereby arrest you." Right there.

W: It's like comic opera.

K: Yeah, but it wasn't that funny. I didn't know, I thought I was going to jail. All it turned out to be, really, he wanted a $500 bond.

We fought this thing throughout and I finally came into the United States legally in December 1946. It took us that long to work it out.

W: As an immigrant? With a visa? As a permanent resident?

K: Yes, exactly. What happened is they had a procedure then. You went to Canada for one day, got the visa and came back. I did it on December 2, 1946.

Authors' Note: Attempts to have Bergson deported had been underway since 1942. With the encouragement of the State Department, this objective had been pressed on the Immigration and Naturalization Service of the Justice Department by various opponents of Bergson, including some American Jewish leaders, Congressman Sol Bloom, and the British Embassy in Washington. Active proceedings to deport him went on through much of 1944 and 1945. Shortly after the end of the war in Europe, the Immigration and Nat-

uralization Service arrested Bergson, released him on bond, and ordered that
he leave the United States by November 1, 1945, or face deportation.

By October 1945, very strong support for Bergson had been communi-
cated to the State Department by a number of prominent Americans,
including especially Senator Guy Gillette and several other members of
Congress, and J. David Stern, the publisher of the Philadelphia Record,
who had close connections with the Truman State Department. In
November, Secretary of State James F. Byrnes informed Gillette and
Stern that arrangements had been made between the State Department
and the Immigration Service to permit Bergson to extend his temporary
stay in the United States, giving him time to apply for a permanent immi-
gration visa. By August 1946, the remaining administrative hurdles had
been removed, the State Department's Visa Division had authorized the
issuance of a visa for Bergson's permanent residence in the United States,
and the U.S. consul in Montreal had approved his papers.

A minor problem remained. Bergson would have to come under the quota
for Lithuania, since he had been born in that country, and the tiny Lithuan-
ian quota of 386 per year was already so oversubscribed that it had a long
waiting list. But the visa division found it was able to make an exception "so
that he will not be required to be put on the waiting list." As Kook pointed out
in the present interview, he received his American visa on December 2, 1946.[6]

K: We didn't know exactly what was going to happen on May 15 [1948,
   when the British were scheduled to withdraw their last forces from
   Palestine]. There were all sorts of things going on. I won't go into them.
   Anyway, I managed to get Hadani, Dr. Rafaeli, to go to London. He had
   an American passport. He and Yitshaq Ben-Ami had volunteered for
   the American army, and when they came out after the war, they were
   granted American citizenship. And we chartered a small British air-
   plane, masquerading as American businessmen in order to get to Palestine with no communications. We rented a little DC-3, which was then
   a—put some bucket seats in it, you know. And on the 14th of May off
   we took, took off to land in Palestine, to keep my promise.

Authors' Note: Bergson had earlier publicly declared "that on the day on
which one square yard of Palestine will be free, I shall be there as a citizen."

By the way, here is a story that has appeared in various versions. We took along, since there were a lot of people around who wanted to go, first of all Ya'akov Meridor, who was deputy commander of the Irgun, who ran away from jail, and who actually took my place for a while. He was then in Europe for a few weeks, and he became the top Irgun man in Europe. He came along. He wrote a long book on the history of his escapes in which he says that he chartered a plane, and he went, and amongst the other passengers was Hillel Kook.[7] Well, it's a question of interpretation, because if you say that Hillel Kook was the head of the Irgun and Hadani worked for him as an Irgun man, why this was done with Irgun money. But you cannot say that Hillel Kook was not Irgun, and then say that he went—the Irgun chartered the plane. This plane was mentioned by three people who were passengers on it as their plane.

W: They were extras.

K: They came along! Anyway, I did it to keep my my vow. We landed in Israel May 15 in the afternoon. We nearly got shot down, because the Egyptians bombed that little airport in Tel Aviv. It was a makeshift airport. And I think around May 20 or 21, I announced that the Hebrew Committee recognizes the provisional government and ceases operations, and that I was going to liquidate it. And dissolve the American League for a Free Palestine as well. Those were our only two organizations that functioned at the time.

Under my plan—one of the fights with Menachem Begin,* not a

---

*The tensions between Begin and Bergson dated back to 1944, when the Irgun launched its revolt against the British in Palestine and Bergson established the Hebrew Committee of National Liberation as the Irgun's de facto American wing. Begin believed that the committee's propaganda campaigns were of little value, and urged that all funds raised in the U.S. be forwarded to the Irgun to aid its military efforts. Bergson rebuffed the request. Begin also opposed Bergson's emphasis on distinguishing between "Hebrews" and Jews, which he felt was provoking needless conflicts within the American Jewish community. Although Bergson was elected to Israel's first parliament, in 1949, as one of the candidates from Begin's Herut Party, new disputes between the two men soon erupted over issues such as the relationship between religion and state in Israel and the country's lack of a constitution. Personality clashes added to political disagreements, and the long-simmering tensions between Begin and Bergson eventually boiled over, resulting in Bergson's decision to leave politics, and Israel, in 1951.

major one, but a fairly major one, one of many conflicts was—I wanted the *Altalena** to arrive on May 14, midnight, and he didn't. So the *Altalena* actually didn't leave—they wanted to make sure, to see what's happening, and I wanted to affect what's happening. Anyway, the *Altalena* was in a state of preparedness to leave, and I didn't know exactly.

The ship was in France and, publicly, nobody knows anything about it. We didn't know there was going to be a [United Nations truce in the Arab-Israeli war], and we didn't know when the *Altalena* would leave. So I said I just have to go back to France and finish a couple of things and liquidate the whole thing, which was exactly my intention. I left a couple of days later, back to Paris, and I was on my way to the United States. When the *Altalena* left France, it was around June 9. The day it left, after it left, a telegram was received from the Irgun in Israel to delay, because the truce came. The contention that this was a kind of a putsch is absolute hogwash, or errant nonsense. The Israeli government knew about the ship, it authorized its leaving, and so forth.

Because Merlin participated in a meeting with Levi Eshkol,[8] who was then head of the defense department under Ben-Gurion. And the whole thing was discussed, the place was decided, the whole thing was done. The ship left. When the ship left, I was finished with it as far as I'm concerned. I would have two days later flown to the States, where I hadn't been in quite a few months, because the last months, most of 1948, I was in Paris.

Then came another telegram instructing the ship to go to Yugoslavia. I tried to convince the man who remained in charge of the Irgun during this time that this was a terrible thing to do because we

---

*Altalena, a pen name used on occasion by the founder of Revisionist Zionism, Vladimir Ze'ev Jabotinsky, was the name given to a ship purchased in 1947 by U.S. supporters of the Irgun Zvai Leumi to ferry weapons from France to the IZL forces in the Holy Land. When the ship reached Israel's coastline in June 1948, Prime Minister David Ben-Gurion initially granted it permission to land, then changed his mind and ordered the Israeli army to sink the ship on the grounds that the IZL might be planning to overthrow his government. Sixteen of the Irgun's men were killed in the Haganah assault.

couldn't do it to the French. Yugoslavia was like China in the 1950s—Yugoslavia was the most doctrinaire Communist country—and the French were quite shaky [in the face of rising Communist political strength in France at that time].

We had got the French to cooperate, some of them—I don't think this was on the level of a Cabinet decision, I mean. This was done with the help of one or two ministers, as far as I'm concerned, and some little mirror tricks about American support, which was not all that efficient. We had a couple of them go to America, and we organized receptions and luncheons and dinners for them with senators and congressmen, and they became affected by the power, by the political power that we have in the United States, you know, popular power. But it would have been a terrible thing to do to them, to take the boat to Yugoslavia, because the whole thing leaked out.

Earlier, when the boat was being loaded with all these arms, the stevedores were mostly Algerians. They made a strike. Then the French sent a battalion of troops to surround the boat to make sure there was no sabotage, and to help load it and get out. The ship left in haste at night, that same evening, you know, to prevent local problems. But the thing was, there were stories in the papers, "a ship of arms sails for Israel." So to then delay the ship, and then to have it come back. They didn't want it to come back because they were afraid the French would take the arms back, or change their mind or something, since the whole thing leaked out.

Ben-Eliezer was a member of the Emergency Committee whom we had sent to Palestine in 1943 to reorganize the Irgun, but then he was arrested by the British and was in jail for a long time. And we brought him to Paris on May 1, 1948, on a French battleship, because there was no other way to get him out of Djibouti [the African port city where he had been hiding after escaping from a British detention camp in Kenya] without falling into British hands. So he went to Palestine, I mean to Israel already, and he was supposed to come back to France, and he didn't come.

Anyway, I decided to fly to Israel and convince Begin not to tell the ship to go to Yugoslavia. As it happened, Ben-Eliezer sent a telegram

that he was arriving in France, but it came after I left. Communications were very bad then. By the time I came to Israel, he wasn't there.
He was flying to Paris while I was flying to Israel. And when I arrived,
they told me that the *Altalena* is arriving on Saturday. I arrived there
on a Thursday. And the government agreed to supply the [unloading
equipment], and it's coming in, and everything's fine.

Being there already, I decided to stay a few days, wait until the ship
comes. All the people got off, and some of the arms were taken. And
when [Ben-Gurion went back on his agreement, and the Haganah
began objecting to the unloading of the arms], this conflict started
developing. I got into a very bitter argument with Begin [about how to
respond]. Ben-Ami was there, he was on the ship as a representative of
the Hebrew Committee. Merlin and I were there because we happened to be in Israel at the time. Captain [Jeremiah] Helpern[9] was
there because he happened to be in Israel at the time. And Begin
ignored us, and I got mad and I bawled the hell out of him. And he
told us what he had told some United Nations guy who came snooping
around asking, "What's there?," and he pretended that he's a sergeant
or something, and he thought it was very funny.

So I left with one guy, figured out a way—there was a little river
there not far away—figured out a way that there would be no army
people behind the river, because it's a natural barrier, you know. And
through the dunes we got to the road, and he was in uniform—the
Irgun was half in the army then, you know, and [he was] without a
revolver, which officers were carrying then, but he was in khaki
clothes, in a simple uniform. So I said, "Look, you go one way, I go the
other way." And I rested a little, because I spent a restless night, a
night on the beach. And then I decided to go to Tel Aviv and try and
see Ben-Gurion, and sort of try and make some head or tail out of it,
because I felt some sort of involvement with the ship and I had
absolutely nothing to say [about] what was going on—nothing! No
more than you did.

By the time I had something to eat in a little place there on the road
and rested up a little bit, I found some sort of a jitney that was going to
Tel Aviv. We passed this place—they started checking people going by,

and stupidly I gave my name. Because my name was Hillel Kook, this guy asked, "Are you related to such and such a Kook?" And I said, "Yes, my cousin." He said, "Then, oh, you are of this famous Kook family." I said, "Yeah." "What are you to Peter Bergson?" Instead of saying, "He's another cousin," like an idiot I said, "I'm Peter Bergson." So, he said I must tell my commander, and his commander told his commander, and to cut a long story short, in the middle of all this waiting for what to do, they started shooting on the beach. They didn't tell me a thing. They took me to a home of this—distant relatives in this village (that's why he knew the name Kook, because there was a Kook living in the village). And then, horn to horn, as the Arabs say, from here and there, the next time I was out was three months later. They kept me in various kibbutzim, and finally, we won a habeas corpus, which in Israel has to go to the Supreme Court, there's no habeas corpus. But the Supreme Court fined the government ten pounds for detaining me illegally, and ordered them to release me or detain me legally.

Some people came over from America, Congressman Somers came over, Fowler Harper came over. They were afraid they'll kill me, which they probably would have. Because they said they didn't know where I was, they didn't say they'd detained me. I disappeared, you see. I made a hunger strike for two days. When they lost the appeal to the court, then they issued a warrant for my arrest under the British Emergency Regulations, which were still in force. Later they released all of us. They then arrested about four hundred people on the beach. There was some shooting, and a number of Irgun men were killed. I wasn't there with them. That's when Merlin was wounded, yes. And Abrasha Stavsky was fatally wounded.[10] He was the man who was doing all the technical work on our immigration things. And they detained—finally they released everybody except four people. And these four were put in a jail somewhere, an old British jail. And I was kept in this kibbutz. And they lost us when the Supreme Court ordered them to release me. Then in the middle of the night some guy wakes me up and starts reading to me an order for my arrest under the Emergency Regulations, signed by the chief of staff. "For ten days," he said, "you are detained for ten days." So I started laughing, and he says, "Why are you laughing?" I said, "I've been already detained twelve days." And then they moved me to their jail. And we were there, five of us, including this fellow Meridor, who came on my plane and who said that I came on his plane. I got out of jail after three months.

*   *   *

K: Jews could have been saved.[11] The proof is very simple. When the whole horror was over, hundreds of thousands of Jews had survived. If we, the Jews, would have done our job better, if even we on the [Emergency] Committee would have done our job better. We tried our utmost, obviously we could have done more. If the Jewish leadership would have acted, if the Jews would have acted, the number of the survivors could have been doubled. I don't want to make conjecture, but I think that it's important to know that the number of people who survived was [in part] up to us, and it was so small, because of the inadequacy of our activities. If I were a Jewish leader, dead, I'd probably be turning in my grave. And if I was alive, I would probably have a very guilty conscience.

W: How could the annihilation have happened?[12] And how could the world let it happen?

K: The world is still letting it happen. Humanity is going to pay a price, unfortunately. I think that the whole course of humanity—many of the mean and barbaric things that are happening, maybe even subconsciously come from the fact that people grew up with the knowledge that it was possible to deliberately exterminate millions of people, and there was no reaction. There is no reaction till today. [Nearly tearful.]

I think the extermination of the Jews provided an example that you can destroy 6 out of 7 million people [the number of Jews in Europe], over 80 percent, and life goes on. When it has come to millions of people, what difference is it if you kill 6 million Jews, or 60 million Russians, or 50 million others? I think it has a dehumanizing effect on humanity. I think the only way to deal with it is to deal with it.

APPENDIX:
DOCUMENTS

"REPORT TO THE SECRETARY ON THE ACQUIESCENCE
OF THIS GOVERNMENT IN THE MURDER OF THE JEWS," DRAFTED BY
JOSIAH DUBOIS AND INITIALED BY RANDOLPH PAUL FOR THE
FOREIGN FUNDS CONTROL UNIT OF THE TREASURY DEPARTMENT,
JANUARY 13, 1944.
(FRANKLIN D. ROOSEVELT LIBRARY,
MORGENTHAU DIARIES, BOOK 693, PAGES 212–29.)

REPORT TO THE SECRETARY ON THE ACQUIESCENCE
OF THIS GOVERNMENT IN THE MURDER OF THE JEWS.

One of the greatest crimes in history, the slaughter of the Jewish people in Europe, is continuing unabated.

This Government has for a long time maintained that its policy is to work out programs to save those Jews of Europe who could be saved.

I am convinced on the basis of the information which is available to me that certain officials in our State Department, which is charged with carrying out this policy, have been guilty not only of gross procrastination and wilful failure to act, but even of wilful attempts to prevent action from being taken to rescue Jews from Hitler.

I fully recognize the graveness of this statement and I make it only after having most carefully weighed the shocking facts which have come to my attention during the last several months.

Unless remedial steps of a drastic nature are taken, and taken immediately, I am certain that no effective action will be taken by this Government to prevent the complete extermination of the Jews in German controlled Europe, and that this Government will have to share for all time responsibility for this extermination.

The tragic history of this Government's handling of this matter reveals that certain State Department officials are guilty of the following:

(1) They have not only failed to use the Governmental machinery at their disposal to rescue Jews from Hitler, but have even gone so far as to use this Government machinery to prevent the rescue of these Jews.

(2) They have not only failed to cooperate with private organizations in the efforts of those organizations to work out individual programs of their own, but have taken steps designed to prevent these programs from being put into effect.

(3) They not only have failed to facilitate the obtaining of information concerning Hitler's plans to exterminate the Jews of Europe but in their official capacity have gone so far as to surreptitiously attempt to stop the obtaining of information concerning the murder of the Jewish population of Europe.

(4) They have tried to cover up their guilt by:

(a) concealment and misrepresentation;

(b) the giving of false and misleading explanations for their failures to act and their attempts to prevent action; and

(c) the issuance of false and misleading statements concerning the "action" which they have taken to date.

Although only part of the facts relating to the activities of the State Department in this field are available to us, sufficient facts have come to my attention from various sources during the last several months to fully support the conclusions at which I have arrived.

(1) State Department officials have not only failed to use the Governmental machinery at their disposal to rescue the Jews from Hitler, but have even gone so far as to use this Governmental machinery to prevent the rescue of these Jews.

The public record, let alone the facts which have not as yet been made public, reveals the gross procrastination and wilful failure to act of those officials actively representing this Government in this field.

(a) A long time has passed since it became clear that Hitler was determined to carry out a policy of exterminating the Jews in Europe.

(b) Over a year has elapsed since this Government and other members of the United Nations publicly acknowledged and denounced this policy of extermination; and since the President gave assurances that the United States would make every effort together with the United Nations to save those who could be saved.

(c) Despite the fact that time is most precious in this matter, State Department officials have been kicking the matter around for over a year without producing results; giving all sorts of excuses for delays upon delays; advancing no specific proposals designed to rescue Jews, at the same time proposing that the whole refugee problem be "explored" by this Government and Intergovernmental Committees. While the State Department has been thus "exploring" the whole refugee problem, without distinguishing between those who are in imminent danger of death and those who are not, hundreds of thousands of Jews have been allowed to perish.

As early as August 1942 a message from the Secretary of the World Jewish Congress in Switzerland (Riegner), transmitted through the British Foreign Office, reported that Hitler had under consideration a plan to exterminate all Jews in German controlled Europe. By November 1942 sufficient evidence had been received, including substantial documentary evidence transmitted through our Legation in Switzerland, to confirm that Hitler had actually adopted and was carrying out his plan to exterminate the Jews. Sumner Welles accordingly authorized the Jewish organizations to make the facts public.

Thereupon, the Jewish organizations took the necessary steps to bring the shocking facts to the attention of the public through mass meetings, etc., and to elicit public support for governmental action. On December 17, 1942, a joint statement of the United States and the European members of the United Nations was issued calling attention to and denouncing the fact that Hitler was carrying into effect his oft-repeated intention to exterminate the Jewish people in Europe.

Since the time when this Government knew that the Jews were being murdered, our State Department has failed to take any positive steps reasonably calculated to save any of these people. Although State has used the devices of setting up inter-governmental organizations to survey the whole refugee problem, and calling conferences such as the Bermuda Conference to explore the whole refugee problem, making it appear that positive action could be expected, in fact nothing has been accomplished.

Before the outcome of the Bermuda Conference, which was held in April 1943, was made public, Senator Langer prophetically stated in an address in the Senate on October 6, 1943:

"As yet we have had no report from the Bermuda Refugee Conference. With the best good will in the world and with all latitude that could and should be accorded to diplomatic negotiations in time of war, I may be permitted to voice the bitter suspicion that the absence of a report indicates only one thing--the lack of action.

"Probably in all 5703 years, Jews have hardly had a time as tragic and hopeless as the one which they are undergoing now. One of the most tragic factors about the situation is that while singled out for suffering and martyrdom by their enemies, they seem to have been forgotten by the nations which claim to fight for the cause of humanity. We should remember the Jewish slaughterhouse of Europe and ask what is being done--and I emphasize the word 'done'--to get some of these suffering human beings out of the slaughter while yet alive.

"****Perhaps it would be necessary to introduce a formal resolution or to ask the Secretary of State to report to an appropriate congressional committee on the steps being taken in this connection. Normally it would have been the job of the Government to show itself alert to this tragedy; but when a government neglects a duty it is the job of the legislature in a democracy to remind it of that duty.*** It is not important who voices a call for action, and it is not important what procedure is being used in order to get action. It is important that action be undertaken."

Similar fears were voiced by Representatives Celler, Dickstein, and Klein. Senator Wagner and Representative Sadowski also issued calls for action.

The widespread fears concerning the failure of the Bermuda Conference were fully confirmed when Breckinridge Long finally revealed some of the things that had happened at that Conference in his statement before the Committee on Foreign Affairs of the House on November 26, 1943.

After Long's "disclosure" Representative Celler stated in the House on December 20, 1943:

"He discloses some of the things that happened at the so-called Bermuda Conference. He thought he was telling us something heretofore unknown and secret. What happened at the Bermuda Conference could not be kept executive. All the recommendations and findings of the Bermuda Conference were made known to the Intergovernmental Committee on Refugees in existence since the Evian Conference on Refugees in 1938 and which has been functioning all this time in London. How much has that committee accomplished in the years of its being. It will be remembered that the Intergovernmental Committee functions through an executive committee composed of six countries, the United States, the United Kingdoms, the Netherlands, France, Brazil, and Argentina. True, no report of the Bermuda Conference was made public. But a strangely ironical fact will be noted in the presence of Argentina on this most trusted of committee, Argentina that provoked the official reprimand of President Roosevelt by its banning of the Jewish Press, and within whose borders Nazi propagandists and falangists now enjoy a Roman holiday. I contend that by the very nature of its composition the Intergovernmental Committee on Refugees cannot function successfully as the instrumentality to rescue the Jewish people of Europe. The benefits to be derived from the Bermuda Conference like those of the previous Evian Conference can fit into a tiny capsule."

One of the best summaries of the whole situation is contained in one sentence of a report submitted on December 20, 1943, by the Committee on Foreign Relations of the Senate, recommending the passage of a Resolution (S.R. 203) favoring the appointment of a commission to formulate plans to save the Jews of Europe from extinction by Nazi Germany. The Committee stated:

"We have talked; we have sympathized; we have expressed our horror; the time to act is long past due."

The Senate Resolution had been introduced by Senator Guy M. Gillette in behalf of himself and eleven colleagues, Senators Taft, Thomas, Radcliffe, Murray, Johnson, Guffey, Ferguson, Clark, Van Nuys, Downey, and Ellender.

The House Resolutions (H.R.'s 350 and 352), identical with the Senate Resolution, were introduced by Representatives Baldwin and Rogers.

The most glaring example of the use of the machinery of this Government to actually prevent the rescue of Jews is the administrative restrictions which have been placed upon the granting of visas to the United States. In the note which the State Department sent to the British on February 25, 1943 it was stated:

"Since the entry of the United States into the war there have been no new restrictions placed by the Government of the United States upon the number of aliens of any nationality permitted to proceed to this country under existing laws, except for the more intensive examination of aliens required for security reasons."
(Underscoring supplied)

The exception "for security reasons" mentioned in this note is the joker. Under the pretext of security reasons so many difficulties have been placed in the way of refugees obtaining visas that it is no wonder that the admission of refugees to this country does not come anywhere near the quota, despite Long's statement designed to create the impression to the contrary. The following administrative restrictions which have been applied to the issuance of visas since the beginning of the war are typical.

(a) Many applications for visas have been denied on the grounds that the applicants have close relatives in Axis controlled Europe. The theory of this is that the enemy would be able to put pressure on the applicant as a result of the fact that the enemy has the power of life or death over his immediate family.

(b) Another restriction greatly increases the red tape and delay involved in getting the visa and requires among other things two affidavits of support and sponsorship to be furnished with each application for a visa. To each affidavit of support and sponsorship there must be attached two letters of reference from two reputable American citizens.

If anyone were to attempt to work out a set of restrictions specifically designed to prevent Jewish refugees from entering this country it is difficult to conceive of how more effective restrictions could have been imposed than have already been imposed on grounds of "security".

It is obvious of course that these restrictions are not essential for security reasons. Thus refugees upon arriving in this country could be placed in internment camps similar to those used for the Japanese on the West Coast and released only after a satisfactory investigation. Furthermore, even if we took these refugees and treated them as prisoners of war it would be better than letting them die.

Representative Dickstein stated in the House on December 15:

"If we consider the fact that the average admission would then be at the rate of less than 58,000 per year, it is clear that the organs of our Government have not done their duty. The existing quotas call for the admission of more than 150,000 every year, so that if the quotas themselves had been filled there would have been a total of [one and] one-half million and not 580,000 during the period mentioned.

"But that is not the whole story. There was no effort of any kind made to save from death many of the refugees who could have been saved during the time that transportation lines were available and there was no obstacle to their admission to the United States. But the obstructive policy of our organs of Government, particularly the State Department, which saw fit to hedge itself about with rules and regulations, instead of lifting rules and regulations, brought about a condition so that not even the existing immigration quotas are filled."

Representative Celler stated in the House on June 30:

"Mr. Speaker, nations have declared war on Germany and their high-ranking officials have issued pious protestations against the Nazi massacre of Jewish victims, but not one of those countries thus far has said they would be willing to accept these refugees either permanently or as visitors, or any of the minority peoples trying to escape the Hitler prison and slaughterhouse.

"Goebbels says: 'The United Nations won't take any Jews. We don't want them. Let's kill them.' And so he and Hitler are marking Europe Judentun.

"Without any change in our immigration statutes we could receive a reasonable number of those who are fortunate enough to escape the Nazi hellhole, receive them as visitors, the immigration quotas notwithstanding. They could be placed in camps or cantonments and held there in such havens until after the war. Private charitable agencies would be willing to pay the entire cost thereof. They would be no expense to the Government whatsoever. These agencies would even pay for transportation by ships to and from this country.

"We house and maintain Nazi prisoners, many of them undoubtedly responsible for Nazi atrocities. We should do no less for the victims of the rage of the Huns."

Again, on December 20, he stated:

"According to Earl G. Harrison, Commissioner of the Immigration and Naturalization Service, not since 1862 have there been fewer aliens entering the country.

"Frankly, Breckinridge Long, in my humble opinion, is least sympathetic to refugees in all the State Department. I attribute to him the tragic bottleneck in the granting of visas.

"The Interdepartmental Review Committees which review the applications for visas are composed of one official, respectively, from each of the following Departments: War, Navy, F.B.I., State, and Immigration. That committee has been glacierlike in its slowness and coldbloodedness. It take months and months to grant the visas and then it usually applies to a corpse.

"I brought this difficulty to the attention of the President. He asked Long to investigate at once. No, there has been no change in conditions. The gruesome bottleneck still exists."

(2) State Department officials have not only failed to cooperate with private organizations in the efforts of these organizations to work out individual programs of their own, but have taken steps designed to prevent these programs from being put into effect.

The best evidence in support of this charge are the facts relating to the proposal of the World Jewish Congress to evacuate thousands of Jews from Rumania and France. The highlights relating to the efforts of State Department officials to prevent this proposal from being put into effect are the following:

(a) On March 13, 1943, a cable was received from the World Jewish Congress representative in London stating that information reaching London indicated the possibility of rescuing Jews provided funds were put at the disposal of the World Jewish Congress representation in Switzerland.

(b) On April 10, 1943, Sumner Welles cabled our Legation in Bern and requested them to get in touch with the World Jewish Congress representative in Switzerland, whom Welles had been informed was in possession of important information regarding the situation of the Jews.

(c) On April 20, 1943, a cable was received from Bern relating to the proposed financial arrangements in connection with the evacuation of the Jews from Rumania and France.

(d) On May 25, 1943, State Department cabled for a clarification of these proposed financial arrangements. This matter was not called to the attention of the Treasury Department at this time.

(e) This whole question of financing the evacuation of the Jews from Rumania and France was first called to the attention of the Treasury Department on June 25, 1943.

(f) A conference was held with the State Department relating to this matter on July 15, 1943).

(g) One day after this conference, on July 16, 1943, the Treasury Department advised the State Department that it was prepared to issue a license in this matter.

(h) The license was not issued until December 18, 1943.

During this five months period between the time that the Treasury stated that it was prepared to issue a license and the time when the license was actually issued delays and objections of all sorts were forthcoming from officials in the State Department, our Legation in Bern, and finally the British. The real significance of these delays and objections was brought home to the State Department in letters which you sent to Secretary Hull on November 24, 1943, and December 17, 1943, which completely devastated the "excuses" which State Department officials had been advancing. On December 18 you made an appointment to discuss the matter with Secretary Hull on December 20. And then an amazing but understandable thing happened. On December 18, the day after you sent your letter and the day on which you requested an appointment with Secretary Hull, the State Department sent a telegram to the British Foreign Office expressing astonishment with the British point of view and stating that the Department was unable to agree with that point of view (in simple terms, the British point of view referred to by the State Department is that they are apparently prepared to accept the possible—even probable—death of thousands of Jews in enemy territory because of "the difficulties of disposing of any considerable number of Jews should they be rescued"). On the same day, the State Department issued a license notwithstanding the fact that the objections of our Legation in Bern were still outstanding and that British disapproval had already been expressed. State Department officials were in such a hurry to issue this license that they not only did not ask the Treasury to draft the license (which would have been the normal procedure) but they drafted the license themselves and issued it without even consulting the Treasury as to its terms. Informal discussions with certain State Department officials have confirmed what is obvious from the above mentioned facts.

Breckinridge Long knew that his position was so indefensible that he was unwilling to even try to defend it at your pending conference with Secretary Hull on December 20. Accordingly, he took such action as he felt was necessary to "cover up" his previous position in this matter. It is, of course, clear that if we had not made the record against the State Department followed by your request to see Secretary Hull, the action which the State Department officials took on December 18 would either never have been taken at all or would have been delayed so long that any benefits which it might have had would have been lost.

(3) State Department officials not only have failed to facilitate the obtaining of information concerning Hitler's plans to exterminate the Jews of Europe but in their official capacity have gone so far as to surreptitiously attempt to stop the obtaining of information concerning the murder of the Jewish population in Europe.

The evidence supporting this conclusion is so shocking and so tragic that it is difficult to believe.

The facts are as follows:

(a) Sumner Welles as Acting Secretary of State requests confirmation of Hitler's plan to exterminate the Jews. Having already received various reports on the plight of the Jews, on October 5, 1942 Sumner Welles as Acting Secretary of State sent a cable (2314) for the personal attention of Minister Harrison in Bern stating that leaders of the Jewish Congress had received reports from their representatives in Geneva and London to the effect that many thousands of Jews in Eastern Europe were being slaughtered pursuant to a policy embarked upon by the German Government for the complete extermination of the Jews in Europe. Welles added that he was trying to obtain further information from the Vatican but that other than this he was unable to secure confirmation of these stories. He stated that Rabbi Wise believed that information was available to his representatives in Switzerland but that they were in all likelihood fearful of dispatching any such reports through open cables or mail. He then stated that Riegner and

Lichtheim were being requested by Wise to call upon Minister Harrison; and Welles requested Minister Harrison to advise him by telegram of all the evidence and facts which he might secure as a result of conferences with Riegner and Lichtheim.

(b) State Department receives confirmation and shocking evidence that the extermination was being rapidly and effectively carried out. Pursuant to Welles' cable of October 5 Minister Harrison forwarded documents from Riegner confirming the fact of extermination of the Jews (in November 1942), and in a cable of January 21, 1943 (482) relayed a message from Riegner and Lichtheim which Harrison stated was for the information of the Under Secretary of State (and was to be transmitted to Rabbi Stephen Wise if the Under Secretary should so determine). This message described a horrible situation concerning the plight of Jews in Europe. It reported mass executions of Jews in Poland; according to one source 6,000 Jews were being killed daily; the Jews were required before execution to strip themselves of all their clothing which was then sent to Germany; the remaining Jews in Poland were confined to ghettos, etc.; in Germany deportations were continuing; many Jews were in hiding and there had been many cases of suicide; Jews were being deprived of rationed foodstuffs; no Jews would be left in Prague or Berlin by the end of March, etc.; and in Rumania 130,000 Jews were deported to Transnistria; about 60,000 had already died and the remaining 70,000 were starving; living conditions were indescribable; Jews were deprived of all their money, foodstuffs and possessions; they were housed in deserted cellars, and occasionally twenty to thirty people slept on the floor of one unheated room; disease was prevalent, particularly fever; urgent assistance was needed.

(c) Summer Welles furnishes this information to the Jewish organizations. Summer Welles furnished the documents received in November to the Jewish organizations in the United States and authorized them to make the facts public. On February 9, 1943 Welles forwarded the horrible message contained in cable 482 of January 21 to Rabbi Stephen Wise. In his letter of February 9 Welles stated that he was pleased to be of assistance in this matter.

Immediately upon the receipt of this message, the Jewish organizations arranged for a public mass meeting in Madison Square Garden in a further effort to obtain effective action.

(d) Certain State Department officials surreptitiously attempt to stop this Government from obtaining further information from the very source from which the above evidence was received. On February 10, the day after Welles forwarded the message contained in cable 482 of January 21 to Rabbi Wise, and in direct response to this cable, a most highly significant cable was dispatched. This cable, 354 of February 10, read as follows:

"Your 482, January 21

"In the future we would suggest that you do not accept reports submitted to you to be transmitted to private persons in the United States unless such action is advisable because of extraordinary circumstances. Such private messages circumvent neutral countries' censorship and it is felt that by sending them we risk the possibility that steps would necessarily be taken by the neutral countries to curtail or forbid our means of communication for confidential official matter.

Hull (SW)"

Although this cable on its face is most innocent and innocuous, when read together with the previous cables I am forced to conclude it is nothing less than an attempted suppression of information requested by this Government concerning the murder of Jews by Hitler.

Although this cable was signed for Hull by "SW" (Sumner Welles) it is significant that there is not a word in the cable that would even suggest to the person signing it that it was designed to countermand the Department's specific requests for information on Hitler's plans to exterminate the Jews. The cable appeared to be a normal routine message which a busy official would sign without question.

I have been informed that the initialled file copy of the cable bears the initials of Atherton and Dunn as well as of Durbrow and Hickerson.

(c) Thereafter Sumner Welles again requested our Legation on April 10, 1943 (cable 877) for information, apparently not realizing that in cable 354 (to which he did not refer) Harrison had been instructed to cease forwarding reports of this character. Harrison replied on April 20 (cable 2460) and indicated that he was in a most confused state of mind as a result of the conflicting instructions he had received. Among other things he stated: "May I suggest that messages of this character should not (repeat not) be subjected to the restriction imposed by your 354, February 10, and that I be permitted to transmit messages from R more particularly in view of the helpful information which they may frequently contain?"

The fact that cable 354 is not the innocent and routine cable that it appears to be on its face is further highlighted by the efforts of State Department officials to prevent this Department from obtaining the cable and learning its true significance.

The facts relating to this attempted concealment are as follows:

(i) Several men in our Department had requested State Department officials for a copy of the cable of February 10 (354). We had been advised that it was a Department communication; a strictly political communication, which had nothing to do with economic matters; that it had only had a very limited distribution within the Department, the only ones having anything to do with it being the European Division, the Political Adviser and Sumner Welles; and that a copy could not be furnished to the Treasury.

(ii) At the conference in Secretary Hull's office on December 20 in the presence of Breckinridge Long you asked Secretary Hull for a copy of cable 354, which you were told would be furnished to you.

(iii) By note to you of December 20, Breckinridge Long enclosed a paraphrase of cable 354. This paraphrase of cable 354 specifically omitted any reference to cable 482 of January 21--thus destroying the only tangible clue to the true meaning of the message.

(iv) You would never have learned the true meaning of cable 354 had it not been for the fact that one of the men in my office whom I had asked to obtain all the facts on this matter for me had previously called one of the men in another Division of the State Department and requested permission to see the cable. In view of the Treasury interest in this matter this State Department representative obtained cable 354 and the cable of January 21 to which it referred and showed these cables to my man.

(4) The State Department officials have tried to cover up their guilt by:

(a) concealment and misrepresentation

In addition to concealing the true facts from and misrepresenting these facts to the public, State Department officials have even attempted concealment and misrepresentation within the Government. The most striking example of this is the above mentioned action taken by State Department officials to prevent this Department from obtaining a copy of cable 354 of February 10 (which stopped the obtaining of information concerning the murder of Jews); and the fact that after you had requested a copy of this cable, State Department officials forwarded the cable to us with its most significant part omitted, thus destroying the whole meaning of the cable.

(b) the giving of false and misleading explanations for their failures to act and their attempts to prevent action.

The outstanding explanation of a false and misleading nature which the State Department officials have given for their failures to work out programs to rescue Jews, and their attempts to prevent action, are the following:

(i) The nice sounding but vicious theory that the whole refugee problem must be explored and consideration given to working out programs for the relief of all refugees--thus failing to distinguish between those refugees whose lives are in imminent danger and those whose lives are not in imminent danger.

(ii) The argument that various proposals cannot be acted upon promptly by this Government but must be submitted to the Executive Committee of the Intergovernmental Committee on Refugees. This Committee has taken no effective action to actually evacuate refugees from enemy territory and it is at least open to doubt whether it has the necessary authority to deal with the matter.

(iii) The argument that the extreme restrictions which the State Department has placed on the granting of visas to refugees is necessary for "security reasons." The falsity of this argument has already been dealt with in this memorandum.

The false and misleading explanations, which the State Department officials gave for delaying for over six months the program of the World Jewish Congress for the evacuation of thousands of Jews from Rumania and France, are dealt with in your letter to Secretary Hull of December 17, 1943.

A striking example is the argument of the State Department officials that the proposed financial arrangements might benefit the enemy. It is of course not surprising that the same State Department officials who usually argue that economic warfare considerations are not important should in this particular case attempt to rely on economic warfare considerations to kill the proposed program.

In this particular case, the State Department officials attempted to argue that the relief plan might benefit the enemy by facilitating the acquisition of funds by the enemy. In addition to the fact that this contention had no merit whatsoever by virtue of the conditions under which the local funds were to be acquired, it is significant that this consideration had not been regarded as controlling in the past by the State Department officials, even where no such conditions had been imposed.

Thus, in cases involving the purchase, by branches of United States concerns in Switzerland, of substantial amounts of material in enemy territory, State Department officials have argued that in view of the generous credit supplied by the Swiss to the Germans "transactions of this type cannot be regarded as actually increasing the enemy's purchasing power in Switzerland which is already believed to be at a maximum". It is only when these State Department officials really desire to prevent a transaction that they advance economic warfare considerations as a bar.

(c) the issuance of false and misleading statements concerning the "action" which they have taken to date.

It is unnecessary to go beyond Long's testimony to find many examples of misstatements. His general pious remarks concerning what this Government has done for the Jews of Europe; his statement concerning the powers and functions of the Intergovernmental Committee on Refugees; his reference to the "screening process" set up to insure wartime security, etc., have already been publicly criticized as misrepresentations.

A statement which is typical of the way Long twists facts is his remarks concerning the plan of a Jewish agency to send money to Switzerland to be used through the International Red Cross to buy food to take care of Jews in parts of Czechoslovakia and Poland. Long indicates that the Jewish agency requested that the money be sent through the instrumentality of the Intergovernmental Committee. I am informed that the Jewish agency wished to send the money immediately to the International Red Cross and it was Long who took the position that the matter would have to go through the Intergovernmental Committee, thereby delaying the matter indefinitely. Long speaks of an application having been filed with the Treasury to send some of this money and that the State Department was supporting this application to the Treasury. The facts are that no application has ever been filed with the Treasury and the State Department has at no time indicated to the Treasury that it would support any such application.

The most patent instance of a false and misleading statement is that part of Breckinridge Long's testimony before the Committee on Foreign Affairs of the House (November 26, 1943) relating to the admittance of refugees into this country. Thus, he stated:

"***We have taken into this country since the beginning of the Hitler regime and the persecution of the Jews, until today, approximately 580,000 refugees. The whole thing has been under the quota, during the period of 10 years--all under the quota--except the generous gesture we made with visitors' and transit visas during an awful period."

Congressman Emanuel Celler in commenting upon Long's statement in the House on December 20, 1943, stated:

"***In the first place these 580,000 refugees were in the main ordinary quota immigrants coming in from all countries. The majority were not Jews. His statement drips with sympathy for the persecuted Jews, but the tears he sheds are crocodile. I would like to ask him how many Jews were admitted during the last 3 years in comparison with the number seeking entrance to preserve life and dignity. ***One gets the impression from Long's statement that the United States has gone out of its way to help refugees fleeing death at the hands of the Nazis. I deny this. On the contrary, the State Department has turned its back on the time-honored principle of granting havens to refugees. The tempest-tossed get little comfort from men like Breckinridge Long. ***Long says that the door to the oppressed is open but that it 'has been carefully screened.' What he should have said is 'barlocked and bolted.' By the act of 1924, we are permitted to admit approximately 150,000 immigrants each year. During the last fiscal year only 23,725 came as immigrants. Of these only 4,705 were Jews fleeing Nazi persecution.

*   *   *

"If men of the temperament and philosophy of Long continue in control of immigration administration, we may as well take down that plaque from the Statue of Liberty and black out the 'lamp beside the golden door.' "

ASSISTANT SECRETARY OF STATE BRECKINRIDGE LONG TO STATE
DEPARTMENT OFFICIALS ADOLF BERLE AND JAMES DUNN,
JUNE 26, 1940.

(LIBRARY OF CONGRESS, BRECKINRIDGE LONG PAPERS,

BOX 211, VISA DIVISION,

GENERAL, 1940.)

A-L

June 26, 1940.

A-B—Mr. Berle

PA/D—Mr. Dunn

Attached is a memorandum from Mr. Warren. I discussed the matter with him
on the basis of this memorandum. There are two possibilities and I will discuss
each category briefly.

Nonimmigrants

Their entry into the United States can be made to depend upon prior authori-
zation by the Department. This would mean that the consuls would be divested of
discretion and that all requests for nonimmigrant visas (temporary visitor and
transit visas) be passed upon here. It is quite feasible and can be done instantly.
It will permit the Department to effectively control the immigration of persons in
this category and private instructions can be given the Visa Division as to nation-
alities which should not be admitted as well as to individuals who are to be
excluded.

This must be done for universal application and could not be done as regards
Germany, for instance, or Russia, for instance, or any other one government
because it would first, invite retaliation and second, would probably be a violation
of some of our treaty arrangements. The retaliation clause is in connection with
Germany because it could mean the closing of our offices in almost all of Europe.

Immigrants

We can delay and effectively stop for a temporary period of indefinite length
the number of immigrants into the United States. We could do this by simply
advising our consuls to put every obstacle in the way and to require additional

evidence and to resort to various administrative advices which would postpone and postpone and postpone the granting of the visas. However, this could only be temporary. In order to make it more definite it would have to be done by suspension of the rules under the law by the issuance of a proclamation of emergency—which I take it we are not yet ready to proclaim.

Summing up

We can effectively control nonimmigrants by prohibiting the issuance of visas unless the consent of the Department is obtained in advance, for universal application.

We can temporarily prevent the number of immigrants from certain localities such as Cuba, Mexico and other places of origin of German intending immigrants by simply raising administrative obstacles.

The Department will be prepared to take these two steps immediately upon the decision but emphasis must be placed on the fact that discrimination must not be practiced and with the additional thought that in case a suspension of the regulations should be proclaimed under the need of an emergency, it would be universally applicable and would affect refugees from England.

The Canadian situation and travel across that border we can handle through an exception to the general rule and so advise our consuls in Canada.

STEPHEN EARLY, SECRETARY TO THE PRESIDENT, TO BILLY ROSE,
MARCH 4, 1943, REGARDING THE "WE WILL NEVER DIE" PAGEANT.
(FRANKLIN D. ROOSEVELT LIBRARY,
FRANKLIN D. ROOSEVELT PAPERS,
OFFICIAL FILE 76-C.)

March 4, 1943

Dear Billy Rose:

Dave Niles has forwarded to this office your letter of February twenty-second, requesting a message from the President in connection with the memorial pageant you and Ben Hecht as co-chairmen are arranging to take place in Madison Square Garden on next Tuesday evening. I wish it were possible for the President to comply with your request, particularly so because of the splendid cooperation you have given in support of good works very near and dear to the President's heart.

I am sure that you are aware of the fact that the President has a dozen times spoken out fearlessly in behalf of oppressed Jews everywhere. This he has done in public utterances and in statements sent to various conventions and deliberative bodies. His views, in fact, have been given such repeated and widespread expression that they are very well-known.

But the President has many times asked to be excused from sending messages in connection with dramatic pageants and other presentations similar to this one to be given in Madison Square Garden. It would be difficult to make an exception in this instance. I am sure, upon reflection, you will understand why it is not possible for the President in these times of stress and pressure to do many things which in different circumstances he would be very glad to do.

Very sincerely yours,

STEPHEN EARLY
Secretary to the President

Mr. Billy Rose,
33 Beekman Place,
New York, N. Y.

REPORT ON ATTEMPTS TO STAGE "WE WILL NEVER DIE,"
UNDATED [EARLY 1944].

(YALE UNIVERSITY LIBRARY,
PALESTINE STATEHOOD COMMITTEE PAPERS, BOX 13.)

REPORT ON ATTEMPTS TO STAGE "WE WILL NEVER DIE"
IN KINGSTON, ROCHESTER, BUFFALO, BALTIMORE, GARY,
AND PITTSBURGH

On December 31, 1943, we succeeded in setting up a committee in Kingston, N.Y. for the presentation of "We Will Never Die". Everything was worked out in detail and seemed to go very well. The committee undertook to underwrite the cost. Important town's people, not only from Kingston, but also from neighbouring towns, volunteered for the committee, but all of a sudden, through the intervention of the American Jewish Congress and the Zionist Organization of America, we received a short letter from Kingston, saying: "We are not going to have 'We Will Never Die' ".

In Gary, Indiana, where Mr. Richard S. Kaplan had worked for long weeks and had succeeded in setting up a committee, (in fixing the date for the presentation) we were already preparing promotion and the printing of propaganda material when, all of a sudden, we received a letter from Mr. Kaplan, stating: "It is with considerable regret that I must advise you that the "We Will Never Die" pageant cannot be presented in the city of Gary. I wish I could tell you something different, but circumstances make it impossible to present it. As I have hinted before, considerable agitation was started immediately after it was announced in the papers that the pageant would be presented. Typical of the American Jewish Conference's attitude, all of the Jewish organizations met, this includes the reform Temple, the orthodox Temple, the B'nai B'rith and the Jewish Welfare Board. They unanimously agreed to present a demand to the American Legion that it be stopped."

In Baltimore we engaged Rabbi A.I. Rosenberg, who, under great sacrifices and without any personal profit, succeeded in organizing a luncheon for the purpose of creating a local sponsor committee to present "We Will Never Die". There was considerable enthusiasm among prominent town's people. The Mayor of Baltimore promised to preside at that luncheon. But the Community Council there, on

orders from New York, engaged in a bitter fight against us, using all means of
calumny, slander, smearing of the Emergency Committee, its members, and also
Mr. Ben-Ami, spreading all kinds of vile rumors. The Community Council, under
its executive director, Mr. Leon Sachs, organized a "telephone campaign", calling
every single person liable to help us, and influencing them not to come to the
luncheon. A few hours before the luncheon the Mayor decided not to come.

From all the persons who promised to come, only three or four appeared at
the luncheon and one lady, Mrs. Land, had the courage to get up at her table and
say that she was contacted by the Community Council not to go to the luncheon,
but since she considered herself a free American, she didn't care and had come.
The Community Council also circulated confidential letters against us. They organized meetings of all existing Jewish organizations, including the B'nai B'rith with
the aim of boycotting the pageant. Only the non-Jewish press gave us courage,
telling us to go ahead, that we would receive their support. The same statement
was made by a well-known radio commentator.

In Buffalo we hired former Assembly man Fred Hammer as field secretary.
Together with him, Mr. Wachsman, who went to Buffalo three times, visited about
50 people who promised to participate in the luncheon and to underwrite the cost
of the production. Some of these people used their influence in advance in secur-
ing the Buffalo Memorial Auditorium for the price of $350.00. Rabbi Fink who
was contacted and who, incidentally, attended the New York performance of the
pageant, stated that he was whole-heartedly with us and that we were at liberty
to use his name and influence in connection with the Buffalo performance wherever we thought it fit to do so. The only Jewish Assembly man of Buffalo, Mr.
Harry Ehrlich, said that he is all out for our project. A few presidents of Temples
promised their active support and collaboration. So did the Jewish War Veterans
and some Italian societies who were approached by Miss Taylor Caldwell.

The same enthusiasm was found in the neighbouring towns of Dunkirque and
Niagara Falls. Everything was set for success when the Zionists, or the American
Jewish Congress began to work. The rumor is that they sent down a special emissary from New York. A secret meeting was held, at which Rabbi Fink attended,
(presided by Mr. David Diamond), where the decision was made to interfere and
sabotage all our efforts. A smear campaign worse than that in Baltimore was set
into action and, as one of the participants at the luncheon declared, every single
person who might have helped was contacted and warned not to go to the luncheon. They even managed to produce a scandal at the luncheon itself. All entries
and halls of the Hotel Statler were watched by their men who stopped everyone
going into the luncheon room and succeeded in convincing most of them not to

join us at the luncheon. Before the luncheon, it was said, Mr. Diamond had the intention to put some financial smear questions, but Mr. Wachsman had him know that we would sue him for liable. He dropped that issue, but interfered during the discussions in a manner as to frighten the few who had come, so that these would have nothing to do with us.

Several of the people stated that if we would bring the pageant to Buffalo, we would get their support, but if we persisted on an underwriting committee, they did not think it could be done. Miss Taylor Caldwell, who was very excited, said in the end that she would take over the cost of the auditorium.

After a thorough review of the situation, we came to the following conclusion:

It appears clearly that the Jewish Conference, the Z.O.A., the American Jewish Congress and affiliated organizations are now *organized* in their fight against the Emergency Committee and, though they profess only praise for "We Will Never Die" as such, nevertheless, they are using "We Will Never Die" as the immediate target to attack. In view of this bitter opposition, the task of creating local sponsor committees to underwrite the cost of the presentation in a given city, is next to the impossible.

There is only one alternative left, to present the pageant ourselves. The opposition can exercise its power in preventing the formation of a group of leading citizens to underwrite the cost of a presentation, but they can never exercise that power to stop the general masses of people from buying tickets and attending the performance of the pageant, as they did not succeed in this effort with the previous performances in every city, though they have tried hard, indeed.

We, therefore, recommend to concentrate our efforts and to undertake the presentation of the pageant in the two large cities of Cleveland and Detroit (as far as Pittsburgh is concerned, we are not as yet free to interfere with the efforts of Rabbi Bookstaber, where he still may succeed in forming a sponsors' committee). A small budget of $2000–$3000 will be needed to start the work. A man has to be on the spot and after a short but careful study of the situation in each city, he will

  a) set up an office, rent the auditorium, and set the date for the presentation, meanwhile gathering around him such people who are willing and determined not to yield to any sabotage and outside influence.

  b) organize a non-sectarian sponsor committee of important individuals (but without the demand from them to underwrite the cost of the presentation), organize the immediate sale of tickets, the promotion and publicity, and see to create the necessary atmosphere and collaboration for the successful presentation of the pageant in each city.

This is the "hard way", but there is no other way. Considering the actual state of affairs, the work of first creating an underwriters' committee, to overcome sabotage and ill-minded propaganda, will cost more and may lead to nothing.

However, we have also better news to report. Mr. Ben-Ami's visit to Toronto was completely successful. At the luncheon, which was held there, re: presentation of "We Will Never Die", attended by 17 influential and important men, an organizing committee was created and $2/_3$ of the necessary capital of $15.000 was underwritten then and there. Tentative dates from which to choose one date, were arranged with the Maple Leaf Gardens. This auditorium has a 13.000 seating capacity. We are now to contact two leading Hollywood stars and set the final date for the presentation in Toronto according to the date the stars will be willing and free to come East.

UNDER SECRETARY OF STATE SUMNER WELLES TO MYRON C. TAYLOR, JUNE 23, 1943, REGARDING THE EMERGENCY CONFERENCE TO SAVE THE JEWISH PEOPLE OF EUROPE.

(Franklin D. Roosevelt Library,
Myron C. Taylor Papers, Box 5,
Correspondence 1938–1954.)

Department of State
THE UNDER SECRETARY

June 23, 1943

Mr. Taylor:

I have refused this invitation. Not only the more conservative Jewish organizations and leaders but also such leaders as Rabbi Wise, who was with me this morning, are strongly opposed to the holding of this conference, have done everything they could to prevent it, and are trying to get Bishop Tucker and one or two others who have accepted this invitation to withdraw their acceptances. In a personal letter to Louis Bromfield I have suggested that he drop in to see me when he is in Washington so that I can talk over this matter with him.

U:SW:DMK

MAX LERNER, "WHAT ABOUT THE JEWS, FDR?"

IN *PM*, JULY 22, 1943, PAGE 2.

OPINION

What About the Jews, FDR?

I address you with great reluctance, President Roosevelt. You are a man harried by every group in the country, every issue and every cause in the world. You carry the massive weight of the war on your shoulders. Only an issue of transcending importance can justify adding to your burden.

But I think that the fate of 4,000,000 Jews is not a trifling matter either in the war or in the conscience of Western man. That is the number of Jews who are still left in Europe. At least 2,000,000 have already been murdered by the Nazis and their satellites in the greatest mass slaughter in history.

There is no sense in pulling all the emotional stops on the theme of the massacre of the Jews. Anyone who has not already been moved to the depths of his being by the thought of the European earth soaked with the blood of 2,000,000 innocent and helpless people, will not be moved by rhetoric.

I can speak to you, Mr. President, in a matter-of-fact way. You know who the Nazis are, you know what they have done and are doing. You want to do everything humanly possible to rescue what Jews remain in Europe.

But you are handicapped at the very start. Neither the American nor the British government has a policy on the matter. Neither government recognizes that any Jewish problem exists. Both governments talk of the Jews as Polish nationals, or Czech nationals, or Hungarian nationals. Yet the fact remains that while Czechs are killed by the hundreds, Jews in Czechoslovakia are killed by the tens of thousands. *And they are killed as Jews, not as Czechs.*

Hitler has made out of Europe a charnel-house of the Jews. But the State Dept. and Downing St. avert their eyes from the slaughter and, with a finicky exactitude, insist on giving the Jews in their death the civic national status that Hitler denies them in life.

The problem is there, Mr. President by whatever name you call it. And it is not too late to act on it. We can stop the senseless and criminal slaughter of the remaining 4,000,000.

How? There is a conference meeting in New York—an Emergency Conference to Save the Jewish People of Europe. There are Jews and Christians in it, laymen and clergymen, Democrats and Republicans, reactionaries and liberals. The only things they have in common are a conscience and a will to action.

Several proposals are emerging. One is that the United Nations put pressure on the Axis satellite countries. Out of 4,000,000 Jews in Europe, 1,500,000 are in Hungary, Rumania, Bulgaria. Hitler is trying to crack down on them to hasten the extermination of their Jews. But Hitler can no longer give them unqualified commands.

Thanks largely to your brilliant leadership in the war, along with Churchill and Stalin, the Axis satellites know that their end is near. They will do many things to acquire even a qualified merit in our eyes. To stop the slaughter of their Jews, to send as many as possible into neutral countries, to cease the brutal discrimination against those who remain, are things they would do if we demanded it.

This is not to relent in the slightest from your Casablanca policy of unconditional surrender. It is merely to use the war power we have to save millions of innocent lives. No promises or commitments could possibly be involved.

Then there is Axis-occupied Europe. I do not include Germany itself; that is, as Hitler has put it with a beautiful irony, *Judenrein*—wholly cleansed of its Jews. But the rest of Europe which the Nazi armies occupy still has some 2,500,000 Jews. They can be saved if we act. You, Mr. President, can promise the direst retribution to the Nazi leaders unless they cease the slaughter of Jews. When it was a question of the Nazi use of poison-gas against the Russian armies, Churchill threatened to retaliate in kind. It worked. And this will work too, if the Nazis know you mean it.

Finally there are the neutral countries—Switzerland, Sweden, Turkey, even Portugal and Spain. If we give them financial aid and encouragement, they can become temporary havens for refugees from the Axis—and satellite countries.

The problem is soluble. Not by words, but by action. You, Mr. President, must take the lead in creating a United Nations agency to follow out these lines of action.

The methods are clear. Neither conscience nor policy can afford to leave them unused. And the time is now.

—Max Lerner

HOUSE RESOLUTIONS 350 AND 352 [THE RESCUE RESOLUTION] AS
INTRODUCED INTO THE U.S. HOUSE OF REPRESENTATIVES ON
NOVEMBER 9, 1943. AN IDENTICAL RESOLUTION WAS INTRODUCED
INTO THE U.S. SENATE ON THE SAME DAY.

(U.S. HOUSE OF REPRESENTATIVES,
PROBLEMS OF WORLD WAR II AND ITS AFTERMATH:
PART 2, THE PALESTINE QUESTION
[WASHINGTON, 1976], PAGES 15–16.)

[THE TEXT OF HOUSE RESOLUTIONS 350 AND 352, IDENTICAL RESOLUTIONS, IS AS FOLLOWS:]

Whereas the Congress of the United States, by concurrent resolution adopted on March 15 of this year, expressed its condemnation of Nazi Germany's "mass murder of Jewish men, women, and children," a mass crime which has already exterminated close to two million human beings, about 30 per centum of the total Jewish population of Europe, and which is growing in intensity as Germany approaches defeat; and

Whereas the American tradition of justice and humanity dictates that all possible means be employed to save from this fate the surviving Jews of Europe, some four million souls who have been rendered homeless and destitute by the Nazis: Therefore be it

Resolved, That the House of Representatives recommends and urges the creation by the President of a commission of diplomatic, economic, and military experts to formulate and effectuate a plan of immediate action designed to save the surviving Jewish people of Europe from extinction at the hands of Nazi Germany.

PRESIDENT FRANKLIN D. ROOSEVELT, EXECUTIVE ORDER 9417,
JANUARY 22, 1944, ESTABLISHING A WAR REFUGEE BOARD.
(*FEDERAL REGISTER* 9,
JANUARY 26, 1944, PAGES 935–36.)

FEDERAL REGISTER

VOLUME 9   **NUMBER 18**

Washington, Wednesday, January 26, 1944

THE PRESIDENT

EXECUTIVE ORDER 9417

ESTABLISHING a War Refugee Board

WHEREAS it is the policy of this Government to take all measures within its power to rescue the victims of enemy oppression who are in imminent danger of death and otherwise to afford such victims all possible relief and assistance consistent with the successful prosecution of the war;

NOW, THEREFORE, by virtue of the authority vested in me by the Constitution and the statutes of the United States, as President of the United States and as Commander in Chief of the Army and Navy, and in order to effectuate with all possible speed the rescue and relief of such victims of enemy oppression, it is hereby ordered as follows:

1. There is established in the Executive Office of the President a War Refugee Board (hereinafter referred to as the Board). The Board shall consist of the Secretary of State, the Secretary of the Treasury and the Secretary of War. The Board may request the heads of other agencies or departments to participate in its deliberations whenever matters specially affecting such agencies or departments are under consideration.

2. The Board shall be charged with the responsibility for seeing that the policy of the Government, as stated in the Preamble, is carried out. The functions of the Board shall include without limitation the development of plans and programs and the inauguration of effective measures for (a) the rescue, transportation,

maintenance and relief of the victims of enemy oppression, and (b) the establishment of havens of temporary refuge for such victims. To this end the Board, through appropriate channels, shall take the necessary steps to enlist the cooperation of foreign governments and obtain their participation in the execution of such plans and programs.

3. It shall be the duty of the State, Treasury and War Departments, within their respective spheres, to execute at the request of the Board, the plans and programs so developed and the measures so inaugurated. It shall be the duty of the heads of all agencies and departments to supply or obtain for the Board such information and to extend to the Board such supplies, shipping and other specified assistance and facilities as the Board may require in carrying out the provisions of this Order. The State Department shall appoint special attaches with diplomatic status, on the recommendation of the Board, to be stationed abroad in places where it is likely that assistance can be rendered to war refugees, the duties and responsibilities of such attaches to be defined by the Board in consultation with the State Department.

4. The Board and the State, Treasury and War Departments are authorized to accept the services or contributions of any private persons, private organizations, State agencies, or agencies of foreign governments in carrying out the purposes of this Order. The Board shall cooperate with all existing and future international organizations concerned with the problems of refugee rescue, maintenance, transportation, relief, rehabilitation, and resettlement.

5. To the extent possible the Board shall utilize the personnel, supplies, facilities and services of the State, Treasury and War Departments. In addition the Board, within the limits of funds which may be made available, may employ necessary personnel without regard for the Civil Service laws and regulations and the Classification Act of 1923, as amended, and make provisions for supplies, facilities and services necessary to discharge its responsibilities. The Board shall appoint an Executive Director who shall serve as its principal executive officer. It shall be the duty of the Executive Director to arrange for the prompt execution of the plans and programs developed and the measures inaugurated by the Board, to supervise the activities of the special attaches and to submit frequent reports to the Board on the steps taken for the rescue and relief of war refugees.

6. The Board shall be directly responsible to the President in carrying out the policy of this Government, as stated in the Preamble, and the Board shall report to him at frequent intervals concerning the steps taken for the rescue and relief

of war refugees and shall make such recommendations as the Board may deem appropriate for further action to overcome any difficulties encountered in the rescue and relief of war refugees.

FRANKLIN D ROOSEVELT

THE WHITE HOUSE,

Jan. 22, 1944.

[F. R. Doc. 44-1274; Filed, January 24, 1944; 2:40 p. m.]

STEPHEN S. WISE TO SECRETARY OF THE INTERIOR HAROLD L.
ICKES, DECEMBER 23, 1943, CONCERNING THE EMERGENCY
COMMITTEE TO SAVE THE JEWISH PEOPLE OF EUROPE.
(LIBRARY OF CONGRESS, HAROLD ICKES PAPERS, SECRETARY OF THE INTERIOR FILES,
BOX 124, FOLDER 17, ASSOCIATIONS 1944.)

AMERICAN JEWISH CONGRESS
330 WEST 42nd STREET   NEW YORK CITY

STEPHEN S. WISE, PRESIDENT   CABLE ADDRESS 'CONGRESS'

CARL SHERMAN, CHAIRMAN, EXECUTIVE COMMITTEE   TELEPHONE LONGACRE 5-2600

NATHAN D. PERLMAN ⎫
                   ⎬ VICE-PRESIDENTS
LEO H. LOWITZ   ⎭

LOUIS LIPSKY, CHAIRMAN, GOVERNING COUNCIL

M. MALDWIN FERTIG, CHAIRMAN, ADMINISTRATIVE COMMITTEE

JACOB LEICHTMAN, TREASURER

Office of Dr. Wise
40 West 68 Street
New York 23, N.Y.

December 23, 1943.

Hon. Harold L. Ickes
Department of the Interior
Washington, D. C.

Dear friend Ickes:

I was very sorry to note, as were others among your friends, that you had
accepted the Chairmanship of the Washington Division of the Committee to Rescue European Jews. I enclose copy of a statement about to be issued by the American Jewish Conference, which virtually includes all organized, responsible and
representative Jewish groups and organizations in America.

I do not like to speak ill to you, not of us, concerning a group of Jews, but I am
under the inexorable necessity of saying to you that the time will come, and come

soon, when you will find it necessary to withdraw from this irresponsible group, which exists and obtains funds through being permitted to use the names of non-Jews like yourself.

I wish I could have seen you before you gave your consent. I know that your aim is to save Jews, but why tie up with an organization which talks about saving Jews, gets a great deal of money for saving them, but in my judgment has not done a thing which may result in the saving of a single Jew.

Faithfully yours,

Luish

SSW:S   PRESIDENT
Enc.

SENATOR GUY M. GILLETTE TO HARRY L. SELDEN, AUGUST 1, 1944,
REGARDING STEPHEN WISE AND THE CREATION OF THE WAR
REFUGEE BOARD.

(YALE UNIVERSITY LIBRARY,

PALESTINE STATEHOOD COMMITTEE PAPERS,

BOX 1, FOLDER 12.)

C
O
P
Y

United States Senate
Committee on Foreign Affairs

August 1, 1944

Mr. Harry Louis Selden
American League for a Free Palestine, Inc.
11 West Forty-Second Street
New York 18, New York

My dear Mr. Selden:

On my return to the office today, my secretary called my attention to correspondence had with you during my absence and particularly referring to your letter of July twenty-fifth in which inquiry was made as to whether or not Dr.
Stephen S. Wise was responsible for the introduction of the Gillette—Rogers Resolutions in the Congress which resulted in the creation of the War Refugee Board.

In reply may I say that Dr. Wise had nothing to do with the development of
action looking to the introduction of these Resolutions so far as I am concerned
personally. My part in the matter came as the result of a meeting called by a
group which was organizing a Washington branch of the Emergency Committee to
Save the Jewish people. As a result of conferences held with this group, a decision
was reached to ask for the introduction of a Resolution covering the subject matter and Representative Rogers agreed to sponsor the Resolution in the House of
Representatives and I agreed to sponsor such a Resolution in the Senate. With
this sponsorship, I associated some of my colleagues. I had no conference with Dr.
Wise on the matter until some time after the Resolution was introduced when Dr.
Wise called at my office accompanied by two or three other gentlemen and dis-

cussed the pending Resolutions with me. None of these gentlemen seemed to be enthusiastic for the passage of the Resolution and the tenor of the conversation seemed to suggest their belief that the action as proposed by the Resolution was not a wise step to take, although they professed very strong interest in everything that would look to the saving of the remnant of the Jewish people in Europe from destruction.

Very sincerely,

/s/

GUY M. GILLETTE

GMG:MM

RONALD BRIDGES TO SAMUEL MCCREA CAVERT,
MARCH 10, 1945, CONCERNING THE EMERGENCY COMMITTEE
TO SAVE THE JEWISH PEOPLE OF EUROPE.

(YALE UNIVERSITY LIBRARY,
PALESTINE STATEHOOD COMMITTEE PAPERS,
BOX 1, FOLDER 17.)

(C O P Y)   March 10, 1945

Samuel McCrea Cavert
The Federal Council,
297 4th Avenue
New York 10, N. Y.

Dear Mr. Cavert:

I had hoped to write you much earlier than this on the matter of Mr. Smertenko and his interests so that you might understand the situation that exists between us. Your letter was very well done, thanks to your good sense of tact, so that it did not need any explanation from me on this particular matter. However, I still want to make a few points clear. About a year ago, Mr. Smertenko came to Phoenix, Arizona, to see about forming a chapter or local group of his Emergency Committee to Save the Jews. I was invited and urged to attend the meeting and did so, particularly after the leading Jews in Phoenix made some point of my presence. We heard his story and it was agreed to form such a chapter for giving aid to the emergency situation then prevailing. I was asked to be chairman of it, and though I had little relish for the job I consented.

The developments that ensued puzzled me very much. At first I couldn't figure them out. Ultimately, I could see that great pressure was being brought on the people who had called the meeting to discontinue their efforts in this quarter. After many weeks had gone by and I was on the verge of returning to the East, I finally got a small group together and entertained a motion to discontinue the chapter. Meantime I had been put on the executive board for the national organization and soon I was the recipient of various letters and documents strenuously asserting the pernicious nature of the Emergency Committee. Finally I got a long letter from Carl Voss politely but urgently requesting that I get off the national board of the Emergency Committee and making charges of a very serious nature against some of its personnel.

As a result of this I wrote to about fifteen persons whose names also appeared on the executive board and whom I knew to be persons of considerable repute. The gist of my inquiry was "What goes on?" I told a little of this pressure that had been brought to bear on me, asked if they had been under similar pressure, and inquired explicitly how much they had investigated the committee and what they knew of its nature. Among those I addressed were such diverse persons as Louis Bromfield, Sigrid Undset, Sheldon Glueck, and Governor Martin of Pennsylvania. The replies were a long time coming in, and they ranged rather widely in the evidence they presented. Governor Martin was moved by my letter to make some inquiry, the result of which was his withdrawal from the committee. Two or three of the others expressed uncertainty. The remainder gave a staunch defense of the committee's principles and program, and some specifically told of having investigated the leadership and being satisfied with their integrity.

I should long since have resigned, had it not been for two things: (1) I was anxious lest any action of mine be interpreted as anti-Semitic, and (2) being a staunch Yankee, I dislike being shoved around. After these letters came in, I had conferences with two or three of the executive board, and inquired into it further. I had replied courteously to the request of Dr. Voss and explained that I wanted to see the evidence. Although I have written him and telephoned him in New York, he has never presented me with a scrap of evidence to support the serious charges which he made. On the contrary, I have had every kind of request granted by the Emergency Committee to show me their files and correspondence and certified accounts, etc. I am persuaded that the issues involved here go very deep and that the matter of personal integrity and personality of the leadership of this group is quite secondary to a basic difference in philosophy. I am inclined to believe that this question of basic philosophy relates to the whole business of world peace.

The ramifications of all this cannot be entered into by correspondence, and I covet a chance to go into the matter in full with you next spring when I am in the East. However, I hope that what I have said may lead you to observe as closely as possible what takes place in this area of conflict and that you may retain the open mind which evidently you now have, even though the evidence has seemed one-sided. I would appreciate, then, whatever courtesy you can show Mr. Smertenko and his group without jeopardizing the good name of the Federal Council or running counter to your own principles and good sense. Whatever you would care to write to me on the subject I would read most gladly.

Sincerely yours,

(S) RONALD BRIDGES

rb:gea

DEPARTMENT OF STATE

MEMORANDUM OF CONVERSATION

CONFIDENTIAL   DATE: May 19, 1944

SUBJECT: Attitude of Zionists Toward Peter Bergson.

PARTICIPANTS: Dr. Nahum Goldmann, Chairman of the
                Administrative Committee of the World Jewish
                Congress.
                Mr. Murray, NEA.
                Mr. Alling, NEA.
                Mr. Merriam, NE.
                Mr. Wilson, NE.

COPIES TO: Jerusalem, VD, WRB (Mr. Warren) and Justice
                (Mr. Nemzer).

In the course of a discussion today on Zionist affairs, Dr. Goldmann referred to the accounts appearing in the press of the establishment of a "Hebrew Embassy" by the "Hebrew Committee of National Liberation" under the aegis of Peter Bergson. Dr. Goldmann gave Mr. Murray a copy of the statement which the Zionists had issued to the press in this connection. He said that the activities of Bergson and his colleagues had been a matter of the greatest concern to the official Zionist leadership and that it distressed him to see Bergson received in high places and given facilities by this Government. The entire matter, he said, was a

gigantic hoax which Bergson and his group were perpetrating on the more guile-
less members of the Jewish community, and he drew particular attention in this
connection to the fact that Bergson's committees are especially active in Chicago
and Los Angeles. In other words, Dr. Goldmann said, the chief support of this
group came from persons who had a less close connection with or knowledge of
international affairs or of the Palestine problem, and this was true of non-Jews as
well as Jews. He asserted that Bergson's activities had not resulted in the rescue
of one single Jew or in the saving of a single Jewish life, and he said that now
that the War Refugee Board had been established and had absorbed a great deal
of the rescue work, Bergson and his associates had developed this "fantastic
notion" that they were a government-in-exile, representing the stateless Jews of
occupied Europe and the Jews of Palestine, which latter they regarded as being
under occupation by the "hostile" forces of Great Britain. Dr. Goldmann characterized this reasoning as complete nonsense, and he said furthermore that the
group in question in no way were representative of Jewry either in Palestine or
abroad. He pointed out also that the distinction which Bergson now drew between
the "Hebrew nation" and the American or other assimilated Jews of the world
was undoubtedly devised in order to attract the financial support both of non-
Zionist Jews and of non-Jews. He continued that the Zionist leadership had had
many discussions with Bergson and his associates during the time they had been
evolving their present ideology and that he had finally broken completely with
Bergson, whom he now regarded as no longer a Zionist in any sense of the word
but as simply an adventurer.

The thing which concerned the responsible Jewish organizations, Dr. Goldmann declared, was the fact that Bergson and his colleagues were free to go about
the country collecting large sums of money for which they did not make any
accounting and giving the impression that they were engaged in a vast humanitarian work. He alluded to the fact that Bergson and his associates were in this
country on temporary visitors' visas and he also mentioned their efforts to obtain
draft deferments. He added that he could not see why this Government did not
either deport Bergson or draft him.

Mr. Murray replied that these were matters which were handled by different
Government departments, and he made it clear to Dr. Goldmann that there was
no disposition on the part of the Executive branch to support or assist Bergson or
his associates.

Dr. Goldmann recalled that Eri Jabotinsky, a member of the group, had
recently departed for Palestine and Turkey by air with the ostensible purpose of
engaging in rescue work in behalf of the War Refugee Board. He said that he did

not see how this could contribute in any way to the rescue of Jews from the Balkans, since the Jewish Agency representative in Turkey, Mr. Barlas, was the only person in Turkey who had the right to allot certificates for entry into Palestine and in addition had facilities for engaging in clandestine activities in occupied Europe which Bergson's group did not possess.

A discussion then ensued as to various aspects of Bergson's activities, including the inquiry which the Foreign Agents Registration Section of the Department of Justice is conducting with a view to determining the liability of the various organizations involved to register under the Foreign Agents Registration Act. Dr. Goldmann said that he was quite familiar with this Act as he himself had registered as the representative of the Jewish Agency, and he did not believe that Bergson's registering would in itself curtail his activities. What was needed, he asserted, was for persons in authority to have the facts laid before them and they would then see the light and desist from supporting Bergson or paying any attention to him. Dr. Goldmann mentioned the remaining members of Bergson's committee and declared that he had never heard of most of them, which he cited as showing that their claim to be representative of any element in Jewry was all the more ridiculous.

Dr. Goldmann said that Rabbi Wise while recently on the Pacific Coast had been present with Bergson at a large meeting and had questioned Bergson about his activities until the latter had admitted publicly that none of the funds which they had collected had been sent out of the country or had been employed for any purpose other than to finance the purchase of additional advertising space in the newspapers. In spite of this, however, many misguided persons continued to contribute, being attracted by the prominent names appearing in the list of sponsors of the various committees and their avowedly humanitarian aims. With regard to the sponsorship of these committees by members of Congress, Dr. Goldmann said that he and other Zionists had often discussed the matter with various Senators and Representatives, with the result that almost all members of Congress, except Representative Will Rogers, Jr., had severed their connection with Bergson. This was true even of Senator Johnson of Colorado. He predicted that within the next few days Senator Wagner would issue a scathing denunciation of Bergson and that in addition several Representatives, including Congressmen Celler and Dickstein, would make a public attack upon him. In so far as Representative Rogers was concerned, he said that the Representative was a complete fanatic on the point and that he and Mrs. Rogers harbored a great admiration for Bergson which no amount of persuasion had been able to shake.

In so far as other branches of the Government were concerned, Dr. Goldmann said that today he had addressed a letter to Secretary Morgenthau pointing out that Bergson's committee intended to float a million-dollar bond issue to be redeemed in ten years by the "Hebrew nation". He said that in addition he would try to arrange for a group of prominent Jews to call personally on Mr. Morgenthau to expose the background of Bergson's activities. He mentioned the support which Bergson had been receiving from the War Refugee Board, and he said that he had discussed this several times with Mr. Pehle, the Executive Director of the Board, who had taken the position that Bergson's Emergency Committee to Save the Jewish People of Europe had inspired the introduction of the Gillette-Rogers Resolution, which in turn had led to the creation of the War Refugee Board. In one of their meetings with Mr. Pehle, Rabbi Wise had gone so far as to inform Mr. Pehle that he regarded Bergson as equally as great an enemy of the Jews as Hitler, for the reason that his activities could only lead to increased anti-Semitism. Dr. Goldmann said that only yesterday he had again seen Mr. Pehle and had told him that unless the War Refugee Board disavowed Bergson it would be necessary for the World Jewish Congress to denounce publicly the War Refugee Board. Mr. Pehle had agreed to break with Bergson, but Dr. Goldmann added that if this should not take place, it would be difficult for the Zionists to press the matter in view of their obvious interest in the Board's activities.

Further on this point, Dr. Goldmann said that recently Mr. Ira Hirschmann, the War Refugee Board's representative at Ankara, who is now in this country, had appeared at a reception which Bergson's Emergency Committee had given in New York City and he ventured the opinion that this fact alone was worth fifty to one hundred thousand dollars to the Committee in additional contributions.

Mr. Wilson inquired as to Bergson's purpose in all this activity, and Dr. Goldmann expressed the opinion that it was purely a question of personal ambition on the part of a group of irresponsible young men who had had to leave Palestine because the British authorities were aware of the true nature of their activities, and he asserted that their connection with the Irgun Zvai Leumi was well known.

Mr. Murray assured Dr. Goldmann that there was no question of the Department's recognizing Bergson or any of his colleagues or organizations in any official capacity whatsoever.

NE:EMWilson:MW   NEA

NOTES

CHAPTER 1: INTRODUCTION

1. David S. Wyman, *Paper Walls: America and the Refugee Crisis, 1938–1941* (Amherst, 1968), vii, 155–205, 209; David S. Wyman, *The Abandonment of the Jews: America and the Holocaust, 1941–1945* (New York, 1984), Preface and Chapters 7, 10, and 11.
2. Wyman, *Paper Walls*, 3–9; Wyman, *Abandonment*, 6–9.
3. Wyman, *Paper Walls*, 10–14.
4. Ibid., 14–23; Wyman, *Abandonment*, 9; Charles H. Stember et al., *Jews in the Mind of America* (New York, 1966), 210, 214; *Public Opinion Quarterly*, spring 1942, 56; *The New York Times*, April 11, 1945, 21.
5. Stember, op. cit., 53–55, 121–25.
6. Ibid., 127–28.
7. Ibid., 85, 131–33, 214.
8. Ibid., 7–8, 67, 84–85, 130–33, 214.
9. Lloyd P. Gartner, "The Two Continuities of Antisemitism in the United States," in Shmuel Almog, ed., *Antisemitism through the Ages* (Oxford, 1988), 317–18; Stember, op. cit., 8, 210, 215; Wyman, *Paper Walls*, 14, 17, 20.
10. Ibid., 14–20; Wyman, *Abandonment*, 9.
11. Wyman, *Paper Walls*, 14–21; Wyman, *Abandonment*, 9.
12. Stember, op.cit., 129–33, 214; Wyman, *Paper Walls*, 18–19.
13. Wyman, *Abandonment*, 10–11.
14. Ibid., 14; *Congressional Record*, vol. 90, February 8, 1944, 1418.
15. Stember, op. cit., 132–33; Wyman, *Abandonment*, 311–27.
16. Wyman, *Paper Walls*, 172–78, 182–91; Wyman, *Abandonment*, 124–25, 130–32.
17. Wyman, *Paper Walls*, 143–47, 177–78, 200–201; Wyman, *Abandonment*, 108–9, 190–91. The quotation is from Breckinridge Long to Adolf A. Berle, Jr., and James C.

Dunn, June 26, 1940, Breckinridge Long Papers, Box 211, Visa Division, General, 1940, Library of Congress.

18. Wyman, *Paper Walls*, 191–201; Wyman, *Abandonment*, 125; Fiftieth Meeting of the President's Advisory Committee on Political Refugees, September 4, 1941, James G. McDonald Papers, P65, Columbia University.

19. Wyman, *Abandonment*, 3–5.

20. Ibid., 19–55, 61–62, 321–22.

21. Ibid., 73–76, 97–100, 157–58.

22. Ibid., 61–66, 71–75, 86–89, 104–7.

23. Ibid., 63–73, 93–100, 109–11.

24. Ibid., 84–87, 90–93; Minutes of the Meeting of the Emergency Committee on European Situation, March 6, 1943, American Jewish Committee Archives, Proskauer Emergency Committee; Minutes of the Joint Emergency Committee on European Jewish Affairs, March 15, 1943, American Jewish Committee Archives, Joint Emergency Committee; "Unity in Crisis," *Opinion*, April 1943, 7.

25. Wyman, *Abandonment*, 104–8, 112–22, 168–69.

26. Ibid., 143–50, 152–56, 193–94, 201, 203–4.

27. Ibid., 81, 178–87.

28. Ibid., 187, 203–5, 209.

29. Ibid., 209–15, 240–41, 285, 287, 330, 393.

30. Hillel Kook interview with David S. Wyman, April 13–15, 1973; *New York Post*, July 11, 1944, 29; Gillette to Byrnes, October 11, 1945, Palestine Statehood Committee Papers [hereafter PSC], Yale University, 1:21.

31. Wyman, *Abandonment*, 84–85.

32. Chaim Weizmann (1874–1952), a Russian-born scientist and Zionist leader who lived most of his life in London, played a key role in the British decision to issue the 1917 Balfour Declaration, which pledged to support the creation of a Jewish national home in Palestine. He served as president of the World Zionist Organization (1920–1931 and 1935–1946). After the establishment of the State of Israel, he served as its first president (a largely ceremonial post).

33. This and the ensuing four paragraphs are based on Chapter 1 of Rafael Medoff, *Militant Zionism in America: The Rise and Impact of the Jabotinsky Movement in the United States, 1926–1948* (Tuscaloosa, AL, 2002).

34. Rafael Medoff and Chaim I. Waxman, *Historical Dictionary of Zionism* (Lanham, MD, 1999), 97–98.

35. "Memorandum on the Anglo-American Committee for a Jewish Army," 3, undated [approximately December 1942], FO 371/31380, Public Record Office [hereafter PRO], London, England.

36. Cited in Samuel Halprin, *The Political World of American Zionism* (Detroit, 1961), 268.

37. Vladimir Jabotinsky, "Yes, To Break," *Haint*, November 4, 1932; "Palestine Under Histadruth Rule," 7–9, *The Revisionist* 2 (July 1, 1933), 16-gimel/10, Metzudat Ze'ev (Jabotinsky Institute), Tel Aviv [hereafter MZ].

38. Frankfurter to Wise, December 12, 1934, Box 109, Stephen S. Wise Papers [hereafter SSW], American Jewish Historical Society, Waltham, MA.

39. "Don't Fall for Jabotinsky" (editorial), *The Reconstructionist* [hereafter *Rec*] 1:1 (January 11, 1935), 8; "Rabbis May Plead Guilty" (editorial), *Rec* 1:4 (February 22, 1935), 3–4.

40. Elias Ginsburg, "Is Revision-Zionism Fascist?," *Menorah Journal* [hereafter *MJ*] 22 (October–December 1934), 190–206; Marie Syrkin, "Labor-Zionism Replies," *MJ* 23 (April–June 1935), 66–79. For Stephen Wise's exchange with Jabotinsky about James Wise's anti-Revisionist articles in *Opinion*, see Jabotinsky to Mrs. Wise, October 18, 1934, and Stephen Wise to Jabotinsky, October 29, 1934, Box 102, SSW-AJHS.

41. "Why Zionists Cannot Support Jabotinsky and Revisionism: Excerpts of address delivered before the Free Synagogue at Carnegie Hall—Sunday morning, March 10, 1935 by Dr. Stephen S. Wise," Box 102, SSW-AJHS.

42. Alice Nakhimovsky, in "Vladimir Jabotinsky, Russian Writer" (*Modern Judaism* 7:2 [May 1987], 171), argues that the "fascist" label has been unfairly perpetuated by historians who have erroneously ascribed to Jabotinsky sentiments expressed by one of the characters in his novel *Samson*.

43. Emergency Committee for Zionist Affairs, "Revisionism: A Destructive Force" (New York, 1940). Ironically, the United Palestine Appeal—a leading member-organization of the ECZA—later circulated a fund-raising leaflet featuring a photograph of one of those Revisionist ships, the *Parita*, which had landed 850 unauthorized refugees at Tel Aviv in 1938. See Yitshaq Ben-Ami, *Years of Wrath, Days of Glory* (New York, 1981), 321.

44. Medoff, *Militant Zionism in America*, Chapter 4.

45. Ibid.; Kook interview with Wyman, op. cit.; Wyman, *Abandonment*, 84–85.

46. Ben-Ami, op. cit., 242.

47. The first rally was technically cosponsored by the American Friends of a Jewish Palestine and the New Zionist Organization of America (NZOA), as the formal dissolution of the AFJP had not yet taken place, nor had the final break between the Bergson activists and the NZOA. Benzion Netanyahu, who worked closely with Bergson for several months before returning to the NZOA, was responsible for recruiting van Paassen to the army cause (Benzion Netanyahu interview with Rafael Medoff, March 20, 1997). Also see "Jewish Army Rally Huge Success," *Zionews* 3:18 (June 30, 1941), 6–7; "In the New Zionist Movement," *Zionews* 3:20 (July 28, 1941), 7. *Zionews* was the official publication of the NZOA. See Medoff, *Militant Zionism in America*, Chapter 4.

48. Ben Hecht, *A Child of the Century* (New York, 1954), 540–41; Benzion Netanyahu interview with Rafael Medoff, June 25, 1997.

49. Jabotinsky to Dayag, September 4, 1943 (Palestine Censorship file), FO 371/40129, PRO.

50. Ben-Ami, op. cit., 248; Wyman, *Abandonment*, 157.

51. Halifax to Eden, January 13, 1943, FO 371/35031, PRO.

52. Monty Penkower, *The Jews Were Expendable* (Urbana and Chicago, 1983), 16; *Foreign Relations of the United States—1942*, Volume 4 (Washington, D.C.: 1969), 549–50. Murray's June 2, 1942, memorandum on the subject to FDR is quoted in Joseph B. Schechtman, *The United States and the Jewish State Movement* (New York, 1966), 50.

53. Halifax to Eden, January 13, 1943, and Halifax to Eden, January 15, 1943, FO 371/35031, PRO; Netanyahu interview, June 25, 1997, op. cit.

54. Ben-Ami, op. cit., 284.

55. Hecht, op. cit., 516.

56. Andrew L. Somers (1895–1949), Democrat of New York, served in the House of Representatives from 1925 until his death.

57. Medoff, *Militant Zionism in America,* Chapter 4.

58. Henderson (Foreign Office) to Baker (Colonial Office), November 28, 1945, CO 733/461/75872/14C, PRO.

59. From Baruch Rabinowitz's unpublished autobiography (copy made available to the authors courtesy of Baruch Rabinowitz), 111–112.

60. "A Zionist Army?" (editorial), *The New York Times* [hereafter *NYT*], January 22, 1942, 16; "A Jewish Army" (editorial), *PM,* January 23, 1942, 4.

61. Hecht, op. cit., 547.

62. Stephen S. Wise, "Army Plan Approved" (letters), *NYT,* January 26, 1942, 14; Embassy to Foreign Office, July 2, 1942, FO 371/31379, PRO.

63. Hadassah Minutes, January 14, 1942, 103; January 28, 1942, 113–14; May 5, 1942, 228, Hadassah Archives, New York City.

64. Lourie to Wechsler, January 6, 1942, and January 26, 1942, 1:6, PSC.

65. Wechsler to Lourie, February 9, 1942, 1:6, PSC; Bergson to Levinthal, December 7, 1942, 1:6, PSC; Levinthal to Bergson, January 16, 1943, 1:7, PSC; Merlin to Ziff, May 10, 1943, 1:8, PSC; Bergson to Ziff, June 29, 1943, 1:9, PSC; Bergson to Levinthal, August 30, 1943, 1:9, PSC; Abba Hillel Silver's Confidential Washington Diary, entry for October 11, 1943, 3–4, Abba Hillel Silver Papers [hereafter AHS], The Temple, Cleveland.

66. Wyman, *Abandonment,* 20–24, 42–45, 51, 61.

67. Ibid., 61–62, 321–22.

68. Hecht, op. cit., 518–19.

69. *NYT,* December 5, 1942, 16, and February 8, 1943, 8.

70. "FOR SALE to Humanity: 70,000 Jews, Guaranteed Human Beings at $50 a Piece" (advertisement), *NYT,* February 16, 1943, 11.

71. *Opinion,* March 1943, 14; *New Palestine,* March 5, 1943, 4; *Jewish Frontier,* March 1943, 8; *Congress Weekly,* February 26, 1943, 16; Minutes of ZOA Execuive Committee, March 11, 1943, ZOA Executive Committee, AJHS.

72. See NZOA Press Statement, September 20, 1944, 16-gimel/9, Metzudat Ze'ev [Jabotinsky Archives], Tel Aviv. For a full analysis of the factors leading to the establishment of the Jewish Brigade, see Penkower, *The Jews Were Expendable,* 3–29.

73. "Down with Fascism Forever, Is Cry of 1943" (editorial), *National Jewish Monthly* 57:5 (January 1943), 145; "A People in Mourning" (editorial), *Jewish Spectator,* January 1943, 4–5.

74. It appeared in *Yiddisher Kemfer* on February 12, 1943. For a later English translation, see "6,000,000 and 5,000,000 (Notes in Midstream)," *Midstream* 10 (March 1964), 3-14.

75. *NYT,* February 26, 1943, 14 and March 2, 1943, 1, 4.

76. Ibid., March 2, 1943, 4.

77. Ibid., December 18, 1942, 26; March 3, 1943, 22; and March 4, 1943, 9; *New York Post,* March 6, 1943, 21; *New York Sun,* March 3, 1943, 20; *New York Herald-Tribune,* March 7, 1943, II, 3.

78. Wyman, *Abandonment,* 87–89, 93–94.

79. Rafael Medoff, "'Retribution Is Not Enough': The 1943 Campaign by Jewish Students to Raise American Public Awareness of the Nazi Genocide," *Holocaust and Genocide Studies* 11:2 (Fall 1997), 171–89.

80. Wyman, *Abandonment,* 90–91.

81. Hecht's account of the meeting (op. cit., 553–57) is typically dramatic. A more staid version may be found in Trager to Rosenblum, February 1, 1943, Box 15—War and Peace: Jewish Army 1940–1943, American Jewish Committee Archives.

82. Wyman, *Abandonment,* 90.

83. "Report on Attempts to Stage *We Will Never Die* in Kingston, Rochester, Buffalo, Baltimore, Gary, and Pittsburgh," n.d. (early 1944), 13:57, PSC; Merlin to Ziff, April 23, 1943, 1:8, PSC.

84. The charge was made in the column "Rumor Behind the News," *Hamigdal* III:4 (April 1943), 14; it also appeared in Merlin to Ziff, April 23, 1943, PSC 1:8. Also see "Tuesday to Be Day of Prayer for Jews," *NYT,* March 6, 1943, 8.

85. Israel I. Taslitt, syndicated column "On the Scene" carried by Migdal Features, in *Jewish Review and Observer* (Cleveland), April 23, 1943, copy in PSC, Reel 18.

86. Alexander Rafaeli, *Dream and Action* (Jerusalem, 1993), 109.

87. Halifax to Eden, May 25, 1943, FO 371/35035, PRO.

88. Penkower, op. cit., 110–11.

89. "To the Gentlemen at Bermuda" (advertisement), *Washington Post,* April 20, 1943, 10; *NYT,* May 4, 1943, 17.

90. "Memorandum for Mr. Ladd," May 12, 1943, File: Peter Bergson (Hillel Kook), Federal Bureau of Investigation, made available to the authors under the Freedom of Information and Privacy Acts.

91. Monty Noam Penkower, "In Dramatic Dissent: The Bergson Boys," *American Jewish History* LXX (March 1981), 290.

92. Wyman, *Abandonment,* 168–69.

93. "Rumor Behind the News," *Hamigdal* III:4 (April 1943), 14; "Mass Action" (editorial), Independent Jewish Press Service, March 12, 1943, 4-c.

94. Saadia Gelb, "The Conference to the Rescue," *Furrows* 2:2 (December 1943), 9–11.

95. "Annual Report to the Zionist Organization of America—47th Annual Convention, October 14–17, 1944, Atlantic City, New Jersey," p. 59, Central Zionist Archives, Jerusalem, 1753.

96. Medoff, *Militant Zionism in America,* Chapter 6.

97. Ibid.

98. Murray Everett, "Inside and Out," *The New Leader* 26 (April 8, 1944), 10.

99. "A Year in the Service of Humanity" (New York: Emergency Committee to Save the Jewish People of Europe, 1944), 5–6; Penkower, "In Dramatic Dissent," 291; "U.S. Group Is Named to Save Europe's Art," *NYT,* August 21, 1943, 9.

100. "A Year in the Service of Humanity," 7–8; Wyman, *Abandonment,* 191; Penkower, *The Jews Were Expendable,* 107–8.

101. Wyman, *Abandonment,* 149.

102. Penkower, "In Dramatic Dissent," 294.

103. Embassy to North American Department, Foreign Office, October 14, 1943, FO 371/35040, PRO.

104. Sarah E. Peck, "The Campaign for an American Response to the Nazi Holocaust, 1943–1945," *Journal of Contemporary History* 15 (1980), 381.

105. For the Bergsonites' self-perception as being in a position of weakness, see Fineman to Bergson, January 8, 1943, 1:7, PSC. For details of the negotiations, see "First Proposal Made By The Committee For A Jewish Army To The Emergency Committee on Zionist Affairs," December 3, 1941, 1:5, PSC; Lourie to Wechsler, January 6, 1942, 1:6, PSC; and Lourie to Wechsler, January 26, 1942, 1:6, PSC.

106. Silver's Confidential Washington Diary, entry for October 11, 1943, 3–4, AHS, The Temple, Cleveland.

107. Memorandum of Conversation with Nahum Goldmann, May 19, 1944, 867N.01/2347, National Archives, Washington, D.C.; Department of State Memorandum of Conversation (Waldman, Murray, Alling, Wilson), January 10, 1944, PSC 3:67.

108. Ladd to Tamm, May 23, 1944, Subject: Hillel Kook, alias Peter Bergson; Hebrew Committee of National Liberation, FBI.

109. Hecht, 580–82; Wyman, *Abandonment,* 156; "My Uncle Abraham Reports . . ." (advertisement), *NYT,* November 5, 1943, 14; *New York Herald Tribune,* November 7, 1943, II:2; *Washington Post,* November 8, 1943, 9.

110. Ben-Ami, op. cit., 292.

111. Wyman, *Abandonment,* 193.

112. Henderson (Foreign Office) to Baker (Colonial Office), November 28, 1945, CO 733/461/75872/14C, PRO.

113. In addition to Gillette, the sponsors in the Senate were Elbert Thomas (D-UT), Edwin Johnson (D-CO), Robert Taft (R-OH), Homer Ferguson (R-MI), Bennett Champ Clark (D-MO), Sheridan Downey (D-CA), Allen Ellender (D-LA), Joseph Guffey (D-PA), James Murray (D-MT), George Radcliffe (D-MD), and Frederick Van Nuys (D-IN). In the House, the cosponsor along with Rogers was Joseph C. Baldwin (R-NY).

114. Shalom Wurm, "When the Leaders Fail," *Furrows* 2:3 (January 1944), 14–17.

115. Wyman, *Abandonment,* 168–69.

116. U.S. House of Representatives, *Problems of World War II and Its Aftermath—Part 2: The Palestine Question* (Washington, D.C.: U.S. Government Printing Office, 1976). Kook's testimony appears on pp. 95–139.

117. Ibid., 220–21, 226–27, 231–32, 234–36, 240–42.

118. Wyman, *Abandonment,* 197–98.

119. Ibid., 197–98, 202. Except for Long's testimony, Bloom suppressed publication of the transcripts of the hearings. They did not become available until 1976.

120. Morgenthau Diaries, Book 693, p. 198, and Book 694, p. 88; Penkower, op. cit., 296.

121. Memorandum issued by the Interim Committee of the American Jewish Conference, December 29, 1943, State Department 840.48 Refugees/5025, National Archives.

122. Wyman, Abandonment, 178–89, 203–5.

123. Harry Dexter White (1892–1948) served in the Treasury Department from 1934 to 1947, first as Director of Monetary Research and later as Assistant Secretary of the Treasury.

124. Morgenthau Diaries, Book 692, pp. 289–90.

125. Ibid., Book 694, p. 97.

126. John Morton Blum, ed., *The Price of Vision: The Diary of Henry Wallace 1942–1946* (Boston, 1973), 211, 265, n.1.

127. Morgenthau Diaries, Book 694, p. 97.

128. Ibid., Book 693, pp. 212–29, and Book 694, pp. 190–202; Wyman, *Abandonment,* 187, 203–4, 285, 405–6.

129. Morgenthau Diaries, Book 707, pp. 220–21.

130. Ibid., Book 710, p. 194. See also Book 694, p. 97; Book 735, pp. 24–26; Memorandum of Conversation with Nahum Goldmann, May 19, 1944, 867N.01/2347, National Archives, Washington, D.C.

131. *Christian Science Monitor,* January 24, 1944, 6; *Washington Post,* January 25, 1944, 10.

132. Kook interview with Wyman, op. cit.

133. Wyman, *Abandonment,* 285.

134. Ibid., 213–14.

135. Kook interview with Wyman, op. cit.

136. Wyman, *Abandonment,* 253–54.

137. Medoff, *Militant Zionism in America,* Chapter 6.

138. Wyman, *Abandonment,* 254, 321, 345–46; Thackrey to Bergson, November 22, 1944, 13:57, PSC; Selden to Kampelman, December 22, 1959, 13:59, PSC; *Washington Post,* October 3,4,5,6, and 8, all on page 1, and October 13, page 16 (all in 1944); "Withdrawals and Replies from American League and Hebrew Committee," February 8, 1945, Vertical File: American League for a Free Palestine, Zionist Archives and Library, New York; Independent Jewish Press Service, *News,* February 28, 1944, 8; Bromfield to Bridges, September 16, 1944, 1:13, PSC; Bridges to Cavert, March 10, 1945, 1:17, PSC; Shapiro to Horwitt, November 29, 1944, American Zionist Emergency Council to Adler, November 29, 1944, 13:57, PSC.

139. John Pehle interview with Laurence Jarvik, October 16, 1978; *Federal Register,* vol. 9, no. 18, January 26, 1944, 935; Wyman, *Abandonment,* 232, 312–327.

140. Wyman, *Abandonment,* 263–64; U.S. War Relocation Authority, *Token Shipment: The Story of America's War Refugee Shelter* (Washington, D.C., n.d. [1946]), 13.

141. Wyman, *Abandonment,* 253.

142. Ibid., 252–53.

143. Smertenko to Roosevelt, July 24, 1944, National Archives, State Department 840.48 Refugees/7-2444.

144. Medoff, *Militant Zionism in America,* Chapter 12.

CHAPTER 2: CONFRONTING THE HOLOCAUST

1. This section is from the interview of Hillel Kook by David Wyman on November 20, 1978, in New York City.

2. "2 Million Jews Slain, Rabbi Wise Asserts," November 25, 1942, 6.

3. Adolf A. Berle, Jr. (1895–1971), an attorney by profession, was a member of President Franklin Roosevelt's "Brains Trust" circle of expert advisers and a professor of corpora-

tion law at Columbia University. He served as assistant secretary of state for Latin American Affairs from 1938 to 1945. After World War II, he served briefly as U.S. ambassador to Brazil, then returned to his law practice and the Columbia faculty. He went on to become a founder and chairman of the Liberal Party and an adviser to President John F. Kennedy.

4. In fact, according to Wise's biographer, Melvin Urofsky, Wise was anxious to publicize the news and did not require urging from the State Department to do so. (*A Voice That Spoke for Justice: The Life and Times of Stephen S. Wise* [Albany, NY, 1982], 319–22.) According to Wise's account (cited in David S. Wyman, The *Abandonment of the Jews: America and the Holocaust 1941–1945* [New York, 1984], 51), Undersecretary of State Sumner Welles confirmed the authenticity of the genocide reports during Wise's November 24, 1942, meeting with him, and Welles then withdrew his earlier request to Wise to refrain from publicizing the information. According to Wise, Welles said, "For reasons you will understand, I cannot give these [reports] to the press, but there is no reason why you should not. It might even help if you did."

5. This section begins the main interview of Hillel Kook by David Wyman, conducted on April 13–15, 1973, in Amherst, Massachusetts.

6. Emanuel Neumann (1893–1980) worked for American Zionist organizations throughout his career. He served as education director of the Zionist Organization of America (1918–1920), national director of the U.S. wing of the Keren Hayesod (1921–25), chairman of the executive committee of the United Palestine Appeal (1925–27), and president of the Jewish National Fund (1928–1930). After spending the 1930s in Jerusalem as the director of the Jewish Agency's Economic Department and in related positions, Neumann returned to the United States in 1939 as director of public relations for the Emergency Committee for Zionist Affairs, and later played a key role in elevating Abba Hillel Silver to the leadership of the American Zionist movement. Neumann was elected national president of the ZOA in 1947.

7. The section that follows is from the interview of Hillel Kook by David Wyman on May 5, 1973, in New York City.

8. Louis E. Levinthal (1892–1976), a judge of the Court of Common Pleas in Philadelphia from 1937 to 1959, served as president of the Zionist Organization of America (1941–43), chairman of the executive committee of the Emergency Committee for Zionist Affairs (1941–43), and held other positions in the Zionist movement.

9. Arthur Szyk (1894–1951), a Polish-born illustrator and miniaturist, so impressed British officials with his anti-Nazi caricatures that they sent him to the United States in 1940 to help sway American public opinion to support U.S. military intervention against Hitler. He became the editorial cartoonist for the *New York Post* and contributed to many other publications. Szyk joined the Committee for a Jewish Army in 1941 and was subsequently active in Bergson's other groups as well. His dramatic illustrations frequently adorned the Bergson group's newspaper advertisements.

10. The section that follows is from the interview of Hillel Kook by David Wyman on April 13–15, 1973.

11. Herman Shulman (1897–1945), a prominent New York attorney, was also active in the

Zionist Organization of America and the American Zionist Emergency Council, of which he served as vice chairman during the 1940s.

12. Edward G. Robinson (1893–1973), a prominent movie actor in the 1930s and 1940s, is best known for his role as a mobster in *Little Caesar* (1931).

13. During his stint with the Office of War Information, James Warburg (1896–1969) repeatedly became embroiled in controversy. After the OWI took part in a diversionary scheme to aid the Allied invasion of North Africa, Warburg was horrified by the Allies' initial decision to leave in place the anti-Jewish laws from the previous Vichy regime, and "circulated strong internal denunciations of the pact" that made waves in his department. The following year, Warburg and his colleagues, in London, broadcast sharp criticism of Mussolini's pro-Axis successors, but the Roosevelt administration "wanted to negotiate with these Mussolini sympathizers and repudiated the London broadcasts." Warburg chose to resign. (Ron Chernow, *The Warburgs* [New York, 1993], 520–21.)

14. Henry Monsky (1890–1947), an attorney from Nebraska, became president of the Jewish social service organization B'nai B'rith in 1938, and was reelected in 1941. He was a prime moving force behind the convening of the 1943 American Jewish Conference, which sought to establish a unified American Jewry to address issues such as "the rights and status of Jews in the post-war world" and "implementation of the rights of the Jewish people with respect to Palestine." (Alexander Kohanski [ed.], *The American Jewish Conference: Its Organization and Proceedings of the First Session, August 29–September 2, 1943* [New York, 1944], 325, 332–33.)

15. Abba Hillel Silver (1893–1963) first rose to prominence during the 1930s as leader of the large Cleveland district of the Zionist Organization of America, organizing boycotts of products from Nazi Germany and protests against British policy in Palestine. Silver's growing prominence in the American Zionist movement in the early 1940s coincided with a mood of frustration in the Jewish community stemming from the apathetic Allied response to Nazi genocide and the British refusal to open Palestine to Jewish refugees. Silver both symbolized American Jewish militancy and helped promote it. His speech at the August 1943 American Jewish Conference, calling for Jewish statehood, elicited waves of thunderous applause and catapulted him to cochairmanship of the American Zionist Emergency Council, in effect usurping the leadership role of AZEC chairman Stephen Wise. Under Silver's leadership, American Zionists intensified their lobbying in Washington on behalf of the Zionist cause and mobilized grass roots activists to deluge Capitol Hill with calls and letters urging U.S. support for the creation of a Jewish national home in Palestine. Silver's efforts helped bring about the inclusion of pro-Zionist planks in the election platforms of the Republican and Democratic parties in 1944, setting the precedent for future competition between the two parties for Jewish support. Silver did not focus on the issue of rescuing Jews from Hitler, maintaining that the establishment of a Jewish state in Palestine was the answer to the persecution of European Jewry.

16. In a column on March 26, 1943, David Deutsch, the political gossip columnist for the Independent Jewish Press Service, wondered aloud "if there is any truth in the story that the newly created, super-duper Joint Emergency Committee on European Jewish

Affairs squelched one of Ben Hecht's brain-children that was to see the light of day in one of those eye-catching full page ads. Well, the inside dope is that Mr. Hecht is supposed to have penned a poem saying that there's going to be a very happy Christmas this year because by December there wouldn't be any Jews left for the Christian world to spit at. Those who are in the know say that the piece would have to be printed on asbestos, it was so hot. Anyhow, the new committee is said to have gotten after the Committee on Stateless Jews or more appropriately the Committee on Meeting Your Customers through Morning Advertising, and hushed the whole thing up. Yep, Mr. Hecht, the bad boy, was given an ice-cold shower." (David Deutsch, "Heard in the Lobbies," Independent Jewish Press Service, March 26, 1943, 1—E.)

17. In addition to the AJCongress, the AJCommittee, the Jewish Labor Committee, and Agudath Israel, the Joint Emergency Committee on European Jewish Affairs included representatives from the American Emergency Committee for Zionist Affairs (later known as the American Zionist Emergency Council), the Synagogue Council of America, the Union of Orthodox Rabbis, and B'nai B'rith.

18. According to *The New York Times*, there was "an audience of 21,000 that filled the huge auditorium, while several thousand others were unable to get in." ("Save Doomed Jews, Huge Rally Pleas," *NYT*, March 2, 1943, 1.)

19. Kurt Becher served in the SS Death's Head Equestrian Unit 1, which carried out the mass murder of Jews in Poland and western Russia from 1941 to 1943, for which he was promoted to the rank of SS-Obersturmbannführer (SS Major). Becher served as an aide to Adolf Eichmann during the Nazi occupation of Hungary and conducted negotiations with local Jewish leaders for the release of small numbers of Jews in exchange for bribes. He also negotiated with Jewish leaders and representatives of the War Refugee Board concerning a failed proposal to provide 10,000 Allied trucks and supplies to the Nazis in order to halt the deportations of the Jews. After the war, he prospered as a private businessman and escaped prosecution as a war criminal due to the intervention of one of the Hungarian Jewish leaders from whom he had accepted bribes, Rudolf Kastner.

20. Henry L. Feingold, "The Roosevelt Administration and the Effort to Save the Jews of Hungary," in Randolph Braham, ed., *Hungarian Jewish Studies* (New York, 1969), 211–59.

21. Interview of Samuel Merlin by Laurence Jarvik, July 1980, New York City.

22. The section that follows is from the interview of Hillel Kook by David Wyman on April 13–15, 1973.

23. This paragraph and the one that follows it are from the interview of Hillel Kook by David Wyman on April 13–15, 1973.

24. Walter Lippmann (1890-1975), syndicated columnist and author, was once described by *The New York Times* (December 15, 1974, 1) as "the dean of American political journalism in the 20th century" and "one of the most respected and influential political writers of his time."

25. The section that follows is from the interview of Hillel Kook by David Wyman on April 13–15, 1973.

26. The section that follows is from the interview of Samuel Merlin by David Wyman on April 19, 1973, in New York City.

27. New York: World Publishing Company, 1969. For a more detailed examination of editorial policies at *The New York Times* regarding coverage of the Holocaust, see Laurel Leff, "A Tragic 'Fight in the Family': *The New York Times*, Reform Judaism and the Holocaust," *American Jewish History* 88 (March 2000), 4–51.

CHAPTER 3: BUILDING A COALITION FOR
RESCUE, FROM CAPITOL HILL TO HOLLYWOOD

1. This section is from the interview of Hillel Kook by David Wyman on April 13–15, 1973.
2. This section is from the interview of Will Rogers, Jr., by Martin Ostrow on February 17, 1992.
3. The section that follows is from the interview of Hillel Kook by David Wyman on April 13–15, 1973.
4. Jo Davidson (1883–1952) was a prominent sculptor, best known for his portrait busts of international leaders such as Franklin Roosevelt and Mahatma Gandhi.
5. Adlai E. Stevenson (1900–1965) had a long career in public service, including positions as assistant to the Secretary of the Navy (1941–44) and as a U.S. representative to the United Nations (1946–47) before being elected governor of Illinois in 1949. In 1952 and 1956, Stevenson was the Democratic nominee for president, but both times lost the election to Dwight D. Eisenhower. He later served as U.S. ambassador to the U.N. (1961–65).
6. Frank Knox (1874–1944), the Republican candidate for vice-president in 1936, served as Secretary of the Navy from 1940 to 1944.
7. Robert Wagner (1877–1953), Democrat of New York, served in the Senate from 1927 to 1949. He cosponsored the unsuccessful Wagner-Rogers bill of 1939, which sought to grant nonquota admission to the United States of 20,000 German-Jewish refugee children. He was a staunch supporter of Zionism who worked closely with the mainstream American Zionist leadership.
8. Elbert Thomas (1883–1953), Democrat of Utah, served in the United States Senate from 1933–1951, chairing the Senate Committee on Education and Labor for much of that time. Thomas, a devout Mormon, became a passionate Christian Zionist as a result of his visit to Palestine in 1912. Thomas supported the Committee for a Jewish Army, served as honorary chairman of the Bergson group's July 1943 Emergency Conference to Save the Jewish People of Europe, and cosponsored the Gillette-Rogers rescue resolution. Thomas delivered the keynote address to the second Emergency Conference, in August 1944, timing it to coincide with his weekly CBS Radio address. CBS's censorship of the portions of the speech criticizing the British and referring to the 1944 Republican and Democratic party platforms set off a public controversy that netted considerable publicity for the Bergson group, culminating in a public apology by CBS and a rebroadcast of the full speech. (Sharon Kay Smith, "Elbert D. Thomas and America's Response to the Holocaust," PhD dissertation, Brigham Young University, 1992.)
9. *The New York Times,* May 4, 1943, 17. The three-quarter-page advertisement's bold headline declared: "To 5,000,000 Jews in the Nazi Death-Trap, Bermuda was a 'Cruel Mockery.'"

10. See Medoff, *Militant Zionism in America*, Chapter 10.

11. William Langer (1886–1959), Republican of North Dakota, served in the United States Senate from 1941 to 1959. He was one of the most outspoken critics of the Roosevelt administration's policy regarding European Jewry, and cosponsored the Emergency Conference to Save the Jewish People of Europe. His background as governor of North Dakota and his struggle to remain in the Senate are traced in Glenn H. Smith, *Langer of North Dakota: A Study in Isolationism 1940–1959* (New York, 1979), 23–42; and in *the New York Times*, January 4, 1941, 1; December 19, 1941, 28; March 3, 1942, 26; March 10, 1942, 40; March 17, 1942, 15; and March 28, 1942, I, 30.

12. *Washington Post*, April 20, 1943, 10.

13. Charles MacArthur (1895–1956), the longtime writing partner of Ben Hecht, is best known for his work on such films as *Barbary Coast* (1935) and *Wuthering Heights* (1939). He was married to the actress Helen Hayes.

14. This section is from the interview of Max Lerner by Martin Ostrow on March 5, 1992.

15. This section is from the interview of Hillel Kook by David Wyman on April 13–15, 1973.

16. Interview of Rogers by Ostrow, op.cit.

17. Interview of Lerner by Ostrow, op. cit.

18. The section that follows is from the interview of Hillel Kook by David Wyman on April 13–15, 1973.

19. The section that follows is from the April 19, 1973, interview of Samuel Merlin and Hillel Kook by David Wyman.

20. The section that follows is from the interview of Hillel Kook by David Wyman on April 13–15, 1973.

21. Dr. Syngman Rhee (1875–1965), president of the Korean Provisional Government-in-Exile, spent much of World War II in the United States, seeking political and military support for Korean resistance to the Japanese occupation of his country. After the Allies' defeat of the Japanese, Rhee returned to Korea, where he was elected president in 1948, a position he retained until 1960.

22. John D. Dingell (1894–1955), Democrat of Michigan, served in the United States House of Representatives from 1933 to 1955. He endorsed both the Committee for a Jewish Army and the American League for a Free Palestine.

23. Alexander Wiley (1884–1967), Republican of Wisconsin, served in the United States Senate from 1939 to 1963.

24. Adolph Sabath (1866–1952), Democrat of Illinois, served in the House of Representatives from 1907 to 1952. He endorsed the Committee for a Jewish Army in its earliest phase, but did not associate with the Bergson group subsequently.

25. Arthur Klein (1904–1968), Democrat of New York, served in the House of Representatives from 1941 to 1945 and from 1946 to 1956. He supported the Committee for a Jewish Army in its early stage, but had no later connection with the Bergson group.

CHAPTER 4: THE OPPOSITION

1. This section is from the interview of Hillel Kook by David Wyman on April 13–15, 1973.
2. Rudolph Sonneborn (1898–1986), a wealthy Baltimore industrialist, spearheaded the secret effort from 1945 to 1948 to ship weapons, airplanes, medical supplies, and other materials to the Jewish community of Palestine in anticipation of an Arab invasion upon proclamation of the Jewish state.
3. Isaac Neustadt-Noy, "The Unending Task: Efforts to Unite American Jewry from the American Jewish Congress to the American Jewish Conference," PhD dissertation, Brandeis University, 1976, 358.
4. "The Last Stand" (editorial), *Jewish Frontier*, June 1943, 3.
5. The phrase was derived from the second chapter of Exodus (2:14), in which Moses killed an Egyptian who was beating a Jewish slave. The next day, Moses happened upon two Jews quarreling, and when he attempted to intervene, one snapped, "Who made you [*mi samcha*] a ruler and a judge over us? Do you intend to kill me, as you killed the Egyptian?"
6. Although Silver was close to Republican Senator Robert Taft, he himself was not a member of the Republican Party, and during his years as a leader of the American Zionist movement he refrained from publicly supporting either political party.
7. This section is from the interview of Will Rogers, Jr., by Martin Ostrow on February 17, 1992.
8. This section is from the interview of Hillel Kook by David Wyman on April 13–15, 1973.
9. Maurice Rifkin, proprieter of a business called Global Travel Service, was a leader of the Philadelphia branch of the American League for a Free Palestine.
10. Mrs. Frances Gunther (1897–1964), author and journalist, was active with the Bergson group from its very first phase, when it was known as the American Friends of a Jewish Palestine. She was married (until 1944) to the prominent author John Gunther.
11. Eliezer Silver (1881–1968), the leading Orthodox rabbi in Cincinnati, became president of the Union of Orthodox Rabbis, or Agudat HaRabbanim, in 1923. He was president of the union's Vaad Hahatzala rescue group and was one of the leaders of the Bergson group's October 1943 rabbinical march in Washington.
12. Wolf (Ze'ev) Gold (1889–1956), a prominent Orthodox rabbi in San Francisco and longtime leader of the Mizrachi Religious Zionists of America, served as vice president of the Vaad Hahatzala, and played a key role in the October 1943 rabbinical march in Washington, serving as its spokesman to the media. Rabbi Gold later settled in Jerusalem and was one of the fifteen original signatories on Israel's Declaration of Independence.
13. Philip D. Bookstaber (1892–1964), a Reform rabbi, served as spiritual leader of Temple Ohev Sholom in Harrisburg, Pennsylvania, from 1924 to 1962. He was active in the Emergency Committee to Save the Jewish People of Europe.
14. Louis I. Newman (1893–1972), a Reform rabbi who was ordained by Stephen Wise, was active in the Zionist Organization of America during the 1920s. In 1935, Newman helped organize a faction within the ZOA to oppose endorsement of the Labor Zionists' trade union in Palestine, the Histadrut. When that initiative failed, Newman left

the ZOA and joined the U.S. wing of the Revisionists, the New Zionist Organization of America. He served as president of the NZOA from 1938 to 1940, and in subsequent years continued to publicly identify as a supporter of the NZOA and, to a lesser extent, the Bergson group.

15. This sentence and the two paragraphs that follow it are from the November 20, 1978, interview of Hillel Kook by David Wyman.

16. This section is from the interview of Hillel Kook by David Wyman on April 13–15, 1973.

17. This adage is to be found in the Talmudic tractate *Sanhedrin*, 37-a; and also in the Talmudic tractate *Baba Batra*, 11-a.

18. The advertisement appeared in *The New York Times* on February 16, 1943, 11, under the title "FOR SALE to Humanity: 70,000 Jews—Guaranteed Human Beings at $50 a Piece."

19. The advertisement appeared in *The New York Times* on November 5, 1943, 14, under the title "My Uncle Abraham Reports . . ."

20. This section is from the interview of Max Lerner by Martin Ostrow on March 5, 1992.

21. This section is from the interview of Hillel Kook by David Wyman on April 13–15, 1973.

22. *PM*, July 22, 1943, 2.

23. Dean Alfange (1898–1981), an attorney, ran unsuccessfully for governor of New York in 1942 as the candidate of the American Labor Party, and two years later was one of the founders of the Liberal Party. He served as honorary chair of the Emergency Conference to Save the Jewish People of Europe and was a member of the executive board of the Emergency Committee to Save the Jewish People of Europe from its formation in July 1943 until August 1944.

24. Kenneth Leslie (1893–1974) was a prominent Canadian poet and publisher of *The Protestant Digest*, a left-wing journal of politics and religion.

25. The involvement of Bergson group activists in gun-smuggling for the Irgun came to public attention on two occasions, both in 1948.

On April 27, 1948, Joseph Untermeyer, the nineteen-year-old son of Judge Esther Untermeyer, national treasurer of the American League for a Free Palestine (ALFP), was arrested along with Revisionist Zionist activist Isaiah Warshaw in connection with the discovery in a Manhattan loft of weapons and ammunition awaiting shipment to Palestine. Defense attorney Paul O'Dwyer, a Bergson supporter, moved for dismissal of the charges on grounds that the Irgun gun-smugglers were comparable to the patriots of the American Revolution; Magistrate Frederick Strong agreed, and threw out the case.

Late on the night of November 24, 1948, four young ALFP activists were caught loading weapons onto a truck in upper Manhattan. O'Dwyer was again the defense attorney, and he again launched into a political speech at the boys' first court hearing. Magistrate Vernon Riddick immediately dismissed the charges. ("Large Quantity of Arms in West Side Loft Found Being Hidden in Palestine Parcels," *NYT*, April 28, 1948, 12; "Two in Arms Cache for Palestine Free," *NYT*, May 29, 1948, 2; "5 Youths Seized With an Arsenal," *NYT*, November 26, 1948, 1; "5 Youths Released in Munitions Case," *NYT*, December 10, 1948, 7.)

26. Interview of Lerner by Ostrow, op. cit.

27. This section is from the interview of Hillel Kook by David Wyman on April 13–15, 1973.

28. For more on Hoover's response to the Holocaust, see Rafael Medoff, "The Impact of the Holocaust on Herbert Hoover," in *Holocaust Studies Annual* 1991, 53–67.

29. *NYT*, August 9, 1944, 13; *PM*, August 8, 1944, 16.

30. Joseph Brainin (1895–1970), a member of the Jabotinsky-initiated Jewish Legion that fought in World War I, founded and directed the Seven Arts Feature Syndicate. During the 1920s and 1930s he also served in England and South America as a foreign correspondent for various newspapers. In later years he assumed a prominent role in the Rosenberg atomic espionage case, serving as chairman of the National Committee to Secure Justice in the Rosenberg Case. In addition to encouraging Pierre van Paassen's involvement in the Committee for a Jewish Army, Brainin himself was an early supporter of the Jewish army campaign.

31. *New York Post*, November 9, 1945, 33. Van Paassen stated that "the Zionist leaders and especially the [American Zionist] Emergency Council" were behind the "efforts to drive Bergson out of this country." It was in this context that he referred to the Zionists as acting "in the manner of stool pigeons and *indicateurs de police.*"

32. Lisa Sergio (1905–1989), an Italian journalist, arrived in the United States in 1937, just ahead of a warrant for her arrest issued by Mussolini. She was a prominent radio host and commentator, and later a television host as well. Sergio served on one of the panels of experts at Bergson's July 1943 Emergency Conference to Save the Jewish People of Europe.

33. *PM*, August 8, 1944, 16, and *NYT*, August 9, 1944, 13.

34. Wise's version of the incident differs slightly. According to Wise, Freud asked him to name "the four greatest living Jews." Wise: "Oh, that is easy. Einstein, Ehrlich, Freud, and Brandeis." Freud: "And you." Wise: "No, no, no, no, you cannot include me." Freud: "If you had said 'no' once, I would believe you, but four 'no's leads me to suspect that you protest too much." Wise: "I have gotten a free psychoanalytic reading from the greatest authority on the subject." Wise evidently did not regard the exchange as unflattering, for he repeated it to journalist Nathan Ziprin, who wrote it up as an editorial for the Seven Arts Feature Syndicate on March 9, 1944 (Urofsky, op. cit., 236, 399 n31.).

35. Louis Lipsky (1876–1963), a close associate of Stephen Wise and Chaim Weizmann, was a leader of, among other organizations, the World Jewish Congress, the American Jewish Congress, the United Jewish Appeal, and the Zionist Organization of America, of which he served as president from 1921 to 1930.

36. This section is from the September 6, 1973, interview of Samuel Merlin by David Wyman.

37. This section is from the May 5, 1973, interview of Hillel Kook by David Wyman.

38. This section is from the April 19, 1973, interview of Samuel Merlin by David Wyman.

39. This brief exchange is from the interview of Hillel Kook by David Wyman on April 13–15, 1973.

40. Interview of Lerner by Ostrow, op. cit.

41. This section is from the interview of Hillel Kook by David Wyman on April 13–15, 1973.

42. David Niles (1892–1952) served both Presidents Roosevelt and Truman as a liaison to liberal and labor organizations and minority interest groups, the Jewish community included.

43. *NYT*, March 2, 1945, 1.

44. William D. Hassett, *Off the Record with FDR 1942–1945* (New Brunswick, NJ, 1958), 209.

45. Helen Gahagan Douglas (1900–1980), Democrat of California, served in the United States House of Representatives from 1945 to 1951. Both Douglas and her husband, the actor Melvyn Douglas, were active in the Bergson group.

46. Bergson to Eleanor Roosevelt, August 11, 1943, with enclosures, FDR to Thompson, August 16, 1943, Eleanor Roosevelt Papers, Box 2899, File 190, Franklin D. Roosevelt Library.

47. Interview of Emanuel Celler by Laurence Jarvik, October 4, 1978, New York City.

48. This section is from the November 10, 1978, interview of Hillel Kook by Laurence Jarvik, New York City.

49. This sentence and the remainder of this chapter are from the interview of Hillel Kook by David Wyman on April 13–15, 1973.

50. Elliott Roosevelt (1910–1990), the second child of Franklin and Eleanor Roosevelt and one of the most colorful members of the Roosevelt family, was a heavily decorated World War II combat pilot who later worked as an editor, a business consultant, a breeder of Arabian horses, and mayor of Miami Beach. In between, he was married five times and wrote a series of controversial "tell all" books about life in the Roosevelt family, as well as a number of mystery novels featuring his mother as an amateur detective.

CHAPTER 5: THE RESCUE RESOLUTION

1. This section is from the September 6, 1973, interview of Samuel Merlin by David Wyman.

2. Wise's oral testimony at the hearing is available (along with the transcripts of the rest of the hearings on the rescue resolution) in U.S. House of Representatives, *Problems of World War II and Its Aftermath: Part 2, The Palestine Question*, 217–43 (Washington, 1976). His reference to the resolution as "inadequate" appears on pages 220 and 226.

   Reference to Wise's written statement is made on page 220. A synopsis of the written statement was published in an American Jewish Conference press release of December 2, 1943. (National Archives, Legislative Branch, file 16432.)

3. This section is from the interview of Will Rogers, Jr., by Martin Ostrow, February 17, 1992.

4. This section is from the September 6, 1973, interview of Samuel Merlin by David Wyman.

5. Interview of Rogers by Ostrow, op. cit.

6. This section is from the November 20, 1978, interview of Hillel Kook by David Wyman.

7. This section is from the April 13–15, 1973, interview of Hillel Kook by David Wyman.

8. Interview of Emanuel Celler by Laurence Jarvik on October 4, 1978.

9. Herbert Moore was president of a radio news service, Transradio News Features of New York City. He was also a vice chairman of the Emergency Committee to Save the Jewish People of Europe.

10. This section is from the April 13–15, 1973, interview of Hillel Kook by David Wyman.

11. *Interpreter Releases,* January 10, 1944, 14; *NYT,* December 21, 1943, 10; *San Francisco Examiner,* December 22, 1943, 12; Address of Senator Guy M. Gillette, December 20, 1944, PSC, Box 6, Folder 27; Emergency Committee to Save the Jewish People of Europe, *The Work Is Still Ahead* (New York, 1944), 11–12, copy in PSC, Box 6, Folder 27.

12. Signed by Dean Alfange and Sigrid Undset for the Emergency Committee to Save the Jewish People of Europe, November 13, 1943, National Archives, Legislative Branch, File 16432.

13. Aryeh Ben-Eliezer (1913–1970), a senior activist in the Irgun Zvai Leumi in Palestine in the 1930s, was one of the handful of Irgun emissaries sent to the United States in 1939. He became active in the American Friends of a Jewish Palestine and later was part of Bergson's inner circle in the Committee for a Jewish Army and the Emergency Committee to Save the Jewish People of Europe. Returning to Palestine in 1943, he assumed a leadership role in the Irgun, but in April 1944 was captured by the British. He was held in East African detention camps until 1948, when he escaped and made his way back to Palestine. He was elected to the first Israeli parliament, launching a lengthy political career in Menachem Begin's Herut Party, eventually reaching the post of Deputy Speaker of the Knesset.

14. Dr. Joseph Klarman (1909–1987) was a leader of the Revisionist Zionist movement in Poland from 1934 to 1939. He emigrated to Palestine in 1940, and in 1943 was named the Revisionist representative to the Jewish Agency's Rescue Committee. The following year he was sent by the Revisionists to Istanbul, where he worked closely with Orthodox rescue activist Dr. Ya'akov Griffel in organizing the emigration of Jewish refugees from the Balkan countries to Palestine.

15. Theodore O. Thackrey (1901–1980), a lifelong journalist and newspaper editor, was named executive editor of the *New York Post* in 1943, a post he held until his divorce from the *Post*'s owner, Dorothy Schiff, in 1948. During that time he authored a number of editorials sympathetic to the positions of the Bergson group.

16. Chaim Lieberman, *Forward,* November 26, 1943, 2.

17. Flegelman to Bloom, February 11, 1944, National Archives, Legislative Branch, File 16433.

18. Wilson, Memorandum of conversation with Goldmann et al., May 19, 1944, National Archives, State Department 867N.01/2347.

19. Wyman, *Abandonment,* 195–98.

20. Oscar L. Chapman (1896–1978), an attorney and a Democratic Party activist, served as Assistant Secretary of the Interior from 1933 to 1946, then as Undersecretary of the Interior from 1946 to 1949 and, finally, as Secretary of the Interior from 1949 to 1953. He was one of the key organizers of the Washington, D.C., chapter of the Emergency Committee to Save the Jewish People of Europe.

21. Fowler Harper (1897–1965), a professor of law who taught at a number of universities (including, beginning in 1947, the Yale Law School), served during World War II as a

solicitor general with the Department of the Interior. Harper was active in the Emergency Committee to Save the Jewish People of Europe and later served as vice chairman of the American League for a Free Palestine. He drafted the text of the Gillette-Rogers resolution, frequently spoke for the Bergson group on radio broadcasts, and was a member of the four-man Bergson group delegation that traveled to England in 1945 to meet with Foreign Minister Ernest Bevin about the Palestine situation.

22. This section is from the April 19, 1973, interview of Hillel Kook by David Wyman.
23. Wyman, *Abandonment*, 94–95.
24. *Problems of World War II*, op. cit., 30, 88, 132–33.
25. Interview of Rogers by Ostrow, op. cit.
26. The Women's International League for Peace and Freedom was founded in 1915 by Jane Addams. Detzer joined the Emergency Committee to Save the Jewish People of Europe and worked with it as much as time allowed. In her autobiography, *Appointment on the Hill* (New York, 1948), Detzer reports that a poll of both houses of Congress in mid-January 1944 showed "a sufficient margin of votes to insure passage" (of the rescue resolution). (242)
27. This section is from the interview of Hillel Kook by David Wyman on April 13–15, 1973.
28. Senate Report No. 625, 78th Congress, 1st Session, December 20, 1943.
29. Morgenthau Diaries, Book 693, p. 198, and Book 694, p. 88.
30. Interview of Rogers by Ostrow, op. cit.

Chapter 6: The War Refugee Board

1. This chapter is from the interview of Hillel Kook by David Wyman on April 13–15, 1973.
2. John Ellis van Courtland Moon, "Pressing at the Limits: The Challenge of the Hebrew Committee of National Liberation to Chemical Warfare Policy," *Simon Wiesenthal Center Annual* 2, 139–47.
3. This and the preceding paragraph are based on *American Jewish History* 85 (1997), 337–41; *American Jewish History* 86 (1998), 221–22; and *Journal of Genocide Research* 3 (2001), 507–10.
4. Ansel Luxford (1911–1972) served in the Treasury Department in various capacities from 1935 to 1946. He was actively involved in the investigation of the State Department's obstruction of rescue efforts, leading to the establishment of the War Refugee Board. He became an official of the WRB.
5. Assistant Secretary of War John J. McCloy served as the War Department's liaison with the War Refugee Board.
6. Wyman, *Abandonment*, 286.
7. Morgenthau Diaries, Book 735, pp. 60, 77.
8. William O'Dwyer (1890–1964) served as executive director of the War Refugee Board from January through May 1945. That autumn, he successfully ran for mayor of New York City, a post he held until resigning in 1950 amidst a corruption scandal.

CHAPTER 7: EPILOGUE

1. This section is from the interview of Hillel Kook by David Wyman on April 13–15, 1973.
2. James P. McGranery (1895–1962), Democrat of Pennsylvania, served in the U.S. House of Representatives from 1937 to 1943. He later served as U.S. district judge for the Eastern District of Pennsylvania and became Attorney General of the United States from 1952 to 1953.
3. Hugh D. Scott, Jr. (1900–1994), Republican of Pennsylvania, served in the United States House of Representatives from 1941 to 1945 and in the Senate from 1947 to 1977. He was a supporter of the American League for a Free Palestine.
4. Joseph Sharfsin, who served as the Philadelphia city solicitor and then as the director of the Pennsylvania Public Utilities Corporation, was active in the Philadelphia branch of Bergson's American League for a Free Palestine.
5. Hillel Kook to Sarah E. Peck, February 1, 1978, copy in possession of the authors.
6. Wilson, Memo of Conversaton with Waldman et al., January 10, 1944, Breckinridge Long Papers, Box 200, Palestine; Wilson, Memo of Conversation with Goldmann et al., May 19, 1944, National Archives, State Department 867N.01/2347; Murray to Stettinius, June 1, 1944, Murray to Stettinius, June 2, 1944, State Department 867N.01/6-144; Halifax to Foreign Office, May 24, 1944, FO 371/40131, PRO; Balfour to High Commissioner, Jerusalem, August 9, 1945, Chancery (Washington) to Eastern Department, August 6, 1945, FO 371/45399, PRO; Frank to Guthman, May 19, 1945, 1:18, PSC; Gillette to Byrnes, October 11, 1945, Stern to Byrnes, October 16, 1945, Stern to Russell, October 16, 1945, 1:21, PSC; Byrnes to Stern, November 14, 1945, Stern to Byrnes, November 15, 1945, Byrnes to Stern, November 21, 1945, 1:22, PSC; Byrnes to Gillette, November 1, 1945, Memorandum for J. David Stern [August 2, 1946], Haering to Kook, August 2, 1946, Johnson to Kook, August 12, 1946, 10:9, PSC.
7. Ya'akov Meridor, *Long Is the Road to Freedom* (Hebrew) (Jerusalem, 1950).
8. Levi (Shkolnik) Eshkol (1895–1969), a member of the Haganah high command, went on to become the first director-general of the Israeli Ministry of Defense. He served as Minister of Agriculture (1951–1952) and Minister of Finance (1952–1963) before succeeding David Ben-Gurion as prime minister in 1963, in which office he remained until 1969.
9. Jeremiah Helpern (1901–1962) was a sea captain who was chief of military training for the Betar movement and head of its Jewish Marine League. After the outbreak of World War II, he became a leader of the British division of the Committee for a Jewish Army. He periodically visited the United States and took part in some of the Bergson group's activities there.
10. Avraham Stavsky, a Revisionist Zionist activist, had been indicted, but later acquitted, on charges of taking part in the assassination of Labor Zionist leader Chaim Arlosoroff in Tel Aviv in 1933. He later became active in the Irgun and was in charge of organizing the *Altalena*.
11. This section is from the interview of Hillel Kook by Laurence Jarvik on November 10, 1978.
12. This section is from the interview of Hillel Kook by David Wyman on November 20, 1978.

BIBLIOGRAPHY

Following are interviews used in this work, as well as books, dissertations, and essays dealing in part or whole with the Bergson group.

INTERVIEWS

Celler, Emanuel, by Laurence Jarvik, October 4, 1978, New York City. The Laurence Jarvik interviews of Kook, Merlin, and Celler were made for the film *Who Shall Live and Who Shall Die?*, written, produced, and directed by Laurence Jarvik (1981, distributed by Kino International Corporation, New York City).

Kook, Hillel, by David Wyman, April 13–15, 1973, in Amherst, Massachusetts; April 19, 1973, New York City; May 5, 1973, New York City; November 20, 1978, New York City.

Kook, Hillel, by Laurence Jarvik, November 10, 1978, New York City.

Lerner, Max, by Martin Ostrow, March 5, 1992, New York City. The Rogers and Lerner interviews were made for the American Experience film *America and the Holocaust: Deceit and Indifference*, written, produced, and directed by Martin Ostrow (1994, American Experience, WGBH Educational Foundation, Boston).

Merlin, Samuel, by David Wyman, April 19, 1973, New York City; September 6, 1973, New York City.

Merlin, Samuel, by Laurence Jarvik, July 1980, New York City.

Rogers, Jr., Will, by Martin Ostrow, February 17, 1992, Tubac, Arizona.

PUBLISHED DOCUMENT

U.S. House of Representatives. *Problems of World War II and Its Aftermath: Part 2, The Palestine Question*. Washington: U.S. Government Printing Office, 1976.

BOOKS

Ben-Ami, Yitshaq. *Years of Wrath, Days of Glory: Memoirs from the Irgun*. New York: Shengold, 1983.

Hecht, Ben. *A Child of the Century*. New York: Simon & Schuster, 1954.

Korff, Baruch. *Flight from Fear*. New York: Elmar, 1953.

Lowenstein, Sharon R. *Token Refuge: The Story of the Jewish Refugee Shelter at Oswego, 1944–1946*. Bloomington: Indiana University Press, 1986.

Medoff, Rafael. *The Deafening Silence: American Jewish Leaders and the Holocaust, 1933–1945*. New York: Shapolsky, 1987.

———. *Militant Zionism in America: The Rise and Impact of the Jabotinsky Movement in the United States, 1926–1948*. Tuscaloosa: University of Alabama Press, 2002.

O'Dwyer, Paul. *Counsel for the Defense: The Autobiography of Paul O'Dwyer*. New York: Simon & Schuster, 1979.

Penkower, Monty Noam. *The Jews Were Expendable: Free World Diplomacy and the Holocaust*. Urbana and Chicago: University of Illinois Press, 1983.

Rafaeli, Alex. *Dream and Action: The Story of My Life*. Jerusalem: Achva, 1993.

Rapoport, Louis. *Shake Heaven and Earth: Peter Bergson and the Struggle to Rescue the Jews of Europe*. Jerusalem: Gefen, 1999.

Wyman, David S. *The Abandonment of the Jews: America and the Holocaust, 1941–1945*. New York: Pantheon, 1984; The New Press, 1998.

Zuroff, Efraim. *The Response of Orthodox Jewry in the United States to the Holocaust*. Hoboken, NJ: Ktav, 2000.

DISSERTATIONS

Halasz, Dorottya. 2000. The War Refugee Board and the destruction of Hungarian Jewry. PhD diss., Texas Christian University.

Saidel, Joanna Maura. 1994. Revisionist Zionism in America: The campaign to win American public support, 1939–1948. PhD diss., University of New Hampshire.

Smith, Sharon Kay. 1992. Elbert D. Thomas and America's response to the Holocaust. PhD diss., Brigham Young University.

M.A. THESES

Feinstein, Marsha. 1973. The Irgun campaign in the United States for a Jewish army. Master's thesis, City University of New York.

Levine, Charles J. 1974. Propaganda techniques of the Bergson Group 1939–1948. Master's thesis, University of Texas.

SCHOLARLY ESSAYS

Baumel, Judith Tydor. 1995. The Irgun Zvai Leumi delegation in the U.S.A., 1939–1948: Anatomy of an ethnic interest/protest group. *Jewish History* 9 (spring): 1, 79–89.

Lowenstein, Sharon R. 1982. A New Deal for refugees: The promise and reality of Oswego. *American Jewish History* 71 (March): 3, 325–41.

Medoff, Rafael. 1997. Who fought for the 'right to fight'? The campaign for a Jewish army, 1939–1944. *Journal of Israeli History* 18 (spring) :1, 113–27.

———. 1996. Why Mrs. Brandeis endorsed the *Irgun*: An episode in Holocaust-era American Jewish politics. *American Jewish History* 84 (March): 1, 29–38.

———. 1994. Menachem Begin as George Washington: The Americanizing of the Jewish revolt against the British. *American Jewish Archives* XLVII (fall/winter): 2, 185–95.

———. 1992. The influence of Revisionist Zionism in America during the early years of World War Two. *Studies in Zionism* 13 (autumn): 2, 187–90.

Peck, Sarah E. 1980. The campaign for an American response to the Holocaust 1943–1945. *Journal of Contemporary History* 15:367–400.

Penkower, Monty N. 1981. In dramatic dissent: The Bergson boys. *American Jewish History* 70 (March): 3, 281–309.

———. 1985. American Jewry and the Holocaust: From Biltmore to the American Jewish conference. *Jewish Social Studies* XLVII (spring): 2, 95–114.

Roth, Walter. 1992. 'A Flag Is Born' pageant sought to establish Jewish state in Palestine. *Chicago Jewish History* XVI (fall): 1, 4–7.

Saposnik, Arye Bruce. 1996. Advertisement or achievement? American Jewry and the campaign for a Jewish army, 1939–1944: A reassessment. *Journal of Israeli History* 17 (summer): 193–220.

Whitfield, Stephen J. 1996. The politics of pageantry, 1936–1946. *American Jewish History* 84 (September): 221–51.

INDEX